D0427249

Wild Orchids Across North America

Cypripedium acaule, large clump, New Hampshire.

Wild Orchids Across North America

A BOTANICAL TRAVELOGUE

Text and photographs by Philip E. Keenan

Published by Timber Press, Portland, Oregon

Timber Press, Inc.
The Haseltine Building
133 S.W. Second Avenue, Suite 450
Portland, Oregon 97204, U.S.A.

Printed in Singapore

Library of Congress Cataloging-in-Publication Data

Keenan, Philip E.
    Wild orchids across North America: a botanical travelogue / text and
photographs by Philip E. Keenan.
        p.   cm.
    Includes bibliographical references (p.   ) and index.
    ISBN 0-88192-452-0
    1. Orchids—United States. 2. Orchids—Canada, Eastern. 3. Orchids—
United States—Pictorial works. 4. Orchids—Canada, Eastern—Pictorial
works. 5. United States—Description and travel. 4. Canada, Eastern—
Description and travel. 7. Keenan, Philip E.—Journeys—United States.
8. Keenan, Philip E.—Journeys—Canada, Eastern. I. Title
QK495.064K397 1998   97-43424
584'.4'0973022—dc21   CIP

Contents

Preface

BOTANIZING has been an important part of my life for at least fifty years. Since the age of eleven, I've had a compulsion to know the names of everything I see. The pink lady's-slipper was the first wild orchid I identified, but in those early years I found few orchids on my own. It wasn't until 1958 when I became acquainted with Herman and Hazel Willey of St. Johnsbury, Vermont, that the affliction known as "orchid madness—a very pleasant disease" took hold and never let go.

Like many before me, I was deeply moved by the extraordinary blooms of *Cypripedium acaule* and the striking leaves of *Goodyera pubescens* (rattlesnake plantain). Like the entrepreneur who bought the electric shaver company because he fell in love with the product, I bought the parcel with those goodyeras. Orchid madness indeed! Since then I have driven more than 100,000 miles, walked several hundreds of miles, and flown to all parts of the country while taking thousands of photographs—all in pursuit of the elusive orchid.

Though I have done some scientific research over the years and have a degree in botany and zoology, I am not an academic botanist. I consider myself an amateur in the best sense of the word. Despite our differences in academic training and vocation, however, we all experience similar joys and disappointments in the process of finding, identifying, and learning as much as we can about the largest family in the plant world. The pursuit of our native orchids, for me, is an intellectual and emotional involvement that lends meaning and purpose to my life.

My purpose in writing this book, therefore, is an attempt to whet the appetite of the beginner, while at the same time offering a source of reminiscing for those who have spent time in the field enjoying orchids. If I have succeeded in any way, a great deal of the credit must surely go to the photographs. All were taken in the field, not in the studio or with artificial backgrounds.

In the presentation of these botanical excursions, I have purposely avoided giving explicit directions, in most cases, to the location of the orchids, simply because orchids are not like birds. Nobody shoots or collects birds anymore, but they still pick and dig orchids. Most states have laws protecting orchids but like most laws, some people don't bother to obey them. Harvard's Edward Wilson put it this way, "Each species is a masterpiece, a creation assembled with extreme care and genius." Extinction is forever. It behooves us all to do whatever we can to prevent further destruction.

I have purposely avoided as many technical distractions as possible, realizing at the same time that many readers will want to pursue further information. Therefore, an extensive bibliography is provided, as well as a recommendation of books, an explanation of how the photographs were taken, a current checklist of all Canadian and American orchid species, excluding Florida, together with a derivation guide and pronunciation guide for each species. One must keep in mind when consulting these lists that orchid totals change yearly for a variety of reasons, among them, nomenclatural interpretations, new discoveries, and the extirpation of marginal populations.

I have not mentioned or photographed all the North American species because, in the words of Susan Sontag, "I haven't been everywhere— but it's on my list."

Finally, I have tried to follow the advice of Richard Jeffries: "Those who love nature never can be dull, provided that love is expressed by an intelligent interest rather than a purely sentimental rapture."

> The greatest thing a human soul ever does in this world is to see something, and tell what it saw in a plain way. Hundreds of people can talk for one who can think, but thousands can think for one who can see.
>
> John Ruskin in *Modern Painters*

Acknowledgments

My mother, who started it all.

My wife, Susan, for giving me the encouragement and space to write this book, and for reading, critiquing, and correcting the entire manuscript; our daughter, Barbara, for her expertise in critiquing and, with my wife, for putting me back on track when the word processor was uncooperative; and our sons, Philip, Robert, and Greg, who also helped with computer problems.

The late Herm Willey, for more than thirty years my friend and guide in Vermont, and his wife, Hazel, who treated me as part of the family.

Les Eastman, for his friendship and guidance during the early years in the state of Maine.

Paul Martin Brown, for his friendship, knowledge, and help throughout North America.

Sally Puth and Shirley Curtis, for their camaraderie and slide shows.

Stan Bentley and Bobby Toler, for their help in North Carolina.

Ron Coleman, for guiding me in California and Arizona.

Joseph Welch, for help in Oregon and Arizona.

Alec Pridgeon, Chuck McCartney, and Jim Watson, editors of the American Orchid Society *Bulletin,* for publishing more than twenty-four of my essays and photographs from 1985 to 1997.

The late Albion Hodgdon, former professor of botany at the University of New Hampshire and a source of inspiration.

Garrett Crow, professor of botany at the University of New Hampshire and curator of the Hodgdon Herbarium.

Frankie Brackley, Harry Trowbridge, Dr. George Newman, Hank Tyler, and the late Larry Newcomb, able botanists all.

Anyone I might have missed, who directly or indirectly contributed to the success of this endeavor.

Last but not least, Neal Maillet, executive editor of Timber Press, for his invitation and support to do the book. My sincere thanks.

Introduction

ORCHIDS comprise the largest family of plants in the world—approximately 30,000 species—and the most fascinating, I might add. They account for almost 10 percent of all species of flowering plants. In North America there are approximately 1005 species (Table 1). Only about 205 of these occur north of Mexico, and about 60 are exclusive to the southern half of Florida. Migrants from the Caribbean, these tropical orchids form a unique flora, and to do them justice, a second book is required. Thus, excluding species exclusive to Florida and Mexico, there are approximately 145 orchid species representing thirty-five genera in North America. These species are the focus of this book.

All the native Canadian and American orchids outside of Florida are perennials and monocots. All are terrestrial, except for *Epidendrum conopseum,* the green-fly orchid, which is an epiphyte found as far north as the shores of Lake Waccamaw in North Carolina. Orchids are highly specialized and unique in having one, two, or three stamens (the male part of the flower) united or fused with the pistil (the female part of the flower) into a single structure called the "column." This single feature distinguishes the orchid family from all other plant families. In addition, the ovary in orchids is inferior; that is, it is situated below the whorls of three sepals and three petals. One of the three petals is usually quite different from the other two, forming the distinctive lip petal (Figures 1 and 2). Finally, orchid seeds are the smallest of all plants—dustlike in size—and produced in prodigious amounts, sometimes in the millions. (For a more detailed account of their fascinating morphology, pollination mechanisms, and evolution, consult Dressler 1981, Van Der Pijl and Dodson 1966, and other books listed in the extensive bibliography.)

Table 1. Orchid species totals for selected sites in North America (approximate).

SITE	SPECIES	SITE	SPECIES
United States	205	Rhode Island	37
Alaska	25	Vermont	50
Arizona	25	West Virginia	35
Arkansas	35		
California	32	Canada	75
Colorado	25	Alberta	25
Connecticut	44	British Columbia	35
Florida	110[1]	Keewatin	10
Hawaii	5	Labrador	10
Indiana	40	MacKenzie	15
Kansas	5	Manitoba	30
Kentucky	30	New Brunswick & Nova Scotia	40
Maine	48	Newfoundland	33
Massachusetts	50	Ontario	60
Minnesota	43	Québec	50
New Hampshire	45	Saskatchewan	25
New York	55	Yukon	15
North Carolina	60	Mexico	800

[1] 60 are exclusive to the state

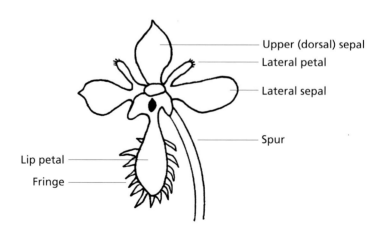

Figure 1. Anatomy of a *Platanthera* flower. Note that the sepals are located outside the petals.

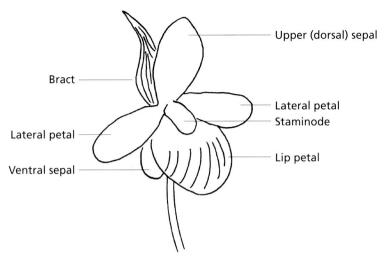

Figure 2. Anatomy of a *Cypripedium* flower. Note that the ventral sepal is formed by two sepals usually united behind the lip.

The two most important factors governing the distribution of orchids are probably temperature and moisture. Soil, topography, and light exposure also play key roles. In what sounds like a contradiction, orchids are extremely adaptable as a group, while at the same time, the specific needs are usually quite exacting, including their so-called mycorrhizal association with certain fungi. Orchid seeds will not germinate and complete their growth without this symbiotic relationship. The fungus provides nutrients to the orchid plant, while the orchid offers a "home" to the fungus. Because orchid seeds are so minuscule in size, they do not have sufficient food storage (as most other plant seeds do) to nourish the developing seedling, hence the critical need for the nutrient-providing fungus. This mycorrhizal association helps to explain why the majority of North American orchids soon die when transplanted from the wild.

One wonders why, with such explosive numbers of seeds, orchids aren't more abundant in nature. A few speculative explanations have been offered over and above human destruction of one sort or another, such as lack of sufficient capsule formation in many populations. However, I recall one large population of *Epipactis helleborine* in central Vermont having a capsule success ratio of nearly 100 percent on several hundred robust plants; every capsule had split open and burst with the whitish gray mass of seeds. Such extraordinary fecundity probably explains this orchid's remarkable expansion in North America in a little over 100 years.

Orchids are found in every conceivable environment except the driest deserts of the Southwest. Where they do occur in the dry, semidesert areas of the Southwest, they are very dependent on moisture and, in consequence, restricted to the proximity of streams, springs, and seepages usually in higher, cooler elevations. Even inside the Arctic Circle at least a dozen species survive very well thanks to the dependable snow cover. *Amerorchis rotundifolia, Coeloglossum viride, Corallorhiza trifida, Cypripedium guttatum* and *C. passerinum, Goodyera repens, Listera borealis* and *L. cordata, Platanthera dilatata, P. hyperborea,* and *P. obtusata, Spiranthes romanzoffiana,* and even *Calypso bulbosa* cross that line at some point.

The geographic areas with the fewest species are Hawaii and the prairies of the Great Plains states. The greatest number of species is to be found in the eastern United States and Canada where the greatest diversity of habitats and concomitant temperature, moisture, soil, and topography is found. Table 1 presents a selective example of this relative distribution, and Appendix 1 presents a current checklist of all Canadian and American orchid species excluding Florida.

One of the most interesting anecdotes in the geographic distribution of orchids, and other plants as well, concerns the similarity of the floras of eastern Asia and eastern North America. More than a dozen species have their counterparts in China and Japan, including *Arethusa bulbosa, Cypripedium acaule, C. arietinum, C. reginae, Galearis spectabilis,* all the listeras except *Listera caurina* (which is endemic to the Pacific Northwest), *Platanthera flava, P. orbiculata,* and *Pogonia ophioglossoides.* What is the explanation for this? Billions of years ago the continental land masses were essentially united in what is called Pangaea, a protocontinent. Since that time, the continents slowly drifted apart to their present locations as the result of plate tectonics, a scientific theory about the movement of the earth's crust through the process of volcanism and earthquakes. The interior of our planet is a hot, molten, mobile mass, as exemplified by the so-called Pacific Rim of Fire, the hotbed of today's geologic activity. The earth has always been on the move and still is.

Cypripedium guttatum, clump with raindrops, Alaska.

ALASKA

CHAPTER 1

Kodiak Island and the Palomino Lady's-slipper

OUR Boeing 737 makes the steep ascent into the murky sky and is quickly assimilated in the leaden gray clouds overhanging Anchorage, Alaska, at seven o'clock in the morning. Two hundred fifty-two miles (403 km) southeast of us, in the Pacific Ocean, Kodiak Island awaits. Since childhood, I have been familiar with this island through an interest in geography, but little did I know then that one day I would actually fly there, not to fish or hunt for grizzlies as most visitors do, but to see and photograph the subtly beautiful *Cypripedium yatabeanum,* the yellow and green lady's-slipper. It is my birthday, 20 June 1995, the day after my daughter's twenty-eighth, two days after Father's Day, and five days before my thirty-fifth anniversary—all four momentous events in the same week, interrupted this year by a once-in-a-lifetime trip to Alaska.

It takes about forty minutes to fly to Kodiak Island, which is as big as the state of Connecticut and the second largest island in the United States after Hawaii. Ordinarily, mountains are visible from the window of the plane, and, of course, the Pacific Ocean. This morning nothing is visible. "Prepare for 'possible' landing," the pilot breaks in. Sally Puth, my seat partner, and I look out the window and see a vast basin of dark gray deck paint slopping miserably up and down, masquerading as the cold Pacific Ocean, and what is more foreboding, only 200 feet (60 m) or so, it appears, below the behemoth in which we are buckled up. At this moment, the deafening roar of engines, like that on the takeoff, thrusts the plane from the horizontal to the vertical, in an attempt to abort the landing. "Oh, my God," I take a deep breath, "this is it, we are going to crash. We're too close to the water to abort now!"

Cypripedium yatabeanum, with raindrops, Kodiak Island, Alaska.

Moments later, safe again in the clouds, the pilot explains he is unable to see the lights on the runway and cannot land. Kodiak is a tiny airstrip with no radar facilities. It requires visual flight rules (VFR) in the soupy fog and rain, which is the norm about 50 percent of the time according to our flight attendant—a bit scary when you consider the many mountains surrounding the airport. Conditions are even worse and more hairy

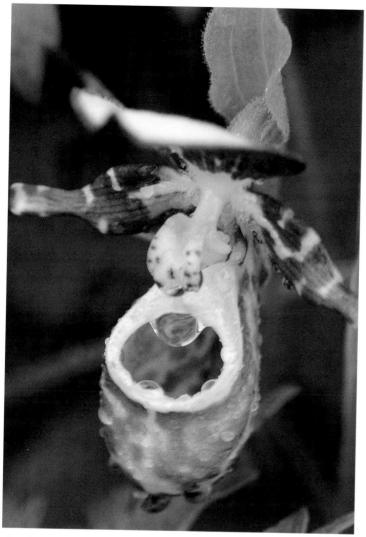

Cypripedium yatabeanum, with raindrops, Kodiak Island, Alaska.

the further out you fly in the western Aleutians, the flight attendant also attests, in places like Attu and Adak, where Carlyle Luer picked up the little yellow *Platanthera tipuloides* for his well-known book, *The Native Orchids of the United States and Canada Excluding Florida* (1975), the "bible" of native orchids in North America. However, there are six flights a day to Kodiak from Anchorage, and we manage to catch a successful flight later the same day when the ceiling lifts enough to see the landing strip and the base of the surrounding mountains.

Kodiak, an Inuit word for island, is also known as the Emerald Isle because the majority of the island is clothed completely in green, with grasses and wildflowers mostly, and pockets of alders and willows, but essentially no trees. Only in the northeastern corner are conifers present and these are exclusively Sitka spruce (*Picea sitchensis*), a coastal fog-belt species found only within 30 miles (48 km) of the coastline in the 2000 miles (3200 km) from extreme northern California to southern Alaska. The largest native spruce, it is also the fourth tallest tree in the world, reaching over 200 feet (60 m) with a girth of more than 3 feet (1 m) at the base. In Abercrombie State Park, in the northeast corner of the island and just outside the only city, Kodiak City, a magnificent Sitka spruce forest represents the westernmost terminus of the great Hudsonian Coniferous forest that stretches clear across the continent, from the Maritimes of eastern Canada to extreme southeastern Alaska, where we stand in the northeastern corner of Kodiak Island. It is a wonderful maritime rain forest, indeed, thickly draped in coats of lush green mosses and lichens. Even the appropriately named nurse logs strewn over the floor are festooned in the same lush, thick padding of mosses, lichens, and seedlings, all in shades of green, of course. This forest reminds me of the famous Hoh rain forest in Olympic National Park in northwestern Washington. Both forests are products of the same type of wet maritime climate that squeezes more than 70 inches (177 cm) of rainfall from the clouds that constantly roll in from the Pacific Ocean.

Great quantities of the green and purple forms of heart-leaved twayblade (*Listera cordata*) abound beneath the Sitka spruce forest. In the boggy, wet low spots, the slender bog-orchid (*Platanthera stricta*) grows like a weed to 3 feet (90 cm). Similar to *P. hyperborea*, as so many greenflowered and white-flowered platantheras are in the difficult *dilatata-hyperborea* complex, this species is distinguished rather easily, in this case, by the short saccate or scrotiform spur behind a linear lip. Later on, we stop for more heavy populations of *P. stricta* in "downtown" Kodiak City. The slender bog-orchid follows the coast from northern California, through British Columbia, into coastal Alaska and the Aleutian Island chain.

Next to this incredible rain forest cliffside, overlooking Monashka Bay and the Pacific Ocean, sits an equally incredible, though small, wildflower meadow filled with an embarrassment of riches for the botanist. In the cool mist and drizzle, we tiptoe along the trail, trying to avoid tramping on any one of thousands of just-opened wildflowers. Some are still in bud, but overall we have timed our arrival perfectly, according to Stacey Studebaker, a very gracious guide who stays with us on her beloved island for three full days.

The list of blooming plants is a long one at Abercrombie with representatives of almost every wildflower growing on the island. Some of the main attractions include the chocolate lily (*Fritillaria camschatcensis*), a deep true chocolate brown unlike anything I have seen before, with colloquial names like skunk lily and outhouse lily because of its smelly flowers; the 3-foot (90-cm) Aleutian or Nootka lupine (*Lupinus arcticus*), a showy blue display of pealike flowers transfigured magically this particular afternoon by silver jewels of water drops on the large palmate leaves; the pretty pink Pacific geranium (*Geranium erianthum*), also with palmate leaves but differently made, precluding a display of the caliber of the lupine nearby; the cream-colored narcissus-flowered anemone (*Anemone narcissiflora*); two species of dwarf cornel or Canadian dogwood, one the same as ours back East (*Cornus canadensis*) and the other with black "flowers" in the center of the white bracts (*C. suecica*), the so-called Swedish cornel; rose-colored shooting stars (*Dodecatheon pulchellum*); and the red-purple Aleutian purple orchis (*Dactylorhiza aristata*), one of several orchids on the island. The incredible diversity and richness of the flora here may be partly the result of the accumulation of ash from the cataclysmic June 1912 explosion of Mount Novarupta, the second largest blast in recorded history, on the Alaska Peninsula.

To me, all these wildflowers pale compared to the object of most of my attention on this island, that unique lady's-slipper, *Cypripedium yatabeanum*, only recently reinstated to its original specific status. The Palomino lady's-slipper is an appropriate common name, marked as it is in similar fashion to the pony of that name and preferable to spotted lady's-slipper, which is more correctly applied, in my opinion, to *C. guttatum*, the mainland species. Both species have a unique lip among cypripediums, in which the top of the pouch is wide open and almost perfectly round, remindful of the genus *Paphiopedilum*. While the ground color of *C. guttatum* is white, that of *C. yatabeanum* is cream. Muted shades of cream, tan, olive, and brown blend on all sides of the pouch, while purple-brown spots dot the narrow, creamy lateral petals, which extend straight out from the sides of the "saddle pouch." Camouflaged is another apt description for this lady's-slipper. Sometimes the lip blotches merge and cover most of the top edge of the lip pouch.

The steady drizzle and mist create a painterly effect on the edge and sides of the polished pitcher, which reminds me of the psalmist's words, "my cup runneth over." Water droplets collect and teeter on the edge of the pitcher and drip down the sides. I hurry to record this sensuous masterpiece in miniature, created by the wonderful alchemy of mist and drizzle, before any breeze or misplaced tripod leg destroys the effect. Of course, everything else is covered in water drops at this moment, but none more beautifully than *Cypripedium yatabeanum*. There is something invigorating about inclement weather, especially in these circumstances, not to mention the opportunity to take advantage of the soft, uniform lighting. To most people, even some photographers, it is something to avoid. Preoccupied by all these thoughts, I am at first oblivious and then thankful—ah, yes, creature comforts—for my Asolo hiking shoes and their Gore-Tex lining that keep my feet perfectly dry.

Cypripedium yatabeanum was discovered and named for Dr. R. Yatabe, who found it on Mount Togakushi in Honshu, Japan, while a professor of biology in Tokyo. This species replaces *C. guttatum* in Japan, as well as on the Kamchatka Peninsula on the eastern edge of the Asian mainland and on the Aleutian Islands of Alaska, including Kodiak. It probably hybridizes with *C. guttatum* on the Alaska Peninsula where we found intermediate forms southeast of Anchorage.

The following day, under more low overcast and drizzle, we drive south for almost two hours on the island's single north-south road. We are headed for Pasagshak Point at the southeastern corner of Kodiak Island. Kodiak City has a population of around 7500, or approximately half the island's total population of 15,000. The city is the sixth largest in the state. The average temperature in the summer is only 53°F (12°C), and it almost never reaches 80°F (27°C). Couple this with mist and rain at least 50 percent of the time and you have a climate hardly suited for people who like the heat and sun. The cost of getting a break from this moisture is $250 per round trip to Anchorage on the mainland, a price most people can't afford more than a few times a year. Two-thirds of the island is a National Wildlife Refuge for protecting the world famous Kodiak brown bear or grizzly, the largest of the grizzlies and land carnivores in the world. There are about 3000 of these remarkable animals on Kodiak—one-fifth the human population. Unfortunately, we have no time for bears on this trip.

On Pasagshak Point, we meet our first buffaloes and American eagles, with splendid panoramic vistas that spread in every direction from the ocean to the mountains. At noontime, the sun begins to appear through cracks and thin spots in the overcast, a welcome relief. The beauty of the wide open green spaces up and down the low mountains slowly intensifies with the brilliant shafts of sun playing down from above, like a vast landscape painting. The emerald green slopes, reminding some of Ireland, are dotted with clumps of the red alder (*Alnus setosa*) and little else, as far as the eye can see. The same wildflower palette that graced the slopes of Abercrombie State Park greets us here; the big difference is sun and warmth. What a perfect way to spend six relaxed hours. Almost a hundred years before, in 1899, the great naturalist-writer John Burroughs spent the first week of July on Kodiak Island, ten days later than us. He was more fortunate weatherwise, but the landscape was the same as today. Listen to him (Burroughs 1901):

> The sky was clear and the prospect most inviting. Smooth treeless, green hills and mountains surrounded us. I warn my reader here, that henceforth I shall babble continually of green fields. There was no end to them. To eyes sated with the wild, austere grandeur of Prince William Sound the change was most delightful.

Half the group choose to climb the nearby mountain slope, in distant company with a pair of buffalo, while Chris Hobbs and I decide to take advantage of a rare opportunity to do some birding. Earlier, on our arrival, sparrows were flying up from the meadow grasses on the edge of the cliff, as we moved up and down from photographic positions in the grassy vegetation. Without binoculars, they appeared to be white-crowned sparrows, the back of the white crown noticeable as they dropped into the grass. Now, with glasses and frontal views, the handsome bright golden-yellow crown stripe shows to advantage, contrasting with the black eyebrow line. A large sparrow, it is a new lifer for me. Savanna sparrows, the color of those back in New Hampshire, and fox sparrows, not the same color as those back home, but darker, are also here. The latter are a uniform dark chocolate, almost black, unlike the eastern subspecies. A few Wilson's warblers hang out among the alders beside the road, and American eagles glide off the cliffs.

Earlier, a young woman jogs up the highland "road." She is a geologist working for NASA, just down the road a bit. When she sees our vehicles, curiosity gets the best of her as almost no one makes it to this remote spot. Stephanie Stockman is studying the effects of subduction, a process in which the Pacific Plate (under the ocean) is slowly pushing up the North American Continental Plate (on land) more than 2 inches (5 cm) a year. Kodiak Island is rising that much on its south coast as a result of this process. Speaking of the remoteness of the place, the ride up here, off the main road, which is gravel, is an experience worth noting. Barely two wheel tracks wide, our two vehicles almost become hung up and stranded by the thick growth of overhanging alders on both sides. Despite a pruning by someone recently we make very slow progress while the branches scrape, bang, and bounce off the vehicles. The destination proves worth the effort and risk, however, as already noted.

In addition to more *Cypripedium yatabeanum,* mostly in bud here, and all the other things we saw at Abercrombie, the Kodiak variety of the Aleutian orchis, *Dactylorhiza aristata* var. *kodiakensis,* with purple-spotted leaves, is a first for all of us. Also a first for us is *Malaxis diphyllos,* formerly a variety of *M. monophyllos,* which we find budded in a sheltered depression beside the "road" in a spot behind the windswept cliffs that is pleasantly quiet this afternoon during the brief interlude of sunshine. Several differences separate it from *M. monophyllos:* twice as many flowers on a larger plant, up to 12 inches (30 cm) tall, with yellow instead of greenish white flowers, according to Luer (1975). A few robust but short-of-stature—as is everything here—frog orchids (*Coeloglossum viride*) are tucked away in the grasses at the very edge of the cliff, requiring constant care and awareness while positioning to photograph. One false step and it is *sayonara.* There are two varieties of this orchid: variety *viride* is circumpolar and mostly Eurasian in distribution, and variety *virescens* is North America's so-called long-bracted green orchis. Long bracted it certainly is. Here the plant is much shorter than in most of its range, I suspect, and is rather hard to make out in the green surroundings. It is one of those plain green orchids with just a touch of pink near the base of the lip, twice as tall as the Eurasian variety, with a wide range of height, between 4 and 36 inches (10 and 90 cm) or so. The sepals and petals almost unite to form a rounded hood, resembling the head of the frog. The hanging lip suggests the tongue of the frog to those with imagination.

In another nearby area, Mariano Ospina, a fellow orchidist from Colombia, South America, makes a remarkable discovery of *Dactylorhiza aristata* var. *kodiakensis* forma *perbracteata,* the leafy, flowerless form of the species that hasn't been seen since 1949, according to our leader Paul Martin Brown. Large purple bracts replace the showy magenta flowers in this form. While waiting our turn to photograph the single plant, Sally Puth and I scout the meadow's edge, surprising a beautiful cross fox that a handsome magpie is scolding. It is interesting that the genus *Dactylorhiza* is so variable and unstable that, despite several centuries of inten-

Coeloglossum viride, Kodiak Island, Alaska.   *Coeloglossum viride,* showing long bracts of var. *virescens,* New Hampshire.

sive study, there is still no agreement on the taxonomy and identification of species in this genus, both here and in Europe. The phenomenon of hybridization or active speciation leads to an unprecedented situation where hybrids and forms outnumber the parents.

On the long drive back to our quarters at the Buskin River Inn, adjacent to the airport, we see an unusual sight: a pair of American eagles sitting side by side in a tree nest right beside the road and staring at us as we drive by, completely unperturbed. What a fitting climax to a memorable day in the field! Someday I must return to this remarkable spot on our fragile earth, one of Alaska's best-kept secrets, rain or no rain.

Dactylorhiza aristata var. *kodiakensis* forma *perbracteata,* flowerless form of the Kodiak orchid, Kodiak Island, Alaska.

CHAPTER 2

The Purple Spotted Lady's-slipper in Alaska

CYPRIPEDIUM *guttatum,* as the name implies, is known as the spotted lady's-slipper in most circles. One Alaskan field guide, however, calls it the pink lady's-slipper, conflicting with the eastern pink lady's-slipper, *C. acaule,* and ignoring the distinctive spotting characteristic.

Cypripedium guttatum is one of the most spectacular lady's-slippers. However, in my reading of the literature it has received little recognition for this, probably because historically Alaska lacks books in the genre of *Our Wild Orchids* (Morris and Eames 1929) and *Bog Trotting for Orchids* (Niles 1904). Correll (1950), who perhaps never saw this orchid, dismissed it with one paragraph in *Native Orchids of North America North of Mexico.* Two or three Alaskan field guides also treat it tersely. Hennessy and Hedge (1989) devoted a full page to this species in their colorful and life-size book, *The Slipper Orchids,* including a pretty but not accurate life-size watercolor. Carlyle Luer (1975), on the other hand, did see this cypripedium and probably has more to say about this "flower of singular beauty" than any other author I have read. An interesting cover painting and article in the Spring 1994 issue of *Wildflower Magazine* by R. W. Tyler of Homer, Alaska, is the only magazine piece I have come across. He writes,

> there are a select few plants whose range, while fairly broad, is limited in ways that make it a very special occasion to encounter them. Surely the lady's-slippers fall into this category. Here in Alaska, two species are fairly common, *Cypripedium passerinum* and *C. guttatum,* the former the more abundant, being found throughout most of the interior of the state.

He goes on to describe his first meeting with *C. guttatum* in the Homer area, on the southern coast.

In any event, *Cypripedium guttatum* was "numero uno" on my list of must-see for almost thirty years, and so, on the afternoon of 19 June 1995, the day of first-hand judgment finally arrives. We leave the Glenn Highway near Sutton, Alaska, late in the afternoon on our way back "home" to Anchorage after a long day in the field near Matanuska Glacier. Miles of gravel roads and intersections, with subdivision signs everywhere, are a challenge but we have good detailed directions and soon pull over to park at the designated spot. Walking up a slight rise we begin to see our first plants scattered beside what appears to be a seldom-used driveway. Some in our group stop and photograph these single plants, but having been told earlier that the main body consists of upwards of five thousand plants, I run to the crest of the knoll and descend on the lake-side slope. I can barely believe my eyes. Beneath the open paper birch (*Betula papyrifera*) overstory and intermingled with the dwarf dogwood or bunchberry (*Cornus canadensis*) are lady's-slippers so thick it is impossible to move without stepping on some of them. On this sunnier (warmer) side of the slope about half of them are past prime and I momentarily wonder if we are too late.

Continuing around the slope, perfect specimens appear, and my eyes are transfixed by the very large, overarching, white-as-snow, red-edged dorsal sepals, which, quite frankly, are almost as beautiful as the remainder of the flower, as you stand over it. Once the eye is able to overcome the almost magnetic pull of this commanding upper sepal, the remaining beauty of the flower can be appreciated and studied at length. I am impressed by the astounding beauty and configuration of purple-red spots and blotches on the lateral petals, which project outward, and on the lip pouch, where they often merge into larger patches, in many instances covering most of the upper half of the otherwise white pouch. The spotting on the conspicuous lateral petals is always uniformly beautiful. Put a few dozen of these flowers in motion with the wind and my mind's eye conjures calico-colored flocks of ruddy turnstones gliding to a landing, in migration on the beaches and rocky shores of New England.

The plant is not large, usually under 10 inches (25 cm) or so, with lips about an inch (2.5 cm) long and half that wide, and only two nearly basal, subopposite leaves. This species and *Cypripedium yatabeanum,* its close-ly related cousin on Kodiak Island, possess a lip pouch (labellum) that opens at the top, somewhat similar to that in *Paphiopedilum,* the larger genus of Asiatic slipper orchids. This opening and the general rounded look of the sides suggest an overall bucket effect, however demeaning that word may be to the remarkable beauty of the flower. The large over-arching dorsal sepal seems to act as a protective roof for the reproductive organs positioned underneath.

Cypripedium guttatum ranges widely from central Russia to eastern Siberia, and from central Alaska into the Yukon Territory of northwestern Canada, as well as in a few well-separated sites near the Seward-Homer area on the south central coast. It is replaced in Japan and the Aleutians by *C. yatabeanum.* Additional Alaskan sites, I would suspect, remain undiscovered over this land that is largely unexplored botanically.

To spend the entire day here would have been frosting on the cake—

Cypripedium guttatum, group from overhead, Alaska.

on my daughter's twenty-eighth birthday and the day before my own. An additional bonus would have been a picture-postcard view of Seventeen Mile Lake: fair weather cumulus clouds floating across a blue ceiling in front of distant snow-covered mountains. Unfortunately, there is little time to savor either view. The two hours seem like minutes, so conscious am I of the limited time. Sooner than later, the horn sounds from the other side of the hill, a reminder that all good things must end. One of the distinct advantages of Alaska in the summertime is the twenty hours of daylight, which drops to six in the winter. Although it is early evening under what is still high and bright sun, we have miles to go before we sleep, not to mention eat.

We see two hundred more *Cypripedium guttatum,* as promised, opposite the hotel in Denali National Park. In contrast to Seventeen Mile Lake, the drizzle and mist here add a desirable prop of water droplets to the sides of the "bucket" pouch. The diffused, dull light of the overcast shifts the colors to the cool blue side of the spectrum and away from the warmer reds; glare and strong contrasts are eliminated, a type of lighting many pros prefer. In my opinion, however, nothing surpasses the beauty displayed on that Seventeen Mile Lake hillside under the dappled sun. To paraphrase the great English poet and writer of the mid-nineteenth century, Elizabeth Browning, in a poem titled "The Best,"

> What's the best thing in the world?
> Pleasure, not in haste to end;
> Memory that gives no pain; . . .
> What's the best thing in the world?
> Something out of it I think.

To my mind, the purple spotted lady's-slipper is the best thing in the world of lady's-slippers. It has often been said that a wish fulfilled is seldom as sweet as its anticipation, but not so with *C. guttatum.*

The Denali site, only a few feet off the parking lot, is most convenient, almost as if a hotel employee or park staff had transplanted the orchids. The question becomes: what will happen to the orchids when inevitably the parking lot is expanded? Apparently, *C. guttatum* is not known anywhere else in this very large park of six million acres (2.4 million ha), the equivalent of the entire state of Vermont.

Alaska is big. How big you ask? Bigger than Texas and California combined! Only a handful of orchids is listed for Denali, which, by the way, lies within 75 miles (120 km) of the geographic center of the state of Alaska. The total number of vascular plant species in Alaska is approximate-

Cypripedium guttatum, showing dramatic dorsal sepal, Alaska.

ly 1500, while twice that number, approximately 3000, occur in New England, an area almost ten times smaller than Alaska. Alaska has about thirty species of orchids, while New England again has about twice that number. Finally, Alaska has fewer species of trees than any other state in the country.

Denali National Park and the "mountain," namely, 20,000-foot (6000-m) Mount McKinley (now Denali), are not the biggest tourist attractions in Alaska. Portage Glacier, 50 miles (80 km) south of Anchorage, near the Gulf of Alaska, claims that honor. More than 650,000 visitors crowd this one glacier each year, a number greater than the total population of the entire state of Alaska, which is around 600,000.

Cypripedium guttatum, pair with raindrops, Alaska.

Unfortunately, our four days in Denali are all the same—low overcast with a combination of periodic light rain and drizzle at a steady temperature of 45° to 55°F (7° to 13°C). This combination of circumstances is not pleasant if you want to experience the mountain. To make matters worse, each day's forecast during the entire week called for clearing skies. Only when we arrived back in Anchorage, however, did the sun come out again. This is not unusual. On average, the mountain is visible only one in three days, and a solid week of unpleasant weather is often the rule. One must be philosophical.

CHAPTER 3

Eklutna Lake and Matanuska River Valley Orchids

PORTAGE Glacier is not on our botanical itinerary, which is just as well, I suspect, in view of the tremendous crowding, especially on weekends. In its place, however, we do spend two of the best days of the entire trip, in terms of weather, at Eklutna Lake in Chugach State Park, and in the Matanuska River valley on the Glenn Highway. In fact these two or three days are the only sunny, warm ones we experience in Alaska.

Between Palmer and Glenallen on the Glenn Highway, about 100 miles (160 km) north of Anchorage, several orchids become common, notably sparrow's-egg lady's-slipper (*Cypripedium passerinum*) at peak bloom, one-leaf orchis (*Amerorchis rotundifolia*), likewise in perfect bloom, and *Calypso bulbosa* var. *americana,* a week or more past flowering except for one fine patch that produces two or three good specimens of the previously unknown (in Alaska) pink-lipped form, or forma *rosea* (first published in the *North American Native Orchid Journal* of March 1995). This section of south central Alaska is scarcely hyped in the guidebooks despite the great mountain scenery and wonderful wildflowers. Of course, Alaska is full of amazing scenery, but I wonder how long this happy state of affairs will last on this stretch of road. Already real estate signs are sprouting and subdivisions staked out amid the orchids, as we feverishly photograph thousands of sparrow's-egg lady's-slipper and one-leaf orchis, a few with a suggestion of the confluent purple lines on the lip as in *A. rotundifolia* forma *lineata,* growing almost like weeds all over the place. The brilliant sunshine, 70°F (21°C), makes everything even more pleasant. The experience is quite a contrast to my other experiences with these two orchids in Ontario and Maine.

It is ironic that the most beautiful and oftentimes rarest orchids choose their homesites on the same basis that humans do: the most fertile of soils and most scenic of views. In this case, "home" directly overlooking the Matanuska Glacier, which glints in the garish backlight of the brilliant summer solstice of the Alaskan summer, on the banks of the wide, wide, wide Matanuska River. Some fortunate people will shortly own a vacation home with a backyard and frontyard covered with wild orchids. On the other hand, the cynic in me suggests a worse fate: the new owners will either be oblivious to the orchids or prefer the artificiality of a lawn. In either case the bulldozer wins.

Almost as plentiful as the more conspicuous orchids, *Platanthera obtusata* is also in prime condition. *Listera borealis* and *L. cordata*, *Platanthera hyperborea* and *Corallorhiza trifida* are scattered further up the side road. Almost as lovely as the orchids, *Pyrola grandiflora*, with its larger raceme of creamy white flowers, stands out among the greenery. Nothing unusual about this habitat, which makes up a good portion of the woody vegetation in this part of Alaska. Consisting of white spruce (*Picea glauca*), trembling aspen (*Populus tremuloides*), and balsam poplar (*P. balsamifera*), the habitat has been previously lumbered, of course.

On most stops in the Alaskan countryside, one is advised to be aware of the possibilities of an encounter with a brown or black bear. Relaxing while photographing in the woods requires vigilance on our part, at the least looking up from the camera every few seconds. No bears are seen here. Another day, on the shores of Eklutna Lake, inside the half-million-acre (200,000-ha) Chugach State Park, the second largest state park in the nation and only 7 miles (11 km) from downtown Anchorage, our luck changes.

We are walking on a trail around Eklutna Lake, within view of the water but in the woods. I happen to be in the lead, some 50 yards (45 m) or so ahead of the group when, suddenly, the biggest grizzly-size black bear I've ever seen ambles out of the brush onto a side trail that connects with the one I am on, only 50 yards (45 m) or so to my right. I stop. He stops. We stare, each deciding his next move, he whether to continue coming my way, and I, momentarily indecisive, whether to slowly raise my camera for a quick picture, or somehow signal the rest of the group behind me without scaring off the bear. I make the wrong decision and the bear

Corallorhiza trifida, Vermont.

moves off in the opposite direction, back into the woods and out of sight.

Any trip to Alaska is enhanced by a reading of John McPhee's classic *Coming Into the Country* (1977). One of the things I remember most in the book is the discussion of life and death, "the all-pervading mesh that holds things together" on the Alaskan frontier. Ecology for most knowledgeable Alaskans "means who's eating whom, and when." This definition is a bit different from the academic definition. When asked if there was anything he feared, one individualist replied that there was nothing for him to fear. He expected that he would die someday and become food for someone else.

Eklutna Lake is a beautiful 7-mile (11-km) long glacially carved body of water with mountains all around it. The mountain backdrop of the same name is made very picturesque by the many white streaks of snow radiating down the slopes. Several bands of Dall sheep are grazing on the newly emerging green "lawns." Because this type of landscape is seen almost everywhere on a sunny day, this particular one rates no more than a sentence in most guidebooks. To us, however, it is one of the few mountains we see completely in the clear and so it rates raves. The Chugach mountains that form the backdrop to Eklutna and the city of Anchorage are the second highest mountain range in Alaska and the highest coastal mountains in the world. The highest point in the range is Mount Baker at just over 13,000 feet (3900 m). Ten percent of the park is covered with glaciers.

Another day at Eklutna Lake is notable for several prime clumps of *Listera borealis,* the northern twayblade. Much smaller than my favorite *L. caurina,* the northern twayblade has a wide distribution across northern Canada, extending into the United States only in the northern Rockies. The lip differs in being oblong, with parallel sides, and significantly

Corallorhiza trifida, bronze form, Alaska.

indented at the apex. *Listera auriculata* more nearly resembles *L. bore-alis.* In fact, close examination is required to identify it when one is botanizing in overlapping territories of the two species such as northern Ontario and Québec. As the name implies, the pair of incurving lobes (auricles) at the base of the oblong lip is diagnostic in *L. auriculata.*

Listera borealis, detail showing straight auricles, Alaska.

Listera auriculata, detail showing incurving auricles at base of lip, New Hampshire.

On the 14-mile (22-km) drive into the park from the Glenn Highway, several interesting other wildflowers keep us company. A lemon-yellow paintbrush (*Castilleja unalascensis*), the prickly rose with very sharp spines (*Rosa acicularis*), and the cow parsnip (*Heraciaum ianatum*) are dominant among the flowers in bloom, as they are along many of the roads of central and south Alaska. Another notoriously formidable adversary that forms an impenetrable dense understory in the shaded forest is the well-named devil's club (*Echinopanax horridum*). The ubiquitous fireweed (*Epilobium angustifolium*), only in bud while we are here, blooms in July and August. It is the one we see in most photographs of the Alaskan landscape, grossly overdone by photographers in my opinion. One other species of fireweed does bloom here in late June, *Epilobium latifolium,* a relatively low, sprawling river beauty under 20 inches (50 cm) in height, in contrast to the 3- to 5-foot (60- to 150-cm) *E. angustifolium.*

CHAPTER 4

North America's Tiniest Orchid

RETURNING to Anchorage around six o'clock in the evening after a rather long and tedious (only because of the drizzle and low overcast) five-hour ride from Denali National Park, study group leader Paul Martin Brown allows a quick stop for changing at our Motel 46 headquarters before we hit the bog in "downtown" Anchorage for the tiniest of all North American orchids, *Malaxis paludosa*, the little bog malaxis.

"You're going to have to lie in 2 feet (60 cm) of water to get the picture!"

"Are you kidding?"

"No! And better wear a bathing suit if you brought one. Or shorts."

"Sure, Paul."

"Mosquitoes are bad, too!"

This caveat deters half the group, already tired, not to make the effort.

"Well," I say to myself, "no point in taking my camera bag along as there will be no place to set it down."

That proves to be a mistake. The water level has gone down in the intervening three days since Paul first scouted the bog, essentially eliminating the water problem. The mosquitoes are no problem, either, but the missing equipment is. I must work with a Canon EOS 10S and 100 mm macro, instead of an Olympus OM 4 with an OM telescoping tube and 80 mm macro lens that allows greater than life-size images. Just what this tiniest orchid needs. I should have at least brought it along in the vehicle, just in case. Instead I simplified, I thought, as Thoreau always advocated.

The bog is filled with quaking mosses, and the Alaskan variety of sweet gale (*Myrica gale*), both sundews (*Drosera rotundifolia* and *D. anglica,* the linear species). Once I see the orchid for the first time, it proves relatively easy to spot again and again. In fact, we find more than a hundred plants in a very compact area. The bog malaxis stands only 3 to 6 inches (7.5 to 15 cm) above the moss bed, which in turn sits on about a foot (30 cm) of water. Without the dual props of moss and other vegetation, the plant would probably be unable to sustain an upright position by itself, it is so tiny and fragile. Any attempt to prop up the stem or do any "housekeeping" on distracting backgrounds will dislodge the superficial bulb that teeters on its soft bed of mosses. Easily jostled by techno sapiens and their equipment, we must be extremely careful moving about. The sun beats down on it most of the day, with no adverse effect, apparently. Now, at seven o'clock in the evening, everything is just about perfect, the movement of air not a factor.

Three darker lime-green stripes on a pale green ground highlight the tiny triangular, uppermost lip petal—another example of a nonresupinate lip—below which the microscopic yellow pollen contrasts sharply. The two lateral petals are almost unnoticeable to the naked eye, so minute are they, as are the slightly larger sepals that flank the lip. The lip is approximately 1.5 by 1 mm in size. There are tiny "bulbils" at the end of the two or three fleshy, ovate-keeled, basal leaves, which sprout new plants when they decay. This unique habit has prompted some taxonomists to put this orchid in a genus of its own. Some even tried to ascribe epiphytic tendencies to it solely on this habit.

Morris and Eames (1929) devoted almost six pages to the challenge of the hunt for this tiny orchid in Ontario near Thunder Bay, hitting the jackpot with nearly 100 plants—as we do today—but after a much greater amount of effort than ours. To these authors, the first encounter with this minute orchid rated a "biggest thrill." Widely dispersed across northern Europe and Asia where it apparently is less rare, *Malaxis paludosa* was first discovered and named in 1800 from Sweden. It took another 105 years, however, to find it in North America, in Minnesota. Shortly after this discovery, more plants were found on a relatively narrow swath of territory northwest to central Alaska, but the plant is elusive and rare almost everywhere in North America.

A block-sized remnant of a much larger original bog and lake in downtown Anchorage is home to this remarkable midget of an orchid whose flowers are not much bigger than the head of a needle. Fortunately,

the few remaining acres of this bog are under at least temporary protection from the
developmental pressures encroaching on all
four sides in a city of 250,000 people. Of the
95,000 native people in Alaska, which represent only about 15 percent of the total state
population of almost 600,000 people, 16,000
of these live in Anchorage while only 6000
call Fairbanks home, further north near the
center of the state.

Another extremely vulnerable Anchorage
bog is not too far from the airport in the
southwest sector of the city. Klatt Bog is located on the road by the same name, which
in turn is off Victor Road and Southport
Road. New housing developments encroach
on all four sides of this bog, too. Wall to wall
with Labrador tea (*Ledum groenlandicum*)
and other tough, stiff heath plants, on a very
thick, bouncy sphagnum moss bed, the 300
yards (273 m) of trudging is difficult and tiring when trying to make time, like walking
on a water bed the size of a football field. The
local native plant society is making a valiant

Malaxis paludosa, showing striped upper lip.

effort to save the remaining acreage from inevitable and complete destruction. What a pity, for this bog harbors several dozen unique intermediate forms of *Cypripedium yatabeanum* and *C. guttatum*. Brown
(1995a), as a consequence, described a new hybrid, *C.* ×*alaskanum*. The
pouch is almost entirely splotched olive-yellow to yellow-brown, on
some specimens. Others are yellow-brown to brown-purple, with more
maroon in the blotches. The lateral petals have some of the purple blotches of *C. guttatum*, while the dorsal sepal is creamy white on the upper
surface and washed out purplish on the under surface. This plant is attractive indeed and unmistakably different from the putative parents.

Klatt is one of the only sites to harbor this hybrid. Will it escape the
bulldozer parked only a few hundred yards away? The next year or two
will decide its fate, I suspect.

CANADA

Corallorhiza striata, Ontario.

CHAPTER 5

Arethusas in the Maritimes and Newfoundland

My wife and I are nearly 2000 feet (600 m) above the Gulf of St. Lawrence, in Cape Breton Highlands National Park, Nova Scotia, on top of French Mountain Plateau. The atmosphere is 100 percent saturated in mist and rain as I kneel in cold water to get in the best position for a picture of that famous water nymph, *Arethusa bulbosa*. There are hundreds of them in this bog, but all are short and runty. Nevertheless, they stick out among the blooming bog laurel (*Kalmia polifolia*), the bog rosemary (*Andromeda glaucophylla*), the Labrador tea (*Ledum groenlandicum*), and that curious frilly white member of the gentian family, the buckbean (*Menyanthes trifoliata*). I am soaked from head to toe, and, as usual, oblivious to the elements. Not one other person walks the boardwalk on this morning of 29 June 1985, the dismal cold and rain discouraging everybody and everything except me and one unexpected butterfly.

The butterfly is about the size of a sulfur or cabbage butterfly, but red! I think I know my butterflies, but this one is new to me. Must be a color phase, I surmise. Unfortunately, there is no ranger around. In fact, not until we get into Fundy National Park two days later do we see a ranger and he knows nothing about butterflies. I look it up to no avail; as I suspect, there just aren't any red butterflies in this part of the world, at least according to the books I have.

The Cape Breton arethusas are forgotten, however, when we stop at another raised bog, 34 miles (54 km) west of St. John, New Brunswick, on the Trans-Canada Highway. Driving alongside this huge bog, edged with Labrador tea in bloom everywhere in the Maritimes, I catch a glimpse of pink, which, at ground level in a bog up here, means only one thing.

Parking on the shoulder of the road, I hurry from the car with camera equipment in hand, jump the narrow water-filled moat separating the bog from the road, race to the clumps of pink, and find myself immersed in water and well over two thousand arethusas, the likes of which I have never seen before. In less than an acre (0.4 ha) I find some specimens more than a foot (30 cm) tall and deep rose to light pink, but no albinos. I do not have time to explore more than a fraction of the bog.

The plants are blowing in a gale. Oh, for a calm moment, I beg, as the minutes tick away. I am determined to get at least a few decent photographs despite the wind, so I wait, and wait, and wait—forty-five minutes of pure frustration. I also stare at the multiple sparkle of sunbeams reflecting off the shallow water below the colorful arethusas; a wonderful background, I sense immediately. Normally, arethusa habitat is more

Arethusa bulbosa, fen, New Brunswick.

typically the edge of a quaking bog, unlike this one, and wet ericaceous (heaths) meadows where the stems are half hidden by mosses, grasses, and woody growth. In such a situation the rosy-pink dragon's mouth barely pokes above the vegetation, and one must look carefully to spot it, but there is no such problem here. I can't recall ever being more excited about an orchid spectacle than this one, even though arethusa is not my favorite orchid or the most beautiful, an opinion that differs from that of many other orchid enthusiasts, I might add.

I steal a quick look far off in the distance, in a corner of the bog. I am flabbergasted by the size of several hundred pitcher plants (*Sarracenia purpurea*), which I am not able to pursue. I am maddeningly aware that I left the emergency lights flashing back at the car with the motor off. I must, therefore, hustle back before I want to. Maybe this particular scenario of haste on the one hand and frustrating wind on the other contributes to my excitement for these arethusas. At any rate, when I race back to the car, the battery is dead. "Now what?" I wonder in the middle of nowhere. I raise the hood of the car, and within five minutes, a car heading toward St. John, in the opposite direction, makes a U-turn and pulls up behind us. The driver removes a set of battery cables from the trunk of his car and has us back on the road in fifteen minutes or so. As we Americans always say, Canadians make the best neighbors.

Though steadily diminishing in numbers throughout New England and many other parts of its range well south of Canada, *Arethusa bulbosa* seems to be holding its own in the Maritimes of eastern Canada, Newfoundland, and northern Minnesota, which "may be a stronghold of the species" (Smith 1993). In North America, however, perhaps nothing matches the populations in Newfoundland. In the second week of July 1996 it was my good fortune to spend several hours with many thousands of arethusas within a four-acre (1.6-ha) area in a wonderful raised bog. If that wasn't enough excitement, consider the fact that complementing this spectacle was the widest variety of colors imaginable for this species—from white (forma *albiflora*) through palest pink and deepest rose-red, as well as the rarest lilac color (forma *subcaerula*), and my first double-lipped monstrosity—all in prime bloom. One rarely experiences such a show as this one was, to be sure.

I once found *Arethusa bulbosa* on the coast of New Hampshire many years ago, and early authors recounted it in Massachusetts, Connecticut, and Rhode Island, but few places remain. On the other hand, Taylor (1915) wrote of Long Island, New York, that "about the end of May this part of the peninsula (Montauk) is aflame with *Arethusa bulbosa.*" As late as 1988 (Lamont and Beitel) listed six extant populations for Long Island, with two still present at Montauk. Morris and Eames (1929) are fre-

Arethusa bulbosa forma *albiflora,* Maine.

quently quoted in the literature regarding the beauty and appearance of the flower, likening it to the face of a dragon or other animal, with ears alert and mouth open.

An interesting sidelight to this trip bears repeating, I think. Cape Breton thrusts itself into the Atlantic Ocean at the northern extremity of Nova Scotia. On an overnight in the tiny fishing village of Pleasant Bay,

Arethusa bulbosa, Maine.

on the Cabot Trail, while looking westward, I watched the sun set over the Atlantic Ocean, completely upsetting my sense of direction. As we all know, the sun rises over the Atlantic in the east, right? The map soon straightens me out; it was setting over the Gulf of St. Lawrence. Nevertheless, in the big picture, the Gulf of St. Lawrence is part of the Atlantic Ocean, isn't it?

Arethusa bulbosa forma *subcaerula*, Newfoundland.

Arethusa bulbosa, double-lipped, Newfoundland.

CHAPTER 6

Orchids and Gannets on Bonaventure Island, Québec

ONE OF THE premier vacation spots on the North American continent as far as combined opportunities for birding, botanizing, and sightseeing are concerned is Bonaventure Island across from Percé on the Gaspé Peninsula, in Québec Province. Much of the Gaspé Peninsula isn't worth the long drive, in my opinion, but between the villages of Gaspé and Percé some of the finest birding and scenery in eastern North America is most accessible. The orchid hunting is a plus, though nothing spectacular in terms of glamour species. Nonetheless, large concentrations of *Corallorhiza maculata, Listera cordata, Platanthera obtusata,* and several others are easily and comfortably accessible.

On the eastern side of Bonaventure Island upwards of 50,000 gannets make their home each summer and, while doing so, entertain almost as many visitors. The island is nearly round in aspect and about 2 miles (3 km) in diameter, with elevations of 250 to 450 feet (75 to 135 m) above sea level. You can ride the boat directly to the dock on the west side, or, preferably, do the longer trip around the island to observe the birds on the eastern cliffs before docking on the western side. From the dock on the west side, it takes about forty-five minutes to walk up and over the 450 foot (135 m) rise and down to the nesting gannets on the ocean-edge of the eastern cliffs. This is the main attraction and visitors should never be satisfied with just the boat trip around the island.

Usually, for a birder-botanist to enjoy both pursuits, they need to be done separately. Because birds are in the trees and plants are on the ground, and both require much concentration, it is difficult to combine the two activities at the same time. At Bonaventure Island, however, the impossible becomes the possible.

Corallorhiza maculata, flower, Maine.

Corallorhiza maculata, yellow form, California.

After docking, visitors must hike the 1³/₄ miles (2.8 km) straight across the island through a boreal forest of white spruce (*Picea glauca*) and balsam fir (*Abies balsamea*), full of *Listera cordata*, the heart-leaved twayblade, *Corallorhiza maculata*, the spotted coralroot, and *Platanthera obtusata*, the small northern bog orchid, with lesser

Platanthera obtusata, Ontario.

amounts of *P. orbiculata*, the pad-leaf orchid, *C. trifida*, the early coralroot, and *P. hyperborea*, the northern green orchid. If, however, you like birds, the anticipation is so great on the first trip out that it is wise to postpone the orchid hunting and make a beeline to the birds. You can do the orchids on your way back or on another day. I made three trips, one with my wife, Susan, and two alone, and I could have done more exploring on one of the two main trails, temporarily closed for repairs.

As you get nearer the nesting area, while still on the trail in the woods, you first hear the birds and then smell them. Then, all at once, one of the truly great, dramatic sights of the entire bird world hits you full force. Nearly 50,000 magnificent, large, black and white, cigar-shaped birds almost twice the size of a "seagull" perform one of the greatest shows on earth: an endless ritual of milling, strutting, necking, billing (that is, affectionately caressing each other's head, neck, and bill), feeding young (one per year), and rearranging nesting material, all within inches of each other. At the same time, the air is whitened with the continuous incoming and outgoing of birds. Landings are made with a thump and a flop, and takeoffs with much labor. Both occur under a constant din of harsh and hoarse grunts and cries. What appears at first like disorganized bedlam is not that at all but rather organized wall-to-wall, good-natured mayhem. One watches all of this eyeball to eyeball on the other side of a rail fence, which is the only thing that separates the spectators from the thousands of "entertainers." I am able to spend several hours in rapt attention and photograph to my heart's content.

The boat ride to the cliffs on the eastern side of the island presents an entirely different spectacle. In front of you are thousands of mostly different species (only the gannets nest on the top of the cliff): black-legged kittiwakes, black guillemots, common murres, razorbill auks, and herring gulls, as well as some gannets, all competing for a niche on the sheer ledges. The captain slows down for pictures and binocular work, approaching quite close to the remarkable scene playing out in front of you. The first day out the waters are quite choppy and it takes me awhile before deciding to go for it.

Bonaventure Island became a Canadian provincial park in 1972 at which time the few human residents had to leave the island. The gannets arrive in April and May, even before the snow is gone. The young are all fledged by September, and the birds depart in October and November. When the young are ready to try flying, they flop and wobble their way to the edge of the cliff and jump off. Most make it to the water but some don't and hit the rocks, where they become fair game for the patient predators. Those who make it to the water do not return to the cliffs until they are ready to breed, about four years later. Their future is always in doubt because of overfishing, mostly herring, which they rely on for food. The potential of a disastrous oil spill and the danger of becoming caught in the gill nets set for commercial salmon harvesting also contribute to their tenuous hold on life.

With the major birding completed, I take the leisurely walk back and concentrate on the orchids, though nesting warblers, evening grosbeaks, and other birds are found in the spruce forest as well as orchids. The heart-leaved twayblade, *Listera cordata,* is prime this first week of July and by far the most common of the orchids here. The flowers, the size of mosquitoes, number in the thousands, and grow in the moss of the sha-

Listera cordata, Vermont.   *Listera cordata,* Vermont.

Listera cordata, Vermont.

dier portions of the forest, together with the small northern bog orchid, *Platanthera obtusata.* There is nothing pretty about the greenish white flowers of *P. obtusata,* the blunt-leaf orchid, but it is so rare below northern Maine that it is nice to see so many here. *Listera cordata,* however, is a pretty little thing especially when one uses a loupe on it. Then the miniature dull purple forked tip of the lip contrasts beautifully with the greenish sepals and petals and the yellow pollen on the column. Mosquitoes are said to be a pollinator, and there are many mosquitoes here today, but none that I see in the act of pollination. Little else grows in the shade, but in the sunnier spots and margins, the twin flower (*Linnaea borealis*), still in bud, is the most common of the non-orchids. The naked mitrewort (*Mitella nuda*) is in full bloom, too, and could easily be mistaken for *Listera cordata,* prompting me on several occasions to get down on my knees to be certain.

Several hours go by sitting on the ground among the orchids, people passing and pausing to wonder what I am doing there; when they see camera equipment some ask what I am photographing, for there is nothing apparent to them on the forest floor. I can't relax completely, however, because the last boat leaves at five o'clock in the afternoon, and I can't swim very well. So, on the path again, I make tracks for the docks. A red fox sprints ahead of me as if to beat me back to the boat.

CHAPTER 7

On the Road to Hudson Bay for the Timmins Orchid

As of this writing, there are three *Dactylorhiza* species in North America. Only one of them is a native, and that just barely—*D. aristata* in the Aleutian Islands of Alaska. The other two come to us from Europe where they form a complex group of intergrades and hybrids under the umbrella name of spotted orchids. One of these European species was first discovered in North America in 1960 in Timmins, Ontario; the other species was discovered in Tilt Cove, Newfoundland, in 1988. The certain identification of the latter two is still up in the air, so to speak, because of the difficulty taxonomists are having with the group. The so-called Timmins orchid was first named *D. purpurella* in 1961, later changed to *D. maculata,* and more recently, British taxonomists, more familiar with this group, have placed it in the so-called *Dactylorhiza* cf. *fuchsii* complex, possibly only temporarily, I might add. The Newfoundland species was first thought to be the same plant as *D. maculata,* then it was changed to *D. incarnata,* then *D. majalis,* and currently *D. praetermissa,* the southern marsh orchid of Europe. The Alaskan species continues to go by the name of *D. aristata,* a species that traveled to North America by way of Asia, perhaps thousands of years ago in company with Native American Indians.

We depart Tobermory in Bruce County early on the morning of 5 July 1992, and arrive in Timmins at ten o'clock in the evening, a distance of about 260 miles (416 km). The ferry ride to Manitoulin Island takes about two hours alone. On Manitoulin, the largest island within a body of fresh water in the entire world, we detour to pick up several interesting new plants, including the endangered pitcher's thistle (*Cissium pitcheri*), with an unusual cream-colored head of flowers. The limestone bedrock of the

Bruce Peninsula and Manitoulin Island changes abruptly to granite on the southern edge of the Canadian Shield, on the mainland near Espanoza and Sudbury, Ontario. We lose the arbor-vitae (*Thuja occidentalis*) vegetation of the alkaline Niagara Escarpment and pick up the acidic, in the form of jack pine (*Pinus banksiana*) and white pine (*Pinus strobus*), all three aspens (*Populus grandidentata, P. tremuloides,* and *P. balsamifera*), and the typical boreal forest elements of white and black spruce (*Picea glauca* and *P. mariana*).

North of Sudbury, Ontario, Route 144 runs pretty straight and smooth all the way to Timmins. Not surprisingly, the dominant roadside plant is the common daisy (*Chrysanthemum leucanthemum*), in full bloom along the entire stretch of road. Next is the gray-foliaged, common everlasting (*Anaphilis margaritacea*), followed by another common "weed," the orange hawkweed (*Hieracium aurantiacum*), a deeper "red" than those back home in southern New Hampshire. The hawkweed, however, peters out before Timmins. In the woods and on the edges, the dominant understory shrub is Labrador tea (*Ledum groenlandicum*); the dominant herb, bunchberry (*Cornus canadensis*).

Dactylorhiza cf. *fuchsii,* leaf markings, Ontario.

Mildly surprising, I find *Cypripedium acaule* as far north as Timmins on the 50th parallel, just about its northern limit. One "tiny" specimen has a lip that measures 1 1/3 inches (3.5 cm) long and 3/5 inch (1.5 cm) wide. The usual dimensions are more than 2 inches (5 cm) long and 1 inch (2.5 cm) wide.

The day of the dactylorhiza dawns cloudy, soggy, and wet, as is typical of most of this trip, but improves slowly, also typical. We greet the Cowells, our gracious hosts, who then lead us down through a dark and dank hollow of balsam poplar (*Populus balsamifera*) and out onto the open edge of the river where 110 purple beacons greet us, quickly perking up our wet and dreary spirits. An intense purplish-reddish-pink describes the color of the lip, petals, and sepals, which are marked with darker purple scriggly lines. The stem is 1 to 2 feet (30 to 60 cm) tall with up to 50 densely packed flowers. The narrow, green, basal leaves are marked with horizontal blotches of purple. The flower color is remarkably similar to that of the self-heal (*Prunella vulgaris*). After more than an hour of taking turns photographing the orchids, we climb back up the steep bank, pose with our hosts for a few pictures, extend our heart-felt appreciation and good-byes, and head southwest.

In 1996 I had the opportunity to see the so-called Tilt Cove dactylorhiza, *Dactylorhiza praetermissa*. In my opinion, this (recently discovered in Newfoundland) European is no match in beauty with the Timmins orchid, *Dactylorhiza* cf. *fuchsii*. The latter is a deeper red-purple with darker lines and scriggles on the lip petal. The Tilt Cove species is a much

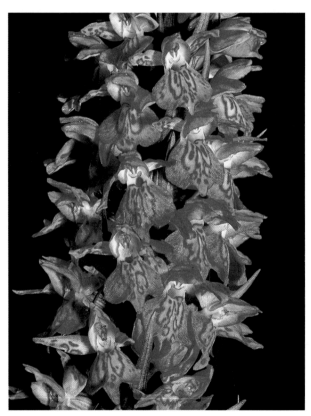

Dactylorhiza cf. *fuchsii*, Ontario.

paler, pinker version of the striking Timmins orchid. I was frankly disappointed with it, but must admit that on our visit only a few plants were in full bloom. Most were just beginning to open during the third week of July, later than usual, apparently.

Another all-day drive to Wawa, Ontario, brings us to the town with the famous oversized statue of the Canada goose. Everywhere we stop enroute for lunch and ferns, the ubiquitous olive-backed thrush (Swainson's) sings ecstatically under cover of the great Canadian boreal forest. This magnificent forest provides the classic backdrop to a multitude of picturesque lakes and ponds: tier after tier of spired balsam fir (*Abies balsamea*) and black and white spruce (*Picea mariana* and *P. glauca*) in this realm of the Christmas tree. If that isn't sufficient pleasure, more comes at a roadside gas and restaurant stop somewhere between Timmins and Wawa, where I taste the best rhubarb pie I've ever had. It is so good, I have a second piece, while the rest of the group check some ferns up the road.

Paul Martin Brown is having a field day on this trip with ferns, particularly the succulent ones known as grape ferns (*Botrychium* species). Here again, the genus is very variable in form and habit, and, as with the orchids, the total number of species depends on the authority doing the classifying. Moonwort (*B. lunaria*) receives most of Paul's attention today along the Trans-Canada Highway, with one stop producing more than a hundred plants. A single leaf halfway up a 6-inch (15-cm) or smaller stalk is divided into a half dozen pairs of unusual looking half-moon or fan-shaped leaflets, followed at the top of the stalk by slightly drooping clusters of spores. According to Boughton Cobb (1975), it is an extremely rare fern "more common in folklore and fable than 'in person.'" Here on the Canadian Shield, it appears to be relatively common in spots. Many other specimens of *Botrychium* are examined and collected for Warren H. Wagner Jr., the current fern authority, of the University of Michigan. Frequent stops for rock ferns also produce other rarities like the alpine woodsia (*Woodsia alpina*), the woolly, rusty woodsia (*W. ilvensis*), and my favorite, the northern holly fern (*Polystichum lonchitis*).

Is this long, somewhat tedious side trip halfway to Hudson Bay worth it? A very rare life-list orchid prompts an affirmative answer, and don't forget the marvelous rhubarb pie, a rarity in itself, anywhere.

CHAPTER 8

Sparrow's-egg Lady's-slipper on Lake Superior, Ontario

"In wildness is the preservation of the world," Thoreau wrote. Most people, however, prefer to stick to the roads—hard-surfaced ones at that —and are satisfied to get out and stretch their legs or take a look around at a scenic pull-over or rest stop. Driving through all sorts of scenic areas, they have little thought or interest, apparently, in spending any serious time getting to really see or know an area. These thoughts come to mind while driving to Pukaskwa National Park on the north shore of Lake Superior, where the Canadian Shield and the southern edge of Ontario's boreal forest meet, "a wild shore on an inland sea." I am prepared and primed to see one of the southernmost North American stations for *Cypripedium passerinum,* also known as Franklin's lady's-slipper and sparrow's-egg lady's-slipper. Little do I realize that the extraordinarily veined leaves of the diminutive *Goodyera repens* will end up stealing the show.

Pukaskwa (pronounced puck'-a-saw) is a wilderness park that opened to the public in 1983. I arrive less than ten years later, on 8 July 1992 at six in the morning, under a heavy layer of fog and showers. Minutes later, as if by pre-arrangement, the low clouds part, the fog lifts, and the sun streams down, turning the surface of Hattie's Cove into millions of tiny sparkling mirrors, while warming my chilled body. No other humans are here so early on a rainy morning. The visitor's center is closed, and even the park personnel have yet to come to work, making the hushed stillness even more noticeable, until the ethereal strains of a Swainson's thrush float across the water. Only it and two other relatives, the hermit and veery, can make such glorious sounds. A loon joins in with an entirely different offering, a haunting yodel that is the very evocation of wilderness and for my ears alone. A magnificent pileated woodpecker bounds across the cove and disappears in the trees. For too brief an interlude my wilderness world excludes all human distractions. Then reality returns: the sun is again engulfed in clouds, the fog floats back silently "on little cat's feet," the dismal drizzle drips, and others in our group arrive on the scene.

For the next twenty minutes, we walk with difficulty in the ruts of a jeep path over soft sand dunes, with the greatest of all the lakes—Superior—on our left. Though hidden from view by the thick fog, the lake assures its presence with the sound of waves rhythmically lapping the shore. A steep climb follows to the top of a dune ridge, covered on the lee side by a thick growth of red-osier dogwood shrubs (*Cornus stolonifera*) and scattered white spruce (*Picea glauca*). We pause to catch our collective breaths while scanning such an unlikely spot for the object of our search. Three or four hundred inconspicuous sparrow's-egg lady's-slippers, growing in sand, in full bloom and covered with rain drops, stop us in our tracks. I quickly drop to my knees in admiration. The flower, quite frankly though, is probably the homeliest of the cypripediums, and it certainly is not graceful in bearing. This is because of the smallness of the flower and the disproportionately larger leafy stem, but it is beautiful, notwithstanding some minor flaws.

A head-on shot of the flower reminds me of the old, soft, tight-fitting, football helmets in the days of Red Grange, who was appropriately known as the "Galloping Ghost from Illinois" in the 1930s: the clasping dorsal sepal represents the top of the helmet; the two clasping lateral petals, the ear protectors of the helmet; and the round lip pouch, the bulging face of the player. Or, nicer, perhaps is the way Preece (1937) expressed it: "An aura of mystery surrounds these hooded blooms; with helmet visors down and half-hidden amid the foliage, they keep their life-long vigil in the forest depths."

Reading this, however, I must admit a certain charm in this lady's-slipper that is quite different from all other cyps. It is the only lady's-slipper in which the upper sepal is all green and actually clamps down over the pouch opening, essentially closing it off to all insect visitors, as well as orchid lovers. For this reason, it apparently is self-fertilizing, another difference. One must lift the sepal to get a look at the beautiful purple mark-

Cypripedium passerinum, Ontario.

ings on the floor of the pouch. The creamy white, narrow, flat, and straight lateral petals project out from the side of the pouch but remain close to the lip, even clasping it early on. The two green lateral sepals are usually united under and behind the pouch but sometimes they are separate, as in the ram's-head (*Cypripedium arietinum*). The prominent green upright bract stands almost 3 inches (7.5 cm) above the flower. The

Cypripedium passerinum, Ontario.

staminode is quite different also: pale white at its base with purple spotting on the edges, and increasingly yellow from its mid-point to the apex,
the yellow spotted with rusty-brown or maroon. Further, the base of the
lip is flared into two "ears" or lobes, which also are spotted with purple,
as is the front rim of the pouch. A hand lens reveals white hairs emanat-
ing from the two large purple spots on the floor of the pouch. Finally,
under the upper or dorsal green sepal, the green color glows with fine
whitish lines or veins. As you will see, a hand lens opens up a whole new
perspective on what at first view is taken for a homely flower. Incidentally, it is this purple spotting that leads to the more common name of
sparrow's-egg lady's-slipper.

First discovered by Dr. John Anderson on a polar sea expedition in
1820, *Cypripedium passerinum* was named Franklin's lady's-slipper for

the leader of that expedition, Sir John Franklin. This orchid likes to follow streamsides and lakesides in northwestern Canada, from Hudson Bay to Alaska, and well inside the Arctic Circle. It is one of only two cyps hardy enough to break that barrier; the other is *C. guttatum*. The shore of Lake Superior is a disjunct site for this orchid, meaning it is widely separated from the main population. This remote site was first discovered in 1964 by Dr. John Soper, almost a hundred fifty years after the original discovery farther north. The cool breezes from the cold waters of Lake Superior help this orchid to survive so far south of its normal range. Other flowers testify to the same cooling effects of the lake: the corn lily (*Clintonia borealis*), bunchberry (*Cornus canadensis*), and Canada mayflower (*Maianthemum canadense*), to name a few, are still in bloom at this late date, while in Rossport, further west on the Trans-Canada Highway, lilacs and crabapples are also blooming, six weeks later than back home in southern New Hampshire. The mossy floor of the forest is full of bunchberry (*Cornus canadensis*) and naked mitrewort (*Mitella nuda*), a member of the saxifrage family, with five fantastic, deeply fringed petals that are geometrically arranged like perfect snowflakes, almost microscopic in size, requiring a hand lens to really appreciate. The 4- to 8-inch (10- to 20-cm) stem is difficult to see, as is *Listera cordata,* the heart-leaved twayblade.

While searching for the elusive northern twayblade, *Listera borealis,* along the forest edge of the sand dunes, still within hearing range of the lake and still in the fog, I am mesmerized by hundreds of *Goodyera repens* tucked in the soft bed of mosses that stretch as far as the eye can see over the sand dune, like a padded quilt lying on sand, designed with tiny bouquets of dark green rosettes. What a charmer, thanks to the remarkable crystalline, silvery white reticulations, which here are whiter and sharper than any I have seen on a goodyera. Close examination shows a paler green stripe down the center of the white markings, dividing the white in two. Stated in more botanical terms, the strikingly marked rosettes of three to seven ovate leaves, only 1 or 2 cm wide and 3 or 4 cm long, make the difference between an otherwise ordinary groundcover and this one of exquisite beauty. The temptation is to roll the quilt up and take it home. I am facetious. (Preoccupied with the artistic qualities of the individual leaves and the hurried time, I do not discover until I get back home my failure to include an overall picture of this beautiful green quilt—a not altogether unusual occurrence during hurried daily shoots.) The species is said to intergrade and hybridize with *G. tesselata,* a frequent companion in the Great Lakes and northern New England regions, where some individuals are extremely difficult to identify with certainty. The flower is in tight bud two weeks, perhaps, before bloom, but the evergreen leaves are the attraction then as now. The loosely flowered spike of fifteen or twenty florets is the smallest of North American goodyeras and can be found in the boreal forests that stretch clear across the Northern Hemisphere, one of the widest ranges of any orchid.

As we reluctantly leave the park boundaries, a spruce grouse in its usual tame mode stands motionless in the middle of the road and flies up only when I get out of the car to approach for a portrait. Down the road a bit we leisurely pull over to photograph more wildflowers, notably the Indian paintbrush (*Castilleja septentrionalis*). We do not see any of the animals the park is noted for, the likes of woodland caribou, moose, black bear and wolf, all the so-called glamour species, but the orchids are what we have come to see and who could ask for anything more glamorous?

Goodyera repens, large clump of rosettes, Ontario.

Goodyera repens, showing dramatic veining, Ontario.

CHAPTER 9

The Garden of Eden
on Flowerpot Island, Ontario

FLOWERPOT Island is part of Canada's only marine national park, the Fathom Five Marine National Park, located at the north end of the Bruce Peninsula in Ontario. People who live on the peninsula or who have known it well call it simply the Bruce. Plants are one of the things that have made the Bruce world famous and the reason so many botanists and plant enthusiasts love the peninsula. There, thousands of yellow lady's-slippers (*Cypripedium parviflorum*), a few weeks out of bloom on our arrival, the elusive eastern prairie fringed-orchid (*Platanthera leucophaea*), unfortunately two weeks early for us, the European twayblade (*Listera ovata*), in full bloom as we will see momentarily, the beautiful little bird's-eye primrose (*Primula mistissinica*), and the magnificent hart's-tongue fern (*Phyllitis scolopendrium*) are but a few of the Bruce's delights. The main object of my intentions and attention, however, is the splendid *Corallorhiza striata,* the peppermint-striped coralroot.

The peninsula is part of that famous geologic formation known as the Niagara Escarpment, the same formation the Niagara Falls plunges over 200 miles (320 km) to the southeast. On the northern end of the peninsula lies the picturesque harbor of Tobermory in Bruce County. Throughout the county, an extensive limestone and marble pavement laced with countless cracks and crevices covers the ground with little or no soil cover, making for some potentially treacherous walking. In the Baltic States these pavements are called alvars, a term only relatively recently used in North America. A unique ecosystem and a top priority of the Nature Conservancy, alvars are most common in the Great Lakes region, just south of the granitic bedrock of the Canadian Shield Upland, especially from the north shore of Lake Michigan, east to the islands of Lake Huron, across Manitoulin Island, and south to Georgian Bay. These flat limestone rock slabs harbor the rare American hart's-tongue fern (*Phyllitis scolopendrium* var. *americanum*), with fronds to 2 feet (60 cm) long, strap-shaped, smooth and shiny on one side, and thickly covered with fruit dots on the underside that look like black, scribbly worms. The hart's-tongue is one of the "big things" on the Bruce. *Coreopsis lanceolata* and *Zigadenus glaucus,* both in bloom, and *Cypripedium arietinum* and *C. parviflorum,* both past bloom, are other specialties here.

Our party is guided by the Greenops, a very hospitable couple who live on the Bruce, to a northern hardwood forest of sugar maple (*Acer saccharum*), mountain maple (*Acer spicatum*), and white ash (*Fraxinus americana*), with a very dense canopy above. Hidden in cracks on the shaded labyrinthine surface of the limestone pavement are hundreds of the hart's-tongue fern with several holly ferns (*Polystichum lonchitis*) and male ferns (*Dryopteris filix-mas*) to boot. One must step with care to avoid the deep cracks and crevices that can easily cause a sprain or broken leg.

Corallorhiza striata, Ontario.

The Bruce is famous for its orchids, too. Approximately 35 species grow here. Most of them are past bloom or still in bud on our arrival the first week of July 1992. The yellow lady's-slipper is everywhere in the cracks and elsewhere for that matter. It is clearly the most abundant orchid and one could easily imagine what it looked like a week or two before our arrival. Much fewer numbers of the queen lady's-slipper (*Cypripedium reginae*) bloom at the Petrel Preserve a little further south, on the west coast of the Bruce. Interestingly, the grass-pink orchid (*Calopogon tuberosus*) is normal in size and rich in color at this preserve, but the rose pogonia (*Pogonia ophioglossoides*) is small and runty. Some of the rose pogonias are less than 3 inches (7.5 cm) tall, and the flowers, too, are small. Perhaps the lime content is too much for these plants.

This preserve is a limestone fen, similar to Bergen Swamp in upstate New York. Yes, the Massassauga rattlesnake, once common on the Bruce, still exists, though W. S. Fox (1952) claimed that no human had ever died from its bite, at least on the Bruce. The rare Indian plantain (*Cacalia plantaginea*) is an extremely unusual composite with multiple umbels on a stem 3 foot (90 cm) high and tubular fluted florets of creamy white color; long-petioled leaves complete the picture in the ditch beside the road. Snipe are still absorbed in their nuptial displays aloft as we are in photographing below.

Even more impressive to me are the European twayblades, *Listera ovata,* at Red Bay. They are impressive in size—up to 2 feet (60 cm) tall—the tallest, largest, and easiest to photograph of all the listeras. The lip is more yellow with a curious raised line down the middle of it. The plants grow along a brook on the edge of a dirt road with arbor-vitae (*Thuja*

occidentalis) and an undergrowth of horsetail (*Equisetum* species) and sensitive fern (*Onoclea sensibilis*). *Listera ovata* is generally considered a weed in Europe and the most common orchid of Great Britain. It has followed another European, the helleborine (*Epipactis helleborine*), to North America almost 100 years later, 1879 to 1968 to be exact. All three sites are in Ontario. It will be interesting to see if it follows the fortunes of the helleborine and spreads into the United States.

The highlight of the Bruce, for me at least, has to be the day spent on Flowerpot Island, a fifteen-minute boat ride out of the harbor of Tobermory. Flowerpot is part of the marine national park I mentioned earlier and derives its

Listera ovata, Ontario.

Listera ovata, tall clump, Ontario.

name from the picturesque cylindrical columns of dolomitic limestone just offshore, the work of glaciers during the Pleistocene Epoch, which covered the Great Lakes as well as most of the Northeast. Rain, wind, frost, and tides have continued the job since.

On arrival, the first things to get our attention are two dozen garter snakes sunning on the horizontal branches of a low, ground-hugging balsam fir (*Abies balsamea*). It is a chilly morning and snakes require a warm-up before tending to their daily chores. Hardly a snake muscle moves as

I take a picture, but the snakes are merely a distraction. It is the striped coralroot, *Corallorhiza striata,* for which I am looking. I find it very quickly just ahead, hidden under dense spruces, 20 feet (6 m) off the trail. These plants prove to be past prime as the season here is getting late for this orchid.

On the north end of the 500-acre (200-ha) island, however, I soon discover it is just enough cooler in the shade to extend the season a few days. Scanning carefully both sides of the trail, my eye catches a single specimen near the base of a beautiful, moss-covered limestone ledge, about 50 feet (15 m) off the trail. The problem is how to get into position to set up my tripod and camera without tearing off pieces of moss from the gorgeous carpet that drapes the rock surface. The desire to get this orchid on film is so strong that I persist, taking care to avoid as much damage as possible. Some chunks of moss do become dislodged, like turf divots in a football or golf game. Looking up through the canopy of trees, I wait for a shaft of sunlight to penetrate a crack in the canopy and transform, with backlight, what a moment before was an inconspicuous, nay, even dull, flower, into a peppermint-candy-striped beauty of shimmering garnets and rubies. Remember, in photography, as in Nature, light is the key ingredient. In the immortal words of Morris and Eames (1929), "Until he has seen them in sunlight no one has any idea how beautiful these orchids can be. . . . we have known it passed by with indifference." The moment is transitory as the sun travels across its trajectory quickly,

Corallorhiza striata, Ontario.

and the orchid resumes its nondescript status again, but not before I get the picture. I sit for an hour, savoring the moment and writing in my journal.

The Alaska orchid, *Piperia unalascensis,* common in certain areas is only in bud today, and the same is true of several handsome rosettes of *Goodyera oblongifolia.* I unexpectedly discover an unusual juxtaposition: a single budded *Goodyera oblongifolia,* a blooming northern bog orchid (*Platanthera obtusata*), and a full bloom heart-leaved twayblade (*Listera cordata*). The north-

Corallorhiza striata, selective focus, back lighting, Ontario.

ern bog orchid occasionally produces two basal leaves instead of the usual one, a phenomenon we see later in Pukaskwa National Park. Several other orchids are done blooming, including calypso (*Calypso bulbosa*) and ram's-head (*Cypripedium arietinum*). The best nonorchid flower on Flowerpot, in my opinion, is the pretty little bird's-eye primrose (*Primula mistissinica*), an umbel of pink and lavender notched petals with a yellow "eye," on a 6- to 12-inch (15- to 30-cm) stem, growing beside the stairway to the "Cave," under the cool mist of a nearby waterfall.

On another day the Greenops take us back down the spine of the Bruce in hopes of showing us the increasingly rare eastern prairie white fringed-orchid, *Platanthera leucophaea*. A long drive through private property (with permission) takes us to the side of a lake, which is "prairie" on cracked limestone pavement. We find many, probably hundreds of prairie fringed-orchids, but all of them in tight bud, perhaps as much as two weeks from opening. This is a major disappointment, but one taken in stride because we expect it.

The last day on the Bruce concludes with a delicious whitefish dinner at the Grandview Restaurant, overlooking the delightful harbor of Tobermory. Early the next morning we line up for the big ferry ride to Manitoulin Island. The ride takes two hours but is worth it in saving precious time to points on the north shore of Lake Superior, notably Sault Sainte Marie and Pukaskwa National Park.

Goodyera oblongifolia, Ontario.

Listera cordata, Platanthera obtusata, Goodyera oblongifolia, from left to right in an unusual juxtaposition, Ontario.

CHAPTER 10

The Prairie Fringed-orchid in Easternmost Ontario

THE EASTERN prairie fringed-orchid, *Platanthera leucophaea*, continues to lose habitat to the point where it is now, or shortly will be listed as federally threatened. Welby Smith (1993) stated the case succinctly in Minnesota: "orchid habitats statewide have been reduced by perhaps 75 percent . . . many like prairies by as much as 95 percent." A hundred years ago this orchid was listed as abundant in areas of prairie as large as 15,000 square miles (38,850 sq km) (yes, you read correctly). Today these areas support nothing but farms. Fred Case (1987) has written that the only hope for the salvation of this orchid in most of its range "is the establishment of a natural shoreline prairie preserve sufficiently deep to provide for the orchid's nature of moving inland or shoreward as the water table fluctuates." Orchid preserves are not a novel concept, but one that needs more implementation.

The eastern prairie fringed-orchid has been described as elegant, handsome, lovely, and spectacular. Case (1987) wrote that "few American plants in any family could be lovelier than this orchid." Morris and Eames (1929) called it a "glorified form of the Ragged, twice as large, showy and fragrant." My first impression, quite frankly, is one of mild disappointment. The specimens are few-flowered for one thing, and I immediately question the raves in the literature. I missed the blooming of the prairie fringed-orchid four years previously on a trip to the Bruce Peninsula. That season was almost two weeks late, with only tight buds showing. This time, 10 July 1996, I am "guaranteed" peak bloom, in the extreme eastern corner of Ontario. I need only make the eight-hour drive (one-way) up Interstate 89 to Burlington, Vermont, westward to Malone in upstate New York, across the St. Lawrence River at Ogdensburg to connect with Canada's Highway 401.

Early the next morning I arrive at the designated fen. It is semi-open on one side of the road and heavily wooded on the other, a situation that bodes ill for such a sun-loving, open prairie orchid surviving for long. Semi-dwarf tamarack (*Larix laricina*) and black spruce (*Picea mariana*) are the dominant, albeit small trees here, with the following shrubs: the bog laurel (*Kalmia polifolia*), sweet gale (*Myrica gale*), and cinquefoil (*Potentilla fruticosa*). Purple loosestrife (*Lythrum salicaria*) and narrow-leaved cattails (*Typha angustifolia*) grow in the ditch adjacent to the road,

Platanthera leucophaea, Ontario.

while marsh fern (*Thelypteris palustris*), royal fern (*Osmunda regalis*), buckbean (*Menyanthes trifoliata*), and several grasses and sedges keep company in the open spaces, joined by hundreds of rose pogonias (*Pogonia ophioglossoides*) and grass-pink orchids (*Calopogon tuberosus*), and dozens of relatively small pitcher-plants (*Sarracenia purpurea*) (too alkaline?). My attention, of course, is lavished on the lovely prairie white fringed-orchid. I notice in the literature that the word *white* has been dropped from the common name by modern authors. Why? Maybe to prevent confusion with the other white fringed-orchid, *Platanthera blephariglottis,* which in reality is quite different from *P. leucophaea.*

After the initial impression, represented by the relatively poor specimens mentioned above, another section of the fen produces many, more typical examples. Standing 3 feet (90 cm) tall and mostly alone, these plants carry as many as twenty splendid, cream-colored flowers on long pedicels, with tremendous spurs up to 2 inches (5 cm) long. Obviously contributing to my change of heart is the wonderful fragrance I enjoy for the next four hours. Being alone, I have the added luxury of spending as much time as I want with this, yes, lovely orchid. Most authors emphasize the nocturnal nature of this fragrance, but here under the noontime sun it is quite strong, even to someone like me who has lost much of his sense of smell in recent years.

Platanthera leucophaea, Ontario.

The flowers are not as crowded or as plentiful as those of the other fringed-orchids, but they are larger and more charming. Morris and Eames (1929) and some other authors described the color of the flower as white, but here today there is a distinct cream wash, carried particularly on the backs of the sepals and petals, which connive over the large three-parted lip. It is more noticeable looking down from the top of the raceme—a view, incidentally, that displays the marvelous symmetry of the perfectly spaced pedicellate flowers, typical of all the other fringed orchids, too. Later, I notice a definite chartreuse tint on the conniving tepals in the evening under artificial light, but under the sun it is creamy yellowish. Interesting.

Fred Case (1987) documented stations that have persisted for sixty years, including one in his meadow garden (moved ahead of an industrial site intrusion) that has bloomed for thirty years! This longevity occurred on sites that lacked tree and shrub competition, a very important factor. In many situations, plant succession decimates large populations of orchids.

Incidentally, the prairie white fringed-orchid has been split into two species: *Platanthera leucophaea*, of course, and the new one, *P. praeclara*. The latter is known as the western fringed-orchid and the former as the eastern fringed-orchid. The basis for separation is the larger flower of *P. praeclara*, a more western and smaller distribution centering around the Missouri River drainage (west of the Mississippi River) and a difference in the column structure, making the western an "eye-depositing" pollinator orchid, which, apparently, makes it reproductively less efficient. *Platanthera leucophaea*, in contrast, has a smaller flower, is basically found in the upper Mississippi River drainage (east of the Mississippi River) and the Great Lakes region, and is a "proboscis-depositing" pollinator orchid, making it more efficient reproductively by allowing it to spread into a wider geographic range.

The mid-western prairie moved northeastward following the retreat of the Wisconsin ice sheet during the last ice period, resulting in the disjunct eastern prairie fringed-orchid stations of New York, New Jersey, and Aroostook County, Maine. Sheviak and Bowles (1986) noted that "*Platanthera praeclara* and *P. leucophaea* form a species pair closely related to another evident pair, *P. grandiflora* and *P. psycodes*, and to other species, *P. peramoena* and *P. lacera*. These six species form a natural group."

Platanthera leucophaea, Ontario.

The inevitable long, monotonous drive home soon ensues, assuaged by National Public Radio programming and stops at the Shelburne Museum in Burlington, Vermont, and along the magnificent roadcuts on Interstate 89. These roadcuts, the amateur and professional geologist's delight, are where geologic history is revealed to the interested naturalist. The solo drive allows for much retrospection. Orchid lovers are all brushed with the romantic idealism of Don Quixote. We travel great distances to search and photograph, save and conserve these special species. We recognize and appreciate the natural beauty missed by the maddening crowds more interested in the artificial. We experience the equivalent excitement of big game hunters, mountain climbers, and hybridizers nurturing new varieties, and then we finally pull into our driveway back home and are nudged back into reality. Another successful journey is over—until the next time.

Cypripedium reginae, large clump of paler pink flowers, Vermont.

NEW ENGLAND

CHAPTER 11

A Modern-Day Thoreau and the American Orchis in Maine

BEFORE becoming one of the great names in American conservation, John Muir walked a thousand miles (1600 km) to the Gulf of Mexico and the Florida Keys in the 1860s. On that walk, he met a man in Kentucky, who lived near Mammoth Cave but had never bothered to visit and experience its wonders, because, he said, it was just a big hole in the ground.

The late Martin Rasmussen of Caribou, Maine, was nothing like that Kentuckian. Martin epitomized the person who chooses to study, monitor, and advocate for beauty close to home, especially when native orchids are involved. He played a leading role in Nature Conservancy's success in protecting the beautiful *Amerorchis rotundifolia*, also known as the American orchis or one-leaf orchis, in Aroostook, Maine's northernmost county.

Henry David Thoreau fit the same mold, as have many other less famous naturalists, past and present, including a local compatriot of Rasmussen earlier in the century. I refer to botanist Olof O. Nylander, also of Caribou, who wrote a small publication in 1918 on the orchids of Aroostook County.

Although I did not meet Rasmussen until 1990, I felt I knew him from conversations with Les Eastman and Paul Martin Brown, who were longtime friends of his. Thus, in 1990, on my way to the Gaspé Peninsula, I decided to take the time to meet Martin and renew my earlier acquaintance with one-leaf orchis at the same time. Martin was seventy-seven then. Upon inquiry about his fast walking pace, he said he enjoyed walking and did a lot of it in flower season, but couldn't lift much anymore because it bothered him too much.

Our first day started out on a wrong note. Unable to meet Martin as planned at nine o'clock because of road construction on the way from Houlton, Maine, where my wife and I had stayed the night before, we arrived at the designated meeting place, the corner of a dirt road, and couldn't find the abandoned railroad bed we were to look for on the other side of the paved road. In the meantime, since we were late, Martin and another visitor had gone ahead. I then made a wrong decision and decided to walk up the dirt road looking for a railroad bed, which I found, but in the wrong direction. My wife and I waited there for two and a half hours before deciding to go back to the car. In the meantime, Martin had come out of the bog and back to the car. Not finding us, he left a note on

Martin Rasmussen, 1990.

the windshield and went back into the bog a second time, after saying his good-byes to the first visitor, looking for us in case we had attempted it on our own. Back at the car, I finally recognized the abandoned railroad bed in high grass across the road, and we proceeded to walk down the barely noticeable path. Within a few minutes, Martin was approaching us from the other direction. All's well that ends well, goes the saying. Since too much time had elapsed to make a third trek into the bog, Martin kindly offered to take me back in the next morning. In the meantime, he directed us to an easier-accessed site a few miles down the road, which we could still enjoy that afternoon.

The next morning Martin led us to the one-leaf orchis. I would like to quote from an article I wrote for the *American Orchid Society Bulletin* (Keenan 1991a):

> My guide, who insists on anonymity, is one of the finest gentle-
> men I have ever met. The Woodland Bog, technically a treed fen,
> requires a pleasant half-hour hike, a crossing of a beaver stream—
> which he has to unplug almost every other day—and a squeeze-
> through encounter with black spruce (*Picea mariana*), tamarack or
> American larch (*Larix laricina*), and arbor vitae or northern white
> cedar (*Thuja occidentalis*) before entering a cathedral-like opening,
> carpeted with brown duff from the cedar trees and little else
> except, of course, scattered clumps of the handsome one-leaf
> orchis (*Amerorchis rotundifolia*), she with the purple-spotted lips.
> Here in this peaceful wood, my Thoreauvian friend has built a rus-
> tic table and chair, from nearby fallen branches, against the trunk
> of a tree where he sits and writes in his journal while contemplat-
> ing the beauty before him: *Amerorchis* species this day, *Calypso*
> *bulbosa* earlier in the season, and the others in summer. A clump
> of *Cypripedium reginae* is in full bloom in the sunny peripheral
> openings outside, kept company by a plenitude of other sun-
> worshipers, notably the shrubby cinquefoil (*Potentilla fruticosa*)
> and the very rare *Valeriana uliginosa*. A total of seven species of
> orchids grow here, both inside and outside the 'temple.' Three
> hours in idyllic surroundings, with the perfect companion, and I
> don't want to leave. But, to paraphrase my favorite poet, Robert

Frost: the woods were lovely, dark, and deep, but I had promises to keep and miles to go before meeting up with my wife, Susan, at a predetermined time in the village.

The Nature Conservancy has since bought this bog and another in the vicinity to preserve them for future generations. Martin Rasmussen had much to do with the ultimate success of this endeavor. Conservationists will forever be in his debt. Not many towns have had the likes of a Nylander or a Rasmussen. Today Nylander is remembered by a quaint little museum in Caribou, Maine. It is my hope that someday the *Amerorchis* bog will commemorate Rasmussen's name. Martin Rasmussen died at home rather suddenly in December 1994.

North America's freckle-face, *Amerorchis rotundifolia,* has a dominant three-lobed white lip rather heavily marked with small red-purple spots. Sometimes the purple pigment is entirely lacking, or at the other extreme, the dots merge into two bands of rich color. The former variation is formally recognized as forma *beckettiae* and the latter as forma *lineata.* The one-leaf orchis is typically a small plant with a single basal leaf below a 6- to 12-inch (15- to 30-cm) stem surmounted by a loose raceme of a few to a dozen or more flowers. It prefers living in the open spaces and tundra of northern Canada from Newfoundland to Alaska, where it is often abundant and exposed to the elements, but further south, it becomes increasingly rare and seeks the cool shelter of coniferous bogs. It crosses into the lower 48 states only in restricted portions of northern Maine, Michigan, Minnesota, and Montana.

The original generic name of this species—*Orchis*—was changed in 1968 to *Amerorchis,* because of taxonomic changes involving American orchids with European affinities. The genus *Orchis* is a very large and complicated European group of very similar orchids that have posed many problems over the years to taxonomists trying to find order in that genus. The word *orchis* comes from the Greek word of the same spelling and means "testis," in reference to the double testiculate tubers (roots). Orchids (orchis) figured strongly in the herbal medicines of the Middle Ages because of the so-called Doctrine of Signatures, which taught that cures resulted from using plant parts that resembled the particular part of the diseased human anatomy (e.g., the walnut for the brain, bloodroot for anemia, members of the *Orchis* genus for sexual dysfunctions).

Here in the northernmost county of Maine hundreds if not thousands of specimens of *Amerorchis rotundifolia* hide out in some of the plenti-

Amerorchis rotundifolia, Alaska.

ful coniferous bogs. My first visit to these bogs of Aroostook County occurred in the 1970s in the company of Les Eastman and Dr. George Newman. After a late supper, we all retired early in anticipation of breakfast at five o'clock the next morning and an early departure for the bog. By midnight the heavens opened up and all I could hear in bed the remainder of the night was the heavy downpour. This did not dissuade Les and George, and we headed out under a deluge of cold black rain with the temperature hovering in the forties. We were in the bog at daybreak. In those years I had no waterproof boots and became soaked quickly from head to toes, but the orchids were prime, and we got our pictures despite the cold, miserable rain. Alas, the life of an orchid hunter is often punctuated with these kinds of days.

CHAPTER 12

Calopogon and Rose Pogonia in Maine and New Hampshire

ON FIRST thought, the back of a shopping mall is hardly the place to see rose pogonia, *Pogonia ophioglossoides*. My directions, nonetheless, lead me there. I drive behind a facade of buildings, where only delivery trucks go and school kids, who take a short cut to a mobile home park nearby. At the edge of the hot top, there is an 8-foot (2.5-m) high chain-link fence with an open gate about halfway down the length of it. On the other side of the fence I cross a ditch of shallow water on a few well-placed boards. The path cuts through a sandy heath bog filled with leatherleaf (*Chamaedaphne calyculata*), mountain holly (*Nemopanthus mucronata*), rhodora (*Rhododendron canadense*), chokeberry (*Pyrus melanocarpa*), blueberry (*Vaccinium corymbosum*), and other typical heath plants. A power line intersects the middle of this boggy habitat. The ditch, path, and power line are all strewn with the usual collection of litter some unthinking people always seem to toss in wetlands. On the other side of the power line a cluster of mobile homes backs up to within a few feet of the wetland, which explains the well-worn path to the mall. No sign of pogonias so far, but some open grassy and sedgy areas under the power line look hopeful.

I walk down an extremely bumpy and muddy rut. Mauled and scarred by four-wheel-drive pickups and other all-terrain type vehicles, the rut is partially under water. A dog discovers me and commences to bark. As he does, I note the first hints of pink hidden among the grasses and sedges. Closer inspection reveals hundreds, maybe thousands, in a small area on both sides of the watery rut. They turn out to be the most robust and intensely colored rose pogonias I've ever seen. The color varies, as it does with most pink flowers, from the palest pink to the richest rose.

Pogonia ophioglossoides, New Hampshire.

Pogonia ophioglossoides, with rose chafer, New Hampshire.

"For though the grass was scattered, yet every second spear seemed tipped with wings of color, that tinged the atmosphere," Robert Frost declared in his poem "The Rose Pogonia." Morris and Eames (1929) were similarly smitten by their

delicate charm . . . of almost universal appeal. Like its relative, the Arethusa, it seems by its single blossom and suggestion of a face to have a strange power of attraction that sprays and racemes lack. Everything about it is instinct with modesty, the drooping habit, the softness of color, the delicate fragrance.

Some authors liken the fragrance to raspberries, while others incline toward violets. In either case, the fragrance is pleasant to the nose. The bloom reminds me of a Dutch girl's bonnet, especially in the partially open stage. Here and in most localities it also occasionally produces a pair of bonnets. Albinos are not that rare either, but most of the ones I've seen border on the anemic in terms of size.

The rose pogonia is probably the most common of the trio of so-called bog orchids, which include *Calopogon tuberosus* (grass-pink orchid) and *Arethusa bulbosa*. It often is in the same company with the grass-pink, blooming a few days later and lasting longer than the other two. *Arethusa bulbosa*, of course, blooms several weeks earlier. Henry Baldwin (1884) observed: "I recall no wild flower of as pure a pink unless it is the Sabatia." (There are several different species of *Sabatia*, including those with five petals, and some other larger species that have eight to twelve.)

Incidentally, I must mention my great surprise when carefully lifting a single plant out of a thick bed of sphagnum moss one day to check the roots below. By actual measure, this root was 18 inches (45 cm) long. The fibrous root penetrated the thick moss to reach the moisture below. Off-shoots from such a root produce new plants vegetatively, it is said, just as is true for the large whorled pogonia, *Isotria verticillata*.

When out of bloom, the rose pogonia is hard to see among the greenery, and with the first frosts of late September, the single-leaved stem turns an equally hard-to-see brown. The $1/2$- to $3/4$-inch (12- to 18-mm) capsule is erect with a ribbed or angled surface.

One day in late September in this boggy spot, while checking the rose pogonia for seed capsules, I witness the flight of the beautiful buck moth, *Hemileuca maia*. Hundreds are flying around in every direction, back and forth, high and low. As a result, several are caught in the strong webs of the common garden spider, *Argiope aurantia*. This is bad for the moth but good for me, allowing easy close-ups with my tripod-mounted camera. The moths often allow close approach when they finally alight on some piece of vegetation but not long enough to get a very good portrait. I stand fully absorbed for nearly an hour watching the aerial performance of this beautiful red, white, and black diurnal-flying moth. This mating flight takes place for only a few days in early autumn. It is a phenomenon, surprisingly, that I have never witnessed before, despite a lifetime of observing the natural world. On the other hand, apparently, the buck moth is not common in New England.

The most unusual rose pogonias I've seen were at Petrel Preserve on the west coast of the Bruce Peninsula, Ontario, in a raised limestone fen owned by the Ontario Field Naturalists organization. Here, in early July, amid another aerial flight, this one by the common snipe, the relatively few blooming plants were less than 3 inches (7.5 cm) in height, runty in aspect, and drab in color. Apparently the limy soil has a debilitating effect on the plants, since acidity is preferred, along the Atlantic coast at any rate. At this site, however, *Calopogon tuberosus* is quite normal in size and color. Fred Case (1987) believes "there is no doubt that genetically distinct strains do occur . . . and seem to be characteristic of certain areas."

In a Nature Conservancy preserve in northern Vermont, I once stumbled on the rarest of the rare, a double flower, among several thousand of these orchids in the largest and most prolific stand I've ever seen. The most pogonias, in a small area, on the other hand, occurred in the wet ditches of coastal North Carolina. An occasional clump of spectacular yellow trumpets (*Sarracenia flava*) made a strong statement here, too, as did the graceful and striking white-top sedge (*Dichromena colorata*), higher and drier on the road shoulder. The rose pogonia ranges from Newfoundland to Minnesota, southward to Florida and Texas, but is sporadic in the interior states.

The five species in the genus *Calopogon* (grass-pink) are all endemic to North America, with three species confined to the Southeast, and only one, *Calopogon tuberosus* (grass-pink orchid), occupying the entire eastern United States. *Calopogon barbatus,* a rich pink, and *C. pallidus,* a very pale pink to white, are confined to the coastal plain from North Carolina to Florida, while *C. multiflorus,* another rich pink, sticks mostly to Florida. *Calopogon oklahomensis* (Oklahoma grass-pink), separated from *C. tuberosus* as a result of a critical study by D. H. Goldman (1995), is a mid-westerner restricted to the southern prairie areas of Oklahoma, where it is said to be most abundant, and extends into Missouri, Arkansas, part of eastern Texas, southeastern Kansas, and western Louisiana. Drier habitat, earlier bloom (May and early June), forked instead of spherical corms, and a labellum disc that is pink instead of white are some of the important distinctions.

All the *Calopogon* species are what botanists refer to as nonresupinate; that is, the lip petal takes the uppermost or dorsal position in the perianth. In most other orchids, the ovary and pedicel twist during development, causing the lip petal to assume the bottom or lower position on the flower, the resupinate or normal position. The winged lip above is uniquely "hinged" at its base to the spoon-shaped column below. This lip, with its brush of golden hairs, acts as a landing platform for the pollinating bee. If the bee is heavy enough, like a bumblebee, the lip flops forward like a miniature catapult, landing on top of the column, with the bumblebee's back brushing against and picking up the sticky pollen from the apex of the narrow petal-like column structure. The performance is then repeated on another flower, which completes the pollination cycle. The remaining petals and sepals spread out in a wide-open posture, with none of the conniving or converging of parts that characterize many other North American orchids.

The genus *Calopogon* is more closely related to the genus *Arethusa* than it is to the genus *Pogonia,* but I treat *Calopogon* and *Pogonia* together partly because they are such common associates in a diversity of habitats. The most typical habitats are quaking bogs and wet, acidic, sphagnous prairie or prairielike stretches of meadow and road-shoulder "lawns." As such, they are one of the most familiar sun-loving orchids east of the Mississippi River (with many gaps inland, as is true of *Pogonia*). *Calopogon* gains an advantage over *Arethusa* by producing offsets from a bulbous corm, along with seeds by pollination, whereas *Arethusa* apparently does not reproduce by offsets, thus suffering in late-frost years when no seed is produced. Fred Case (1987) explained that the proclivity of *Calopogon* to produce these offset corms helps to create large colonies and that he once found in northern Michigan "over 1000 plants growing in a spruce-tamarack bog in less than one square yard [0.8 square meter] of sphagnum moss." Wow!

My best stations have always been along the Maine Turnpike. If the conditions are right—no mowing combined with plenty of moisture—the boggy margins and road shoulders are sometimes transformed into a pink haze. Only once or twice have these conditions been optimal for me, which resulted in a glorious display of several thousand blossoms. In most years, however, this doesn't happen, and the numbers drop to a

Calopogon tuberosus, typical flower color, Maine.

few hundred. In almost every year, nevertheless, a few albinos can be found, as well as two or three pale lavender forms. The pretty little crab spider, *Misumena vatia,* white with a pink hash mark on the abdomen, is often found on the flowers lying in wait for its insect prey.

I will never forget one experience with *Calopogon tuberosus* near Portland, Maine. I was coming home from a business appointment when the heavens opened their faucets for an early July downpour. Business suit notwithstanding, I grabbed my pre-set camera and tripod, ran onto the wet, boggy "lawn," and knelt down to photograph the water-drenched flowers. I soon became drenched myself, without rain gear. I often imagine what was going on in the minds of the passing motorists as they looked over at this guy. No one stopped to investigate—too wet for them —but always worth the price for me. I think of Robert Frost's lines again, and "raise a simple prayer before leaving that spot, that in the general mowing, that place might be forgot, or at least obtain such grace for days, while so confused with flowers."

Calopogon tuberosus, lavender form, Maine.   *Calopogon tuberosus,* albino form, Maine.

CHAPTER 13

Calypso in Vermont

THE GREAT American naturalist and conservationist John Muir recalled in his later years the "two supreme moments" of his life: the first, the day he found *Calypso bulbosa* blooming in a Canadian bog, the second, his meeting with Ralph Waldo Emerson in Yosemite National Park. Correll (1950) said he "looked at the flowers (of *Calypso*) with the feeling that at last I was looking upon the most beautiful terrestrial orchid in North America." Morris and Eames (1929) called it "the most rarely beautiful of North American terrestrial orchids," a slight distinction from their description of *Arethusa bulbosa* as "the most exquisitely beautiful."

Beauty is in the eye of the beholder, of course, and not everyone has unstinting words of praise. The late George Aiken (1935), for example, a former senator from Vermont, thought it "one of the most grotesquely beautiful wildflowers. It seems to try to overcome the terrible malformation of its flowers with exquisitely beautiful coloring. They seem like gnomes of the wood, perhaps ashamed of their grotesqueness, which causes them to hide from civilization."

Of all the writers I have read, I think Mabel Osgood Wright (1901) said it best:

> Calypso's shoe, raised on a stem above a single broad leaf, is dull pink and furred inside with soft hairs. It has a curious, overlapped, double-pointed toe of pale yellow; a little rosette of shaded pink and yellow trims the instep, while the narrower petals blow in the breeze like ribbons meant to fasten the shoe about the ankle of its phantom wearer.

Compare Wright's description with Correll's (1978): "The solitary pastel pink-purple flowers touched here and there with white and yellow, diffidently nodded on the tips of short slender stems." Wright's prose is better, I think. She was referring to New England plants, while Correll was recalling hundreds or thousands of plants in northern British Columbia where they still grow in abundance. In New England, however, they were never common and are even less so today. Logging for arborvitae (*Thuja occidentalis*) destroys the habitat by letting in too much sunlight, not to mention the usual clear-cutting, which is even more devastating. In addition, foot traffic by nature lovers and photographers, like myself but especially groups of several individuals, does much damage to the extremely shallow corms. Global warming may also be a factor.

Calypso bulbosa, typical flower color, Vermont.

Calypso bulbosa, pale form, Vermont.

My first experience with the hider-of-the-north came in 1959 when Herm Willey of St. Johnsbury, Vermont, took me into my first cedar swamp. Even if we had not seen the calypso, the unique beauty of the cedar bog was sufficient reward, as unforgettable then as it is today. Everything on the floor of the bog was covered with green mosses, interrupted only by trailing vines of the twin-flower (*Linnaea borealis*) and creeping snowberry (*Gaultheria hispidula*), along with the tiny heart-leaved twayblade (*Listera cordata*) and a few early coralroots (*Corallorhiza trifida*). Two favorite mosses, the feathery mountain fern moss (*Hylocomium splendens*) and the ostrich plume moss (*Ptilium crista-castrensis*), provided a most glorious spread for this orchid. Little wonder that the calypso is associated with the idea of pristine wilderness more than any other North American wild orchid. Optimal conditions exist only during a period of normal or above-normal moisture when dew drops transform the green-golds from ordinary to extraordinary beauty. In dry spells this unique feeling is significantly reduced or lost entirely.

In Vermont, the calypso is often found blooming on the hummocks—the raised area around the swollen base of a multistemmed arbor-vitae (*Thuja occidentalis*)—as well as on the flat ground in between the trees, which is mantled with the brown scalelike leaves of the arbor-vitae and little else. There the showy, single, pendant flower stem rises from a solitary, ground-hugging leaf barely 4 to 8 inches (10 to 20 cm) above the ground. It is very difficult to see, especially when there is other vegetation nearby, like the small white violet (*Viola pallens*). As with so many native orchids, assuming the position of a catcher in baseball, aids in spotting these plants.

The arbor-vitae (*Thuja occidentalis*), also known as northern white cedar, dominates most of the low wet areas in this part of Vermont. I remembered it as a popular cultivated small tree back home, used as screens, hedges, and foundation plants. Like the calypso, it prefers limestone or neutral soil. The term *arbor-vitae* is taken from a French word meaning "tree of life" and was given to this plant because of its many uses in lumber applications, as browse for deer, moose, and rabbits, and in landscaping, to name a few.

Since my initial meeting in 1959, the calypso has disappeared from that particular bog and many others like it. Fortunately, however, a few plants still remain to greet me on my annual pilgrimage to Vermont in late May. I have seen the calypso only in Vermont, but look forward to the day I get to see it out West where both the eastern variety, *Calypso bulbosa* var. *americana,* and the more aggressive western variety, *C. bulbosa* var. *occidentalis,* display their beauty in numbers approaching the thousands in areas where they haven't been pillaged by collectors and commercial operators. The two varieties do not overlap in the West. Variety *americana* occurs well inland from the Rockies to Alaska as well as eastward to Newfoundland, mostly in Canada. Variety *occidentalis* is restricted to the northern coast of California, coastal Oregon, and Washington, as well as the northern tip of Idaho and thence into extreme southeastern Alaska, nearer the coast than the eastern variety. I believe the western variety will eventually attain specific status.

Leonard Wiley (1969) told of a friend who annually picked a huge bouquet of deer head orchids for his wife:

> He was very careful how he picked these flowers for he knew that the stems were more securely attached to the tiny bulbs than the roots were to the moss in which they spend their lives. It is so easy, under these circumstances to destroy the bulbs while picking the stems.

No seeds ripen under these circumstances, and the calypso must produce seeds to survive and thrive. No one should ever purchase this orchid by mail order or any other means. The eastern variety does not survive in the home environment, under any conditions, while the western plant barely does in the best of circumstances for a year or two. Like so many once-common plants, extinction by collection is a serious threat to both of these fragile orchids.

In closing, I offer the following excerpt from an uncredited poem in Henry Baldwin's fine book on *The Orchids of New England* (1884):

> See! where that thoughtless wind the leaves is lifting
> Above her mossy bed
> On lightest tiptoe poised Calypso hovers,
> Her rosy wings outspread.
> I haste; I kneel; for joy I cannot utter
> One stammered word of praise.

CHAPTER 14

The Small Whorled Pogonia in Maine and New Hampshire

A ENDANGERED species biologist for the United States Fish and Wildlife Service, working on an agreement with the U.S. Forest Service to help permanently protect one of the rarest of all North American orchids in the White Mountain National Forest of New Hampshire, summed up the feeling of many people when she was quoted as saying: "Some people just take pure and simple pleasure out of just looking at these plants." She was talking about the small whorled pogonia (*Isotria medeoloides*), perhaps the rarest of all American orchids east of the Mississippi River and north of Florida. She went on to say, "There's one thing we know for sure: we can't grow the small whorled pogonia in a greenhouse. No one's been able to do that."

Some people fret over the U.S. Forest Service policy of protecting endangered species at the expense of a logger's job. Once the logging is done, however, the job is gone and the worker moves on, but the species disappears and extinction is forever. To paraphrase Aldo Leopold, author of *A Sand County Almanac* (1949), considered by some conservationists to be the most important book ever written: The chance to find a small whorled pogonia [substitute any other species] is a right as inalienable as free speech.

We have a better chance of seeing the small whorled pogonia in New Hampshire than anywhere else in North America, for New Hampshire has the largest populations of this pogonia of any state in the United States. First described in 1814, the plant has been seen by few botanists in the intervening one hundred and seventy-five years or so, until the 1980s, when concerted efforts by many state Natural Heritage Inventory programs identified increasing numbers of new stations from Maine to Georgia, and west to Lower Michigan, extreme southern Ontario, and Missouri. Large gaps exist in between, making the distribution of this orchid one of the most difficult to plot on a map. The Ontario station in Canada consisted of only two stems when discovered in the late 1970s, and apparently, the plants have not reappeared for several years.

As early as 1884 Henry Baldwin stated that the small whorled pogonia had been found only once in New England, around New Haven, Connecticut. William Gibson, referring to the northeastern United States about twenty years later, called it "truly a rarity, imperfectly known either

Isotria medeoloides, clump with a dwarf plant, New Hampshire.

here or elsewhere." Grace Niles, however, about the same time called it "frequent" in Connecticut and very rare elsewhere, with a range from Vermont to Pennsylvania. None of these early authors ever saw the orchid. Morris and Eames, on the other hand, traveled from Ontario to William and Mary College in Virginia in the 1920s to visit the most famous historical site of all. Oakes Ames reported seventeen stations as of 1924, and for several decades after that the figures changed little if at all. In 1985, 49 stations and approximately 3200 individual plants were known. In just three years (1988) the number of populations shot up to 74 with 3900 plants, 28 of those stations and 2200 plants in New Hampshire alone. The neighboring state of Maine claims 14 stations and 1000 individuals. Almost 80 percent of the known plants have been found in New Hampshire and Maine. The count is up to 104 stations as of 1993, resulting in a proposal to reduce the federally "endangered" status to one of "threatened."

Frankie Brackley and Tom Rawinski, both former botanists for the Natural Heritage Inventory in New Hampshire and Massachusetts, respectively, determined the typical habitat of this orchid to be one of temporary vernal stream beds that dry up in the summer, usually on a gradual slope, in rather ordinary mixed woods composed of red oak (*Quercus rubra*), red maple (*Acer rubrum*), white birch (*Betula papyrifera*), and

Isotria medeoloides, a pair of flowers, New Hampshire.

hemlock (*Tsuga canadensis*). Friends Sally Puth and Shirley Curtis and I have found two small populations, one with a tight group of four or five plants that bloom every year and one a double, only a half hour's driving time from our homes, at or near the plant's "world" population center.

Hank Tyler of the Maine Critical Areas Program made the date of 18 June 1980 a memorable one for me by a simple telephone call from his office in Augusta, Maine, to mine in Dover, New Hampshire: "*Isotria medeoloides* is in full bloom on the campus of Kent School."

"I'm on my way!"

Such is the advantage to being general manager of a heating company in the summertime. The call came in at eleven o'clock, and I was in Kent's Hill, Maine, two hours later. This station represents the northern limit for the species or did at the time. Fifty to seventy-five plants were scattered through an open white pine (*Pinus strobus*) woodlot on the campus of Kent School. Richard Crane, a faculty member who grew up in St. Johnsbury, Vermont, and a mutual friend of Herm Willey, directed me to the plants, the first I had ever seen. Half of them were in bloom, with four or five doubles.

> It is curious how seldom the mind's eye succeeds in picturing a strange plant correctly . . . in spite of conning carefully over book descriptions. And now, when we were all tuned up to see a rather stunted or impoverished *Isotria verticillata*, behold! a dainty little orchid of an entirely different habit, the flower about the size of a snowdrop and with much the same proportion of outer to inner ring of perianth parts . . . but with nothing of the sprawling almost untidy look of the Large Whorled. The relatively short sepals and pedicel spoke for themselves; they gave an entirely new aspect to the flower . . . it was always the difference that struck—the color of the stem, the shape and set of the leaves, the decorative design of the lip, everything (Morris and Eames 1929).

Despite the above description, in all honesty the flower is a rather small and plain greenish yellow with much white on the lip. The lip also has the traditional or typical pogonia crest on the disc or upper surface of the lip. The five or six leaves in a whorl around the top of the 6-inch (15-cm) stem at first hang down as if wilted, perking up only at full anthesis. As with almost everything else, rarity increases one's interest tenfold.

CHAPTER 15

The Large Whorled Pogonia in Massachusetts

THE LARGE whorled pogonia (*Isotria verticillata*) is always associated in my mind with the late Lawrence Newcomb, who showed me my first one —actually more than a hundred—on 20 May 1980 in his own backyard. Author of the popular *Newcomb's Wildflower Guide,* Lawrence had a very ordinary and typical woodlot of mixed white pine (*Pinus strobus*), with checkerberry (*Gaultheria procumbens*), Canada mayflower (*Maianthemum canadense*), and low-bush blueberry (*Vaccinium angustifolium*) as dominant groundcover. His backyard, then in Sharon, Massachusetts, is close to the highest point in eastern Massachusetts, the 635-foot (182-m) Great Blue Hill, in the Blue Hill Reservation, which is also near the northern limit for this orchid. A site in Burlington, Vermont, is a long distance from all other stations in New England. With this one exception, the large whorled pogonia is essentially absent from northern New England (Maine, New Hampshire, and Vermont), but as soon as one crosses the state line into Massachusetts, it becomes fairly frequent in certain localities.

The 6500-acre (2600-ha) Blue Hill Reservation is part of the great Metropolitan Park system of Massachusetts, just a "stone's throw" from the city of Boston, and one of the most important ecological and recreational resources in the entire Boston area. Another friend, Paul Martin Brown, founder of the North American Native Orchid Alliance in 1995, grew up in this area, down the road in Foxboro, Massachusetts, also the home of the New England Patriots. Paul knows the Blue Hills as well as anybody in the state probably, and he also knows orchids. In fact, I would have to say that he is one of the most knowledgeable field orchidologists and general field botanists I have ever met and the most enthusiastic and intense one to boot. He formerly led field trips for the New England Wild Flower Society but now does the same on his own.

Paul showed me a station of a hundred or more of these exotic "southern" spider orchids in the Blue Hill Reservation on 21 May 1994 almost fourteen years to the day that Larry Newcomb did the initial honors. Dozens of beautiful pink lady's-slippers were also on hand, making it hard to resist "one more photograph." The large whorled pogonia reveals its relationship to *Cleistes divaricata,* sometimes called the spreading pogonia, in the flaring coiffure of green-purple-brown sepals that surround the yellowish green funnel formed by the two lateral petals, which merge and arch over the lip. The lip is peculiarly ridged with a fleshy,

waxy green material that is flanked on the upturned edge with the same green-purple-brown color as the flaring sepals. The apex of the lip barely opens to give a hint of the beautiful multicolored interior. Before the extraordinary open stage, the pale pink-purple, thick, hollow stem rises from the ground with the whorl of five leaves tightly clasped around the petals. It looks like a tapered lance thrusting skyward or the long thin, tapered horn of the narwhal as it comes bursting out of the water, an unusual effect. According to Homoya (1993), the large whorled pogonia

> has a mysterious and foreign appearance seemingly more typical of tropical jungles than of the dry hills of Indiana. This exotic quality is clearly seen in the flower, which, with its long spreading sepals, resembles the threatening pose of some weirdly shaped spider.

Isotria verticillata, spindle stage of emerging flower and leaf whorl, Massachusetts.

Indeed, spider plant is one of several "country" names for this orchid: green adderling (an allusion to a small snake) and purple five-leaved orchid are two others.

This pogonia is neither rare nor common over most of its range, which extends down the Atlantic coastal plain, up onto and across the Cumberland Plateau and the Blue Ridge, into parts of the Midwest. Where it is found, however, large colonies sometimes are the rule and not the exception.

IIsotria verticillata, pair of flowers, Massachusetts.

Both *Isotria verticillata* and *I. medeoloides,* despite what some authors have said, appear regularly every year, but in varying numbers. Fred Case (1987) made an interesting observation about the vegetative reproduction of this pogonia based on eight plants under his care from 1968 to 1984, which increased to 26 stems:

> Between eight and eleven of the plants bloom annually. It is most interesting that some of the current stems are located from several inches to over two feet [60 cm] from where the original plants were placed, indicating not only that this species relies on strong vegetative reproduction to produce its dense colonies, but also that there is considerable underground movement of the plants over the years.

A great deal more investigation and research by both amateurs and professionals is needed to unlock more of the secrets of this and other native orchids that carry out their life histories in relative seclusion.

CHAPTER 16

The Pink Lady's-slipper in New Hampshire

AN ALMOST anthropomorphic relationship exists between some of us and our favorite orchids. This is especially true of the pink lady's-slipper, *Cypripedium acaule*, generally the most familiar and beloved wild orchid in the Northeast. Other of the twelve species of *Cypripedium* are equally loved in other parts of the country, though most of them are less often seen than the pink. This probably accounts for the greater number of colloquial or common names applied to the lady's-slippers than any other of the more than two hundred species of North American orchids. Some of the early settlers who knew the yellow lady's-slipper (*Cypripedium parviflorum*) back home in England used the term moccasin flower for the pink. Noah's ark and whippoorwill-shoe are two other names.

The pink lady's-slipper is perhaps more common in New England than anywhere else in North America. It produces more albino forms in the White Mountains than anywhere else and grows taller and more robust, too. I have measured several specimens with stems in the 20- to 24-inch (50- to 60-cm) range, huge leaves 7 inches (17 cm) wide by 11 inches (27 cm) long, and pouches over 2 inches (5 cm) long by almost 1½ inches (3.5 cm) wide. Plants with a double lip are rarely seen. It took me more than thirty years to see my first one.

Cypripedium acaule has the longest bloom season of any species in the genus, both as a whole population and as individuals within that population. For example, a flower tagged on 17 May 1993 still showed good color (with no staining or wilting) twenty-four days later on 10 June. I must admit, however, that the season was cooler than normal. In an average year, two to three weeks is the norm. A cut stem lasts a week in water.

113

Before anyone jumps to the wrong conclusion, let me assure you that, with few exceptions, I never pick bouquets of any orchid. One exception was in 1976 when my mother was dying of cancer, just before she lapsed into a coma. The pink lady's-slipper was her favorite wildflower. The temptation to pick, of course, has been the undoing of the pink lady's-slipper in many localities. I can understand why the Native Americans of the Northeast picked it for decoration in their hair.

Other singularities of the pink lady's-slipper include a pouch shaped differently from any of the other dozen North American species. Instead of the usual round hole at the top of an inflated pouch, a slit or fissure runs down the front of an elongated drooping pouch, or hanging bag as one imaginative writer described it at the turn of the twentieth century.

Each spring I look forward to checking a site that favors more than

Cypripedium acaule, large clump of white form, New Hampshire.

five hundred of these superb lady's-slippers, a small white pine (*Pinus strobus*) woods within walking distance of my home "where the carpet of pine needles will not hurt her feet." As John Burroughs (1904) so elegantly expressed it, "Most of the floral ladies leave their slippers in swampy places in the woods; only the stemless one leaves hers on dry ground." Here during the first warm days of late May, I sit and enjoy for as long as I desire, a table set with pinks, reds, and whites (albinos) and a highly unusual semipeloric plant whose lateral petals expand to twice their normal size and assume the identical rose color of the lip. This "monstrosity," by the way, appears each year, as do the several albinos, a rarity on the coastal plain. That the peak of the warbler migration in these woods coincides with that of the lady's-slipper is frosting on the cake. Albino forms are not uncommon in the mountains of New Hampshire and make up perhaps as much as 25 percent of the population. Every trip I make to the White Mountains produces several in June.

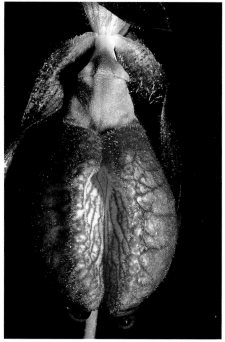

Cypripedium acaule, back of flower, with raindrops, New Hampshire.

Cypripedium acaule, typical flower color, with raindrops, New Hampshire.

Typically, when I am not in the vicinity of a *Cypripedium acaule* woodlot, as when I'm jogging, for example, but would like to check its progress, the best indicator plant for that information is the almost ubiquitous Canada mayflower (*Maianthemum canadense*), which sometimes carpets woodlands like a groundcover. The dense raceme of ten to twenty tiny, white flowers opens from the bottom up over a short period of a few days, by which time the first two or three lower flowers already start to turn brown. The pink lady's-slipper assumes its deepest color before that point, and by the time the Canada mayflower is almost all brown, the pink lady's-slipper is still going strong, like the battery in the TV commercial.

Mrs. William Dana (1910) wrote, "It seems to be touched with the spirit of the deep woods, and there is a certain fitness in its Indian name, for it looks as though it came direct from the home of the red man." Henry Baldwin (1894) quoted T. W. Higginson, who characterized it as "high bred," and added: "I can never resist the feeling that each specimen is a rarity, even when I find a hundred to an acre." Mark Catesby, one of North America's first naturalists, was impressed enough to call it "the most elegant flower of all the Helleborine tribe." Preece (1937), however, was a bit ambivalent in his assessment. He first described the flower as a "grotesque blossom" that, because of "its weird bizarrerie is definitely repulsive" to many people. Later, he described it as "a striking and handsome plant which never fails to attract attention when in bloom."

Cypripedium acaule, a rare double-lipped flower, New Hampshire.

My woodlot is just a remnant of what once was a larger and more pristine bit of wildness, long since destroyed by the familiar stories of woodcutter, bulldozer, and builder. (More than 99 percent of the white pine forest in the Northeast was clearcut during the 1800s and early 1900s, a sad example of poor stewardship. One or two percent for saving is far too small. I believe a figure closer to 10 percent, for many species, is not an unreasonable minimum to expect to save and protect. Unfortunately, not even the redwoods of California are achieving this goal.)

Cypripedium acaule can be found in many (formerly most) dry white pine forests, mixed forests, and oak woodlands in highly acidic soil. It also is found on dry lichen-covered rock ledges (e.g., Bic Provincial Park on the Gaspé Peninsula in Québec, Canada), but almost never in swamps. Having said that, Fred Case (1987) cited sphagnum bogs as a common habitat in the Great Lakes region but on "hummocks and drier areas," not the wetter ones. He also commented on the occurrence of late frosts "that cut down most scapes even though the leaves seem little affected. Following a frost-free blooming season, hundreds of seed pods ripen in the larger colonies." Correll (1978) thought a lack of pollinating agents and elapsed time between actual pollination and fertilization were the causes of poor capsule production. I do not have a strong opinion one way or the other. I do know, however, that I have never seen frost damage in my part of New Hampshire.

The derivation of the generic name *Cypripedium* has an interesting story. According to Niles (1904), it was known as lady's-slipper as early as the 1600s in England. The word *cypripedium* comes from the Latin word *Marianus,* meaning "Our Lady" in reference to the Virgin Mary. Carl Linnaeus, the father of our modern binomial nomenclature system (the naming of plants and animals) objected to honoring the mother of Jesus (he was a noted Lutheran) and chose instead to use the Greek term for goddess of love.

From a pragmatic point of view, because *Cypripedium acaule* is impossible to transplant successfully for more than a year or two, plants should never be purchased at garden centers, nurseries, or by mail-order. There is, however, a better reason: conservation. To me, it is criminal to see "nursery" lists offering the plants in quantities of fifty or more. It is no wonder then that this and other species of native orchids are rapidly approaching the point of no return. If that day does come, the quality of life will not be the same for anyone.

CHAPTER 17

Ram's-head in Vermont

THERE ARE more hard-packed clay-surfaced roads in eastern Vermont than there are asphalt roads. Probably so because of the clay soils and rural nature of the state. Almost all my orchid hunting is done on this type of country road, which, of course, can add to the overall ambience of the hunt. The one I'm on today in this third week in May is more remote than most of them, with no visible houses and no vehicles for which to pull over. I can stop on the side of the road and spend an hour without a single vehicle disturbing the tranquillity, with nothing but a picturesque Vermont sugar maple forest and classic gurgling brook for company.

We are heading for a juicy-rich habitat harboring hundreds of the legendary *Cypripedium arietinum* (ram's-head), gorgeous *C. parviflorum* var. *pubescens,* and four other species of orchids. Hundreds of large, bright, black and yellow-striped tiger swallowtail butterflies gather in crowded groups every 50 yards (45 m) or so in the middle of the roadbed, unmoved by a passing vehicle, which causes the death of many of them. I stop and take their picture. They allow a very close approach before flying off and quickly return to the same spot. Tiger swallowtails are what lepidopterists call mud puddlers—butterflies that spend much time sucking water and minerals from the clay.

All about us mists of pale green to dark green, yellow-green, and mint-green envelop the trees, slowly at first and then in a rush. Welcome to springtime in Vermont, the most enjoyable time of the year! Autumn's blast of brilliant colors is prelude to winter, while spring's symphony of green precedes the sumptuous surge of summer. The only distraction to our elation is an impending downpour brewing in a small black pot of a cloud hidden by the thick canopy of trees. It appears the inevitable will be of short duration, however, and of little consequence to my friend from California, Ron Coleman, who has traveled so far to see the elusive ram's-head.

We leave the car at the corner of an old logging road, impassable in anything other than a high clearance four-wheel-drive vehicle, walk across the same babbling stream that keeps us company all the way up the road, and begin to look for the smallest and rarest of all North American lady's-slippers, *Cypripedium arietinum*. The small size of the flower and plant make it difficult to spot the ram's-head under the best of conditions, so one must not be casual in looking for it or risk walking right by. This advice applies to many other orchids, I might add. Because I have been here several times, we find our prizes quickly, almost seventy-five of them.

Most authors fancy the look of this orchid as that of a charging ram, hence the common name, of course. The late George Aiken, a former Vermont senator and author of *Pioneering with Wildflowers* (1935), considered the flower so grotesquely shaped that "to me they look more like the head of a common housefly." Henry Baldwin (1884), on the other hand, considered it to be the most attractive of all the cypripediums. The flower is indeed shaped like the head of a ram, and the common name will always have a revered place in the folklore of botany. The uniquely crafted lip is the size of a thimble and the shape of a top. Its beauty is greatly enhanced by the interlocking, two-toned purple veining on the sides of the pouch and the frothy, white cotton candy rim surrounding the opening at the top. One must get down to camera level to really appreciate this beauty, and better yet, examine it under a magnifying lens. This, of course, is standard procedure for many orchids.

Though one of the rarest of North American orchids, the ram's-head is actually common in some restricted areas of Upper Michigan and the Bruce Peninsula of southern Ontario. Otherwise, it follows a narrow belt that hugs the Canadian border from north central Maine through north central Vermont, extreme northern New York, extreme southern Ontario, Upper Michigan, and into northern Wisconsin and northeastern Minnesota. In most of these areas it is considered rare.

While Ron photographs, I take a moment to look up and catch a flash of red from a scarlet tanager, joyously proclaiming his arrival, perhaps this very day, with a raspy, racing, queer querit. A rose-breasted grosbeak joins in with a glorious, throaty ca-ree-kio. The echo of a distant drum staccato identifies the exuberant yellow-bellied sapsucker. There is a comfortable feeling that all's well with the world at least at this moment on this day here in the wilds of Vermont.

Cypripedium arietinum, with flash, Vermont.

That delayed thunderstorm finally begins to rumble and the spigot opens. At first we take cover under a large, isolated white pine (*Pinus strobus*) tree, a no-no, and quickly decide to hurry back to the car. It's lunchtime anyway and we might as well stay dry. In a few moments I can't believe what I see. A very large and, fortunately, empty logging truck inches up the road, stops in front of us, and then attempts to turn around. The road is impossibly impassable straight ahead, he sees, and concludes that he has taken the wrong road up. How he got this far is a bit of a mystery to me. The soft-spoken, cigarette-smoking driver asks me to move my car so he can turn around and go back down the ridge. I am happy to oblige but wonder how he can do it. But do it he does!

After the short-lived thundershower, we walk past the ram's-head another few

Cypripedium arietinum, with flash, Vermont.

hundred yards further up the old logging road to lady's-slipper heaven, where more than 500 large yellow lady's-slippers, *Cypripedium parviflorum* var. *pubescens* (formerly *C. calceolus* var. *pubescens*), appear in large clumps of leafy gold goblets. They are not visible from the "road" but hide a short distance above a series of spongy-wet, seepage shelves, in an open sugar maple (*Acer saccharum*) woodland. This lady's-slipper is most attractive in such rich, mesic second-growth forests. Especially abundant companions are maidenhair ferns (*Adiantum pedatum*) and plantain-leaved sedges (*Carex plantaginea*), along with numerous yellow violets (*Viola pennsylvanica*), aging red trillium (*Trillium erectum*), and red baneberry (*Actea rubra*). "How the eye loves to linger upon yellow flowers," Mabel Wright (1901) declared. It is the most dominant flower color throughout the growing season.

Cypripedium parviflorum var. *pubescens*, Vermont.

Cypripedium parviflorum var. *pubescens*, Vermont.

Early the next morning we're off to Green Banks Hollow, one of my favorite spots in this part of Vermont. The hollow is noted for its covered bridge on Joe's River, but our attention is mostly spent admiring and photographing *Galearis spectabilis,* the showy orchis, also in full bloom and again in the hundreds, which seems to be our lucky numbers. The showy orchis is reasonably common in Vermont and at this site produces the forma *willeyi,* named after my friend, the late Herm Willey. Instead of the usual bicolor effect, lavender pink uppers and white lower lip petal, this form is a uniform pink throughout. Luer (1975) is one of the few authors to mention and illustrate this unusual color form. (Incidentally, I might add that the most highly colored specimen I have seen, a red-

Galearis spectabilis, with flash, Vermont.

Galearis spectabilis, with insect, Vermont.

purple, occurred in the aforementioned Taylor Valley area of Strafford, Vermont).

In most clumps in Green Banks Hollow, the showy orchis grows tightly packed, looking all leaves despite only two basal, opposite leaves per plant. The leaves look waxy and "damp" to the touch, a sure sign that they belong to an orchid. A short flowering stem sticks out of some of these crowded clumps, bearing a loose raceme of more than a dozen flowers, but more commonly only a few. Many stems do not flower every year. Mabel Wright (1901) was reminded "of a lovely woman with so short a neck that she cannot turn her head." The showy orchis is sometimes

Galearis spectabilis forma *willeyi*, Vermont.

called preacher in the pulpit, an allusion to the fancied clergyman (anthers) under the canopied pulpit of lavender pink sepals and petals above the white lip. Back at the turn of the twentieth century when picking wildflowers was an annual ritual for country folk and flower lovers, it was said that this orchid was too short to fit very well in a bouquet with other spring ephemerals. How fortunate for the orchids.

The only disappointment of the weekend occurs at our last stop, for the eastern calypso, *Calypso bulbosa* var. *americana*. We find only one in bloom—and that just barely—but at least Ron gets a firsthand look at the difference between our eastern variety and his western variety, *C. bulbosa* var. *occidentalis*. Our two-day weekend has been productive and even though it was threatening at times, Ron is satisfied with a sampling of what the Green Mountain State has to offer in the beautiful month of May.

CHAPTER 18

The Queen Lady's-slipper in Vermont

STANDING on the edge of an almost never used road, I look down into a "hole," about an acre (less than half a hectare) in size, which appears at first glance to be nothing more than an ordinary cattail (*Typha latifolia*) swamp. Veeries complain loudly at my intrusion, uttering yerks from several directions. These alarm notes soon alternate with one of the most unusual songs in the bird world, sounding like the notes of a flute played through a resonant pipe, in a descending, spiraling crescendo. I listen with rapt attention, momentarily distracted from the depression into which I am about to descend.

My timing is right on the mark. I can see several blooming clumps from the rim of the hole. I then begin to brake my way slowly down the almost ninety-degree slope into the muck and water of lady's-slipper heaven. I am surrounded by some 2000 of the largest, and most "sun"-sational of all lady's-slippers, *Cypripedium reginae,* the big pink and white, better known as the showy or the queen. The big, bold upper sepal, which is 1–2 inches (2.5–4.5 cm) long and wide, and the smaller, narrower lateral petals are white as new fallen snow, and provide a perfect foil for the white globular pouch, the sides of which are stained with overflowing purple raspberry juices. "The crowning glory of our northern bogs," Morris and Eames proclaimed (1929). Mrs. Dana (1910) called it the most beautiful North American orchid, a sentiment many others share. "Never have I beheld a prettier sight . . . so gay, so festive, so holiday-looking," wrote John Burroughs (1901).

The stately and aristocratic plant stands almost 3 feet (90 cm) tall and sometimes taller, but usually shorter, making it extremely hard to resist picking or digging. At the turn of the twentieth century, the queen lady's-slipper often graced the altars of many a rural church during the months of June and July. One shudders at how quickly this practice wiped it out in many locales. School children in those days also amused themselves by playing with "boats," floating the inflated lips of this lady's-slipper in a bucket of water. One of the colloquial names for this lady's-slipper is Noah's ark, alluding to this habit. Sometimes two or three buds on a stem add to the glory of the display. Colors range widely from the palest pink to the richest red-maroon. I have seen many pure white albinos, but not in this particular swamp.

A predawn shower creates a third dimension this morning. There is something special about rain drops on a flower, particularly on an orchid. In the shade, I set up my tripod, camera, and reflector, and hurry before the hot sun dries off any more flowers. Then I try back lighting at an angle below the flower to emphasize the translucent quality of the large, wide overarching white sepal, lined with hairs on the edge. Two or three hours are spent slogging over the wet sphagnum and through a

Cypripedium reginae, typical flower color, Vermont.

thicket of willows, which I notice are beginning to shade and crowd out the lady's-slippers, as I look for that perfect picture. That condition eludes me, bringing me back every year. As if compensating for the increased competition in one area, the more open central part of the bog-swamp seems to have more plants this year, including a few white candles of the tall *Platanthera dilatata,* perhaps the most fragrant North American orchid. In one shaded corner each year, dozens of the daisylike golden senecios (*Senecio aureus*) hold forth.

I reluctantly prepare to take leave as my mind returns to the reality of a three-hour drive back home. It is hot and humid, the veeries have long since stopped calling, and few other sounds penetrate the stillness. Retracing my steps to the base of the slope, I inadvertently step into the muddy hole I am trying to avoid. No big deal at first, I think, but as I try to pull my left leg out of the juicy, black, mucky mud, the suction increases. I realize this is going to take some time and energy. The almost quick-sand effect of the mud hole has now sucked my leg all the way up the thigh close to the crotch. I throw off my equipment to lighten the

Cypripedium reginae, vivid red pair, with flash, Vermont.

Cypripedium reginae, albino pair, with flash, Vermont.

Cypripedium reginae, revealing beauty of interior pouch, Vermont.

weight. The road is only 30 feet (9 m) up the slope, but almost no traffic uses this road; in ten or fifteen years I've seen only one or two cars go by. Lying on my side, I manage to take hold of a branch and ever so slowly begin to inch my leg up and out of the hole. With a feeling of relief I scramble up the steep grade, rest my tired body against the car, and take a self-portrait of my black mud-encrusted pant legs to show the world. Such are the occasional hazards of the hobby and one reason why it is good judgment to have a companion along. Of course, this is not always feasible or desirable.

One of the better indicators of the queen lady's-slipper in Vermont, at least, are these lowland willow-cattail swamp-marsh areas commonly adjacent to open pastures, meadows, and arbor-vitae (*Thuja occidentalis*) swamps. I check out as many as time allows. One day I find the finest compact stand of these queens I've ever seen, with the deepest reds and a clump of albinos, all in prime condition. In subsequent years this latter station has quickly deteriorated for some reason I cannot understand. Plant succession does not appear to be the cause. *Potentilla fruticosa* is a common companion plant at this station. Welby Smith (1993) stated that "if left undisturbed the rhizome will continue to grow and produce more stems in successive years. As a result, the large clumps of 20 or more stems may be as much as a hundred years old, possibly much older." I'm not that old but I have seen stands still doing well that I've checked for the last thirty years.

Snowmobile trails are a particularly good niche for these orchids if not disturbed beyond the winter season. Equally good are swaths or paths cut through woodlots for whatever reason. A few of my best stations are of this type, where many companion plants luxuriate as well and add to the decor of the little community. Among them are moisture-loving things like the bog wintergreens (*Pyrola asarifolia* and *P. secunda*), the dwarf cornel or bunchberry (*Cornus canadensis*), the deliciously scented pink, paired bells of (*Linnaea borealis*), and the green *Platanthera huronensis* (often included within *P. hyperborea*), to mention a few. Incidentally, early on in this hobby, it was uncanny how the equally tall and taller false hellebore (*Veratrum viride*) of the lily family looked so much like a cypripedium, at a distance. Unfortunately, there are far more of the lily than the lady's-slipper. Deer frequently browse the 3-foot (90-cm) tall stalks of the lady's-slipper while avoiding the lily, which is also poisonous to humans at maturity.

Cypripedium reginae grows from Newfoundland to Minnesota and Manitoba, keeping close to the U.S.–Canadian border, while detouring south along the Appalachians to Arkansas. It is the state flower of Min-

Cypripedium reginae, double-lipped flower, Newfoundland.

nesota (the only orchid so honored) and the provincial flower of Prince Edward Island in Canada. I have seen it in several other areas, but Vermont will always hold the fondest memories. Of the thousands of photographs I have made of North American wild orchids over the years, the showy lady's-slipper ranks high in the total number of pictures and the end is not in sight. I cannot resist the urge to record ever more portraits. A simple review of my collection proves the point that every year's photographs are different. The transcendent beauty of the flowers, the luxuriant green surroundings and that of the state as a whole, combined with the friendship of the Willeys over nearly thirty years, have left an indelible mark in my mind and heart. We all need a place to get away from the stresses of civilization, to experience Nature on its terms, to see live things, face to face, instead of on a TV screen or in a zoo behind bars. When that place includes wild orchids and good friends, the experience is taken a level higher.

CHAPTER 19

Purple and Green Fringed-orchids in Maine and New Hampshire

LONG drives to distant places can sometimes be boring and tedious without the company of good National Public Radio classical music or talk programs. Better still is good company in the passenger seat, especially someone like Les Eastman, formerly of Old Orchard Beach, Maine, now living and teaching in Lewiston, Maine. Les formerly led the Josselyn Society, a botanical group devoted to Maine botany and founded by Kate Furbish, the state's most famous botanist-painter. Les was my indispensable guide in Maine in the 1970s and early 1980s. He introduced me to the largest stand of *Platanthera psycodes* I ever saw as well as my first orchid hybrid, *P. ×andrewsii,* and many, many more goodies. One of our trips, to Fort Kent in Aroostook County, is almost the equivalent of driving to Washington, D.C., from my home in Dover, New Hampshire. We had plenty of time to talk, and life on the roads of Maine was always interesting with Les. We are both opinionated and interested in a variety of subjects besides orchids, which made the car time go by more enjoyably as well as quickly. Les is also one of those types we call doers. He didn't sit back and wait for the other guy to do it.

In late July 1976 Les showed me a wet meadow in Wilton, Maine, previously used as a horse pasture but beginning to evolve into a classic example of plant succession, with young alders (*Alnus rugosa*) and balsam firs (*Abies balsamea*) taking over. Among this woody growth, however, were more than a thousand small purple fringed-orchids, *Platanthera psycodes.* Many of these plants were standing 3 feet tall (90 cm). The colorful racemes, or soldier's plumes as they are sometimes called, ranged in color from the usual lavender-pink to intense purple-reds, with scattered albinos and bicolors—more color variation than is usually seen.

On one tightly compact raceme I counted the phenomenal number of one hundred and fifty florets. The average stem usually carries closer to forty or fifty individuals.

Two or three hybrids of *Platanthera ×andrewsii* elicited great interest on our part. We could tell instantly that these plants were not the usual *P. psycodes*. The hybrid *P. ×andrewsii* is a delightful combination of pale

Platanthera psycodes, raceme of over 100 pale florets, Vermont.

Platanthera psycodes, showing rectangular spur opening, Maine.

Platanthera psycodes, overhead shot illustrating perfect symmetry of bloom cylinder, New Hampshire.

pink, lavender, white, and green, the latter color derived from the genes of *P. lacera* as are the deeper lacerations. First discovered by Marcus White on 22 July 1899 and named for A. LeRoy Andrews, *P. ×andrewsii* is a cross between *P. psycodes,* the small purple fringed-orchid, and *P. lacera,* the green fringed-orchid.

Suspected crosses between *Platanthera lacera* and *P. grandiflora,* the large purple fringed-orchid, were previously lumped with *P. ×andrewsii* but now are separated as *P. ×keenanii.* Interestingly, this "new" hybrid does not have the rounded spur opening that is so diagnostic in the parent *P. grandiflora,* and the color is a uniformly purplish-pink in the specimens and pictures I have seen, instead of having hints of pale pink, lavender, and greenish white, which often characterize *P. ×andrewsii.* The lack of a round spur opening is a tip-off that the plant is the hybrid rather than the species.

New England and the Maritimes of Canada probably produce more of these two hybrids than any other region because of the availability of both parents. Much to my dismay, when I revisited the Wilton site fifteen years later, the larger alder and fir growth had crowded, shaded, and dried up the meadow to the point of obliterating the remaining orchids. As I have mentioned several times in this book, plant succession is one of the leading causes of orchid loss in Nature.

The flower of the small purple fringed-orchid, *Platanthera psycodes,* is significantly smaller, on average, than that of the large purple fringed, with a denser and more compact raceme. It has a later bloom period by generally two weeks or more and is equally at home in wet, sunny meadows and deep, shaded swamps. The easiest, quickest, and surest way to distinguish the two species, however, is by looking at the shape of the spur opening: round in the large purple fringed-orchid and dumbbell-shaped (horizontal) in the small purple fringed-orchid. This can be noted even without a hand lens.

The large purple fringed-orchid, *Platanthera grandiflora,* stands even taller than the small (*P. psycodes*), up to 4 feet (120 cm), and can be found along trails in the mountains, in wet ditches, and partially shaded thickets, but almost never in fields and open meadows. It is one of North America's most spectacular native orchids in stature, and the color isn't bad either. Thoreau was one of its great admirers, always lamenting that it grew away from the centers of population, out of sight of everyone but the moose and deer in the Maine woods. "A beauty reared in the shade of a convent," he said, "who has never strayed beyond the convent-bell. Only the skunk or owl, or other inhabitant of the swamp beholds it."

My favorite haunt for the large purple fringed-orchid is Evans Notch, just across the New Hampshire border in Maine. Following my intuition, I take the trail "less traveled" one day in the middle of July many years ago, which hints at likely habitat for both the orchid and the moose. I see many moose tracks in the mud but no moose along the way, and then, in the shadows beside the trail, "stand the purple spires with no breath of air nor headlong bee to disturb their perfect poise," in the words of Robert Frost. Sensing there may be more off the trail out of sight, I crash through a wet thicket and come out inside a small, semi-

Platanthera grandiflora, showing round spur opening, New Hampshire.

open meadow of tall grasses and sedges. Here large purple fringed-orchids luxuriate in the hundreds, partially hidden by shoulder-high grass and sedge.

My attention, however, does not remain undivided for long. Three Swainson's thrushes are singing ecstatically and cannot be ignored. This is the thrush whose song is the reverse of the veery, the flutelike notes ascending in a spiral. Ah, what food for the soul. Warblers are everywhere in the trees above me; the young of the season are being fed by their parents. For the next hour I watch seven species of warblers: redstarts, black-throated green, black-throated blue, bay-breast, magnolia, Canada, and my favorite, the little torch, the blackburnian. What an unexpected bonus this is! Finally, the little bands disappear and I walk jubilantly back to the car, having experienced one of those truly rare afternoons in the field where everything seems to fall into place.

Sheviak and Bowles (1986) in an excellent and not too technical article in *Rhodora* made the observation that *Platanthera psycodes* and *P. grandiflora* form a species pair closely related to another pair, *P. leucophaea* and *P. praeclara,* the prairie fringed-orchids, and both pairs are related to a third pair, *P. peramoena* and *P. lacera.* The six species form a so-called natural group. As with the prairie fringed-orchids, the two purple fringed-orchids display a similar pattern in their reproductive pollination structure. Like *P. leucophaea, P. psycodes* is more reproductively efficient as a "proboscis-depositing" pollinator orchid, resulting in a greater range extension than *P. grandiflora,* which is less efficient as an "eye-depositing" pollinator orchid, thus explaining its more restricted geographic range.

The green fringed-orchid, *Platanthera lacera,* is one of the first we New England orchid lovers add to our "life-list." It can be seen in almost every unmown field or meadow whether wet or dry, especially in southeastern New Hampshire and southwestern Maine, where the center of abundance appears to lie. Robust "giants" 2 to 3 feet (60 to 90 cm) tall with well-developed and well-balanced racemes of deeply lacerated greenish white flowers are the order of the day, in contrast to the spindly plants and fewer flowers more typical of areas south and west of Maine and New Hampshire.

George Aiken (1935) aptly described the green fringed-orchid as looking like someone took scissors to it. Morris and Eames (1929) believed the common and popular name of ragged orchis to be "the stuff of which folk names are made, and could hardly be bettered," but they also added, "for many perhaps, it has lost its charm, a flower too often seen to be noticed." Wright (1901) downgraded the green fringed-orchid with these words:

> the dull green Ragged Orchis with the cross-shaped cleft lip . . . has a weedy look and is without any of the dainty fragility of the fringed orchises; consequently it must be classed with the botanist's flowers of purely intellectual interest.

To me, however, it is an old favorite—dependable and comfortable, you might say, like an old shoe, its "torn" fringing and subtle touches of green never boring.

Platanthera lacera, showing green and white colors, New Hampshire.

CHAPTER 20

The Pad-leaf Orchids
in the White Mountains of Maine

THE MORNING of 29 June 1987 finds Shirley Curtis, Sally Puth, and me heading for the mountains. Our destination? South Chatham, New Hampshire, as close to the Maine border as a road can take you, which in this case is Route 113, which weaves back and forth along the state line dividing Maine and New Hampshire. We hug the White Mountain National Forest on its eastern edge. The National Forest is prime habitat for *Platanthera macrophylla,* the large round-leaved orchid. In bud a week or ten days ago, it should be open today, we think. A dirt road breaks off the paved state Route 113, which we follow for 4 or 5 more miles (6 or 8 km), disturbing large numbers of white admiral butterflies (*Limenitis arthemis*) along the way. Like many other butterflies, admirals gather in groups on some dirt roads, apparently for the moisture and salt.

We enter the National Forest under a beautiful canopy of yellow and white birch (*Betula lutea* and *B. papyrifera*), sugar maple (*Acer saccharum*), and beech (*Fagus grandifolia*) that "represents some of our most attractive natural settings," as Correll (1950) pointed out. After an easy ten-minute hike, we begin to see single specimens of one of the most handsome orchids, the large pad-leaf, *Platanthera macrophylla.* Its leaf is significantly larger than that of *P. orbiculata.* "There is perhaps no other orchid that so clearly and emphatically makes its presence known in season and out," Gibson (1905) pronounced. The huge, shiny, ground-hugging, blue-green, opposite leaves almost dinner plate in size are unlike anything else one might come upon in these woods. One I measured was almost round: $6\frac{7}{8}$ inches (16 cm) wide by $7\frac{5}{8}$ inches (19 cm) long. Apparently, a single leaf indicates a seedling that isn't old enough to have a pair of leaves, and not a damaged specimen.

The leaves aren't the only marvel of this plant. The flowers are equally so. Most authors describe a raceme with an average complement of twenty flowers, but here the exception proves the rule. Many plants with huge, perfectly balanced cylinders of up to forty flowers (double the average) all open together on a 19-inch (48-cm) stem and $1\frac{1}{4}$-inch (3-cm) pedicel. The lip is a full inch (2.5 cm) long, while the spur measures al-

Platanthera macrophylla, New Hampshire.

Platanthera macrophylla, New Hampshire.

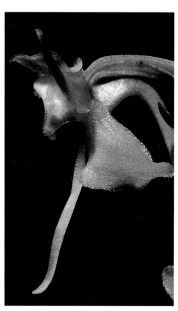

Platanthera macrophylla, close-up of individual flower profile illustrating fanciful shape, Maine.

most 2 inches (5 cm). The sepals are $\frac{3}{8}$ inch (1 cm) by $\frac{5}{8}$ inch (1.5 cm). With the slightest breeze, the raceme of greenish white flowers flutters like a wind chime without the sound. I wonder why they don't get knocked off in a strong breeze.

The most intriguing thing to me is the flower in profile; it looks like the head of a fanciful green elf or miniature gargoyle, dangling on the end of a flexible rod: the column's armlike projection on each side of the spur opening is the face, the yellow anther sac the eye, the inch-long lip petal the chin and beard, and the uppermost sepals and petals the ears and top of the head. Look carefully at the accompanying photograph and you will see what I mean.

For years most authors considered the pad-leaf orchid one species with two varieties, *Pla-*

tanthera orbiculata var. orbiculata and P. orbiculata var. macrophylla, the latter designated as the large round-leaved orchid. Then in 1993 two Canadian researchers, Allan and Joyce Reddoch, proposed specific status for the two varieties. Their studies indicated only two diagnostic characteristics separating the new species: the length of the spur, which is less than 28 mm in P. orbiculata and more than 28 mm in P. macrophylla, and the length of the hemipollinarium, which is less than 4.6 mm for P. orbiculata and more than 4.6 mm for P. macrophylla. The hemipollinarium is an esoteric name for the complex pollen-holding structure in the column of an orchid flower. These differences apparently require two types of moths to pollinate the flower. The Reddochs found no other characteristic as consistently and significantly different, including the comparative size of the leaves. Interesting.

There is also a difference in the distribution of the two species. Both are mesic (rich) forest orchids, with *Platanthera orbiculata* a bit more diverse in habitat choice, often taking up residence in coniferous swamps. *Platanthera macrophylla* has a much more compact distribution, from the Maritimes and northern New England, through extreme southern Québec and Ontario, while P. orbiculata travels further north across Canada to Newfoundland, funneling westward through the prairie provinces and spreading out again in British Columbia. It also follows the Appalachians to North Carolina.

The other so-called pad-leaf orchid is the smaller Hooker's orchid, *Platanthera hookeri.* The leaves are smaller than either of the other two pad-leafs and don't quite hug the ground, and the flowers are yellow-green instead of greenish white. In profile the flowers also have a distinctive, fanciful appearance: like an ice tong, formed by the upper sepals and petals, which connive into a narrow hood above and opposite the lower up-curving lip. In P. orbiculata, on the other hand, the flower is wide open; the sepals and petals flare and the lip hangs down. The accompanying photograph graphically shows this difference.

Morris and Eames (1929) coined the

Platanthera hookeri, close-up of individual flower profile illustrating "ice tongs."

expression "Hooker's hooks" for this orchid as an easy way to remember the difference between *Platanthera orbiculata* and *P. hookeri*. Though neither handsome nor aristocratic in the same sense as its larger cousin, *P. hookeri* is uncommon enough to warrant taking notice whenever one comes upon it. As Morris and Eames (1929) put it:

> No doubt those for whom Hooker's is a familiar orchid will be ready enough to laugh at any one wasting enthusiasm over so ordinary a plant. But try the shoe on the other foot. Where we have hunted in vain for a glimpse of *Habenaria hookeri* [synonym *Platanthera hookeri*] such rarities as striped coral roots, ram's-heads, and the little round-leaf orchis, are common every day sights; and wouldn't you eagerly go a long day's journey and more to clap eyes on one of these?

The range of Hooker's orchid is smaller and more compact than that of the big pad-leaf and stretches from Maine and the Maritimes in a narrow, slightly dipping arc, westward through the Great Lakes region on both sides of the border. It prefers drier mixed or coniferous forests, avoiding the wetter portions. It is particularly common on the Upper Peninsula of Michigan on the south shore of Lake Superior and the north shores of Lakes Huron and Michigan, according to Fred Case (1987). There it keeps company with calypso (*Calypso bulbosa*) and ram's head (*Cypripedium arietinum*). In northern New England I have seen it only in small clumps or singly, well scattered. Michael Homoya (1993) suggested three reasons for its disappearance in Indiana: habitat destruction, habitat alteration, and the fact that Indiana was on the edge of its range. I would suggest that the main reason could be a slow but steady retreat to the colder regions of the north because of global warming, as appears to be happening with several other northern orchids like calypso and the blunt-leaf orchid (*Platanthera obtusata*), to name only two. I have watched a single specimen come up each year in the same spot for more than ten years, with no increase in plants.

CHAPTER 21

The Tall Leafy Northern Orchids

On an herbarium sheet, it is next to impossible to distinguish *Platanthera dilatata* from *P. hyperborea,* but in the field, these twin sisters are singular in color. The former is the tall northern white orchid, and the latter, the tall northern green orchid.

The tall northern white orchid is probably the most fragrant North American orchid. About it Morris and Eames (1929) declared:

> . . . the most delicious of all orchids . . . so perfumes the air as to need no other sign of its presence . . . It is associated in many a mind with a White Mountain flume or a Green Mountain notch . . . a green nook near the limpid pool in which you dipped your hands, or it may have been higher up where white-throated sparrows were whistling through the mist, and icy springs came trickling through beds of moss and snowberry and the bleak summit was almost gained.

Such were the conditions of my first encounter while climbing Mount Willard at the head of Crawford Notch, one of the famous U-shaped, glacially carved valleys in New Hampshire's beautiful White Mountains. Incidentally, the view from the top of Mount Willard is rated as perhaps the best in all the White Mountains for the least amount of effort to get there. Morris and Eames (1929) considered white bog candles the most attractive of all small-flowered orchids in North America, "the gleaming white of its blossoms being even more conspicuous and no less truly beautiful than the gold of the yellow fringeless [*Platanthera integra*] or the flaming orange of the crested [*P. cristata*]."

Regarding *Platanthera hyperborea,* Morris and Eames (1929) expressed the redeeming observation that

> beyond a certain pleasing symmetry, the tall leafy green orchid has nothing remarkable for itself, and yet it is a very general favorite. The fact is, in nearly every orchid-hunter's experience it is so closely associated with the very earliest of his triumphs that the sight of it rouses a strange sense of pleasure and expectancy.

I certainly can vouch for that feeling. Some of the most memorable days afield go way back in the 1970s in the St. Johnsbury–Danville region of northeastern Vermont, the so-called Northeast Kingdom. In early July, the showy lady's-slipper (*Cypripedium reginae*) is in peak bloom, as well as the two tall leafy bog orchids (*Platanthera dilatata* and *P. hyperborea*), and several others, of course. In some of those early years there was so much to see I just had to stay overnight. The Diamond Hill Cabins sat on top of the highest point in the roller-coaster ride that was and still is, for the most part, U.S. Route 2, the main east-west highway in that part of Vermont. The cabins commanded the best view for miles around, encompassing one hundred and eighty degrees of unbroken mountain panorama. I had the "best seat in the house," as it were, on the enclosed front porch during the occasional black thunderstorms that entertained during the early evening hours, followed invariably by an encore of white fog hanging in the valleys the next morning. I never knew that the electrical currents unleashed during one of these wonderful storms are concentrated in a path only a few inches in diameter, heating the air to 20,000°F (11,000°C), which is hotter than the surface of the sun! Wow!

Platanthera huronensis, often included within *P. hyperborea,* is today recognized as a separate species. It is a more robust tall leafy green orchid with densely flowered mint-green to whitish spikes on 3-foot (90-cm) tall plants. The lip is more dilated at the base than in the case of *P. hyperborea,* although the latter is so variable that it, too, presents this type of lip in many specimens, on a more loosely flowered spike of green to yellowish green flowers. In northeastern Vermont, *P. huronensis* and *P. hyperborea* can get pretty big—the size of young cornstalks—in some of the wet ditches along the roadsides. At the same time, when one enters the deeply shaded arbor-vitae (*Thuja occidentalis*) swamps, the plants become smaller and leggy with fewer blossoms. In the city of Anchorage,

Alaska, apparently several varieties of *P. hyperborea* grow in proximity, along the side of the road across from Earthquake Park. Here and elsewhere, the color and shape of the lip, even its posture, as well as the length and shape of the spur, vary a great deal. I find it more plausible to attribute situations like this to individual variations, being more of a

Platanthera dilatata, Vermont.

lumper than a splitter, but these plants certainly offer much to chew on after a long day in the field. As Luer (1975) summed up the situation, *P. hyperborea* is perhaps "best treated as a single polymorphic species" where the problems then "are reduced from the specific to the varietal level, a level of far lower importance."

Both the green and white northern bog-orchids extend well into Canada and Alaska, the green going even further north than the white. Both also extend southward into the Sierras and Rockies. It is in this region of the Pacific Northwest that the current process of speciation is causing much confusion in identification.

The genus *Platanthera* is the most confusing orchid group in North America, I think it is safe to say. All current *Platanthera* species originally were part of the genus *Habenaria*. Then, in 1818, French botanist L. C. Richard segregated *Platanthera* from *Habenaria*. Lindley followed Richard in 1835, as did Carlyle Luer in 1975. At the same time, Luer segregated out two other genera from *Habenaria*, *Coeloglossum* and *Piperia*. The remaining current members of the genus *Habenaria* in North America are restricted to the southeastern United States. Those of the "new" genera *Platanthera*, along with *Coeloglossum* and *Piperia*, have accumulated a huge synonymy over time as the result of the shifting opinions about "what was what and who was who" (see Chapter 38).

Further complicating the situation are intergradations and hybridization, the latter quite common between some of the species and varieties. Schrenk (1978) observed that the North American genera *Platanthera* and *Spiranthes*, like the European genera *Dactylorhiza*, *Orchis*, and *Ophrys*, are in the process of forming and consolidating new species.

> *Platanthera* in North America is an actively evolving genus characterized by a rather high degree of infraspecifc (within species) variability, by the lack of complete interspecific (between species) genetic barriers, and by the gradual fixation and establishment of hybridogenic forms.

He further acknowledged:

> Hybridization, the mixing of preexisting gene pools, of course, is a much faster means toward the achievement of this goal than mutation and subsequent selection of advantageous features, involving de-novo creation of improvements.

In other words, we are witnessing speciation already in progress.

Luer (1975) noted that the whole complex could be treated as one polymorphic species with numerous varieties—the lumper solution. An earlier splitter, on the other hand, recognized twenty-four species in 1901. Luer (1975) then compromised on this wide difference of opinion by recognizing only five variable species as follows:

Platanthera dilatata	*Platanthera limosa*
var. *albiflora*	*Platanthera sparsiflora*
var. *dilatata*	var. *brevifolia*
var. *leucostachys*	var. *ensifolia*
Platanthera hyperborea	var. *sparsiflora*
var. *gracilis*	*Platanthera stricta*
var. *huronensis*	
var. *hyperborea*	
var. *purpurascens*	
var. *viridiflora*	

Brown (1997a) recognized eight species, which included Luer's five plus three of Luer's varieties (*P. dilatata* var. *leucostachys*, *P. hyperborea* var. *huronensis*, and *P. sparsiflora* var. *brevifolia*). Brown, following the original descriptions, also recognizes *P. brevifolia*, *P. huronensis*, and *P. leucostachys* as separate species.

Although the taxonomy of *Platanthera* may sound complicated, just remember that most of these varieties are confined to the Far West. East of the Rockies, only *P. dilatata*, *P. huronensis*, and *P. hyperborea* are found. The latter two green species are the only major problem and can be distinguished by the following points:

Platanthera huronensis	*Platanthera hyperborea*
lip widened at base	lip tapers at base
whitish green flower	yellow green flowers
densely flowered spike	loosely flowered spike
more robust plant	less robust plant

None of these differences are etched in stone—variation again—but most specimens should fit in one column or the other.

CHAPTER 22

Three-birds at Squam Lake, New Hampshire

I AM ON my way to Squam Lake early this morning, at 6:15 to be exact, in hopes of catching the unique three-birds orchid, *Triphora triantho-phora,* in the act of opening from tight bud stage. This amazing orchid opens for only a single day, en masse, in the entire region, repeating this phenomenon about four or five times during the bloom period, which in New Hampshire is from the first week in August to the first week in September. Arriving on the shores of Big Squam Lake an hour and a quarter later, the earliest in my twenty years of observing this remarkable plant, the weather is anything but pleasant, the sky overcast, and the temperature only 50°F (10°C). The saturated beech leaves are not the most comfortable seat either. Nonetheless, here I am sitting beside a clump of seven three-birds, still in tight bud. I am confident they will open this morning because the buds are bright white, with a pink tint if the flower is a highly colored one. The day before this stage the buds are grayish white. This is a subtle but important distinction that took me several years to pin down. Before gaining this knowledge, I spent many fruitless hours driving back and forth, trying to catch the flower open, a very frustrating experience to be sure.

I have time, while waiting, to drive back to Meredith to eat breakfast at a restaurant overlooking beautiful Lake Winnepesaukee in the heart of central New Hampshire's lake country. Winnepesaukee is an Indian name meaning "Lake Land." This largest of New Hampshire's famous lakes was formed during the last ice age when glaciers scoured the relatively soft granite beneath, plugging the southern outlet at Alton Bay with morainal deposits during the slow process of ice melt thousands of years ago. Many of the scenic mountains near the lake, such as the Belknaps and Ossipees, are volcanic in origin, their rocks recording the catastrophic event some two hundred million years ago which resulted in the separation of eastern North America from the continent of Africa.

I am back among the beech trees by 9:00 A.M. The skies are still overcast, the woods dark and dank, but a loon on Squam lifts my spirits with his yodel, the wild wail of the wilderness. Then the clouds begin to break, the sun slips through—9:30 by my watch—and the buds begin to part at the tips, slowly but steadily. By 9:45 the individual flowers are almost half open; 10:00, three-quarters open; and 10:30, all the way open. Less than an hour does the job. For some reason this morning, a few buds never really open completely, the lip retains a keel shape or trough down the center instead of the usual wide-open aspect.

I have spent more time with, written more pages on, and taken more photographs of *Triphora trianthophora* than any other orchid over a twenty-year period. Why? Besides its extraordinary habits and ecology, the colors are a favorite of mine. The triple kelly-green crest on the lip

Triphora trianthophora, large clump, New Hampshire.

lends an almost indefinable *je ne sais quoi* to the beautiful diamond-dusted flower, and the lavender wash that collects at the end of each sparkling white petal melts the heart. I hope I do not commit the sin of sickly sweet here. I must repeat a frequent admonition: get down on your hands and knees, and use a hand lens to see what all the fuss is about.

The entire plant is only 2 to 8 inches (5 to 20 cm) high with tiny "mouse-ears" for leaves. The flower droops after being open for only a day; if pollinated and not eaten by a rodent or grazing deer, the ovary swells rather quickly, becoming upright within a month or so and splitting open for the dispersal of thousands or millions of dustlike seeds. Despite the enormous amounts of seed thus produced, the number of aboveground plants varies a great deal here from year to year, ranging from a few hundred to more than ten thousand. The reason for such swings in numbers from year to year is speculative, but like some other orchids, the three-birds may remain dormant underground for certain periods of time. In my observations, however, there has never been a year without at least several dozen or a few hundred appearing and blooming, in between those extraordinary seasons that produce thousands of plants.

At Squam Lake this orchid starts to bloom around the first day of

Triphora trianthophora, typical flower color, New Hampshire.

August each year, completing its season of bloom generally by the first week in September. During this approximate thirty-six-day season, flowers open on only about six days, and seldom on successive days. This same-day flowering occurs simultaneously throughout New Hampshire, Maine, and Massachusetts, and has been documented (Keenan 1990a). Amazingly, even a flower stem picked and left on a windowsill will recycle the same number of days and open the very same day its counterparts do in the wild. Morris and Eames (1929) apparently saw this orchid in bloom in the wild only once and "were able to follow the life history through to its close by carrying a slab of New Hampshire back to Ontario." This led to a few wrong assumptions on their part, for example, that a single bloom stays open for three or four days. In all my years of experience in the field, this has never been the case. On a rare occasion, such as a cold night, the flower may remain three-quarters open the next day; however, one can notice the difference in freshness and openness. On the windowsill at home, however, on one occasion a single bloom

Triphora trianthophora, highly colored pair of flowers, New Hampshire.

Triphora trianthophora, with raindrops, New Hampshire.

stayed open for three or four days. Why? I do not know. A week may elapse before that next bloom.

In the early years, I spent many hours and many successive days driving back and forth to catch three-birds in bloom. Success eluded me until I unlocked the plant's "secret." The number of buds on a single plant also varies, from one to four usually, with as many as six occasionally, and on one double stem, a grand total of eight buds. On each of the five or six bloom days, one, two, or three flowers open together on the same stem: one or two occur about 95 percent of the time, and three at the same time only about 5 percent of the time, at least here at Squam. This is an extraordinary life history, and yet there is more.

One of the highlights of my annual studies with this orchid occurred on 10 August 1990, when, apparently for the first recorded time, I discovered an all white form, the three green crests on the lip replaced with pure yellow. I named it forma *albidoflava* (Keenan 1992a). There were four buds but only two opened, on different days. Instead of the traditional herbarium specimen, a color print was used, to avoid collecting the single specimen. As Whiting and Catling (1986) noted, "Since pressed and dried flowers fade somewhat, color photographs represent valuable vouchers for rare forms." At this writing, I have seen the albino form three different years.

Triphora trianthophora is the only species of a small genus of ten to occur north of Florida. Though widespread in the United States east of the Great Plains, it is considered generally uncommon but can be locally abundant. I am reminded of an observation made by Maurice Brooks (1965):

> In one respect, at least, it is unfortunate that so much of the good early writing about America's outdoors was done by persons from New England or New York State. Quite naturally, they judged the abundance or scarcity of a plant by what they saw near home. I grew up on botanical literature that listed cranefly and three-birds orchids as among the rarest of their kind. It was always something of a shock to find them both abundant in the woods through which I hiked.

Case (1987) told of a colony in Michigan that has persisted for at least thirty years, noting that

> such documentation of longevity for specific plants or colonies of our native orchids is rare. In my experience, few individuals or colonies of meadow or bog orchids survive the rigors of competition in a given spot for a long time. This behavior of Triphora, however, is consistent with that of

Triphora trianthophora forma *albidoflava*, New Hampshire.

Triphora trianthophora, dehisced seed capsule, back lighting, New Hampshire.

most herbs of the mature forest floor—they are not temporary, successional species, but rather enduring members of the forest community.

The so-called Algonquin station of Morris and Eames at Squam Lake in the 1920s is still producing, as of 1995, marking a total of seventy years under observation, perhaps one of the longest ever for an orchid. However, the increasingly more shaded and darker surroundings have caused a decrease in that population since I started checking the station more than twenty-five years ago. On the other hand, my "new" station of thirteen years is only a few miles away and yet is much more prolific every year, due mostly, in my opinion, to selective cutting which has opened up the canopy, thus providing more light for the orchids. Incidentally, deep shade is not the preferred condition for most orchids.

MID-ATLANTIC &
MIDWESTERN STATES

Platanthera nivea, New Jersey.

The White Lady's-slipper on the Shores of Lake Erie, Ohio

BEFORE the expansion of large commercial farming in the midwestern states, *Cypripedium candidum,* the white lady's-slipper, whitened patches of the prairie for two or three weeks in May. Now it is rare throughout most of its range. Welby Smith (1993) observed that

> only in Minnesota is it still possible to stand in a prairie and see tens of thousands of small white lady's-slippers in a single view. Yet, this seeming abundance represents less than one percent of the original population. The rest was plowed under for the benefit of agriculture, a practice that is continuing unabated.

On the shores of Lake Erie in Erie County, northwest of Cleveland, Ohio, there exists a single wildlife preserve for woodcock situated on one of the largest prairies still remaining in the state of Ohio. Several thousand white lady's-slippers thrive there. On the day Tom Sampliner shows this site to Paul Martin Brown's study group, several acres have apparently been burned over a few weeks before our arrival, a management tool beneficial to both woodcock and lady's-slipper. Staghorn sumac (*Rhus typhina*), red-osier dogwood (*Cornus stolonifera*), and numerous brambles would otherwise soon destroy the value of the habitat by natural plant succession, which is sometimes as damaging as succession caused by human activities. Star-flowered lily of the valley (*Smilicina stellata*) is the most abundant herb everywhere under the warm sun, in company with the small white lady's-slipper, which is the most sun-loving of all North American native lady's-slippers.

The small pure white pouches are bursting through the tops of the plants—like the white button stage on newly emerging mushrooms—

before the leaves have even unwrapped from the stem, barely 6 inches (15 cm) out of the ground. This apparently is typical of its haste to get on with the business of reproduction. Most plants appear as if touched by a late frost, evidenced by the brown tips of most leaves. We speculate on this being the reason rather than the burn-over, since the latter event appears to have occurred just before the plants made their appearance. In either case, few flowers are damaged. Surprising to me, the blooms have a strong mayflower fragrance. Some fragrances I have lost somewhere along the line, but not this one thankfully.

Cypripedium candidum, Ohio.

We discover not one or two but a dozen or more plants of *Cypripedium* ×*favillianum* in bloom, representing *C. candidum* and *C. parviflorum* var. *makasin*. Tom Sampliner accidentally flushes a woodcock hen from her nest and another female sits tight on a second nest, shielding two young ones. Both of these woodcocks are discovered on a part of the preserve recently inactivated agriculturally, where we find no lady's-slippers.

Growing in open, moist, marly meadows and fens around the southern Great Lakes region of extreme northern Ohio, Indiana, and Illinois, southern portions of Michigan, as well as Wisconsin and Minnesota, only small remnants remain of this habitat in these states. A few miles away on Marblehead Peninsula, a 19-acre (7-ha) state nature preserve protects the rarest of more than 200 species currently on Ohio's endangered list. Among these plants is the lakeside daisy (*Hymenoxys herbacea*). The preserve also harbors one of the easternmost sites for *Spiranthes magnicamporum*. We see the daisies but the spiranthes are out of season. Thousands of golden yellow daisies luxuriate on a limestone pavement on the

Cypripedium candidum, Ohio.

shores of Lake Erie, the last major stand of these daisies in the United States. This site became a major tourist attraction many years ago when hundreds of people came to admire the annual floral display in mid-May, until, that is, an extensive quarry destroyed all but the few protected acres remaining today. *Deja vu.*

In another year, Dr. George Newman, Les Eastman, and I make the trek to one of the easternmost outposts for *Cypripedium candidum*, in Bergen Swamp, in upstate New York, south of Rochester. It is a heavily wooded arbor-vitae (*Thuja occidentalis*) swamp, spotted with smallish marly-bog openings or "rooms" as they are called, with open pools of limy water. These pools are punctuated with small hummocks of the familiar oldfield juniper (*Juniperus horizontalis*) within which the famous Massassauga rattlesnake takes cover from the frequent guided visits of orchid lovers during the bloom season of late May. Once inside these "rooms" it is easy to become turned around. One should never venture in alone, for the record shows a number of people have died over the years from the panic that can set in when lost. Les Eastman is ecstatic at finding a coiled Massassauga inside one of the juniper clumps. The story on this rattlesnake is that it bites only when cornered. We quickly leave him alone. After much looking and dozens of spent blooms, we are almost ready to give up the search, but then we find three good specimens of *Cypripedium candidum,* the only bloomin' three in the whole swamp because of the early season that year.

George took us to a few other choice plant sites that weekend, including the famous 300-acre (120-ha) Clark Reservation, near Jamesville, New York, a few miles south of Syracuse. This reservation is considered the fern capital of the United States. Here we not only see the most prolific and robust clumps of the remarkable hart's-tongue fern (*Phyllitis scolopendrium*) that I've ever known—in a remote section of limestone sinks—but also a just-born, curled-up baby fawn, juxtaposed with, of all things, the nefarious alien, the common burdock (*Arctium minus*). Other noteworthy ferns include the walking fern (*Camptosorus rhizophyllus*), silver spleenwort (*Athyrium thelypteroides*), and bladder fern (*Cystopteris bulbifera*). Later, at "Lost Lake" George led us to the magnificent slender cliff-brake (*Cryptogramma stelleri*), which grows in an amazing microclimate of limestone cracks and crevices where the cold air filters up from hundreds of feet below the ground and creates natural refrigeration.

CHAPTER 24

The Appalachian Twayblade in Pennsylvania

"THE twayblades are more curious than beautiful," Fred Case (1987) says. They were always a favorite of Morris and Eames, and they are of mine. Eight species can be counted in North America, including the European import, *Listera ovata,* the largest of the group.

One of the smallest and niftiest twayblades, *Listera smallii,* occurs only in the Appalachian Mountains from central Pennsylvania to northern Georgia. Here at their northern limit, on the northwestern edge of the Appalachians, where the mountain ridges curve northeastward through eastern Pennsylvania—the so-called ridge and valley geologic province of the state of Pennsylvania—the bedrock is composed of folded sandstone and conglomerate. The remainder of the state belongs to the Appalachian plateau province. Looking at a map you see the amazing conformity of the valley roads that parallel this northeasterly curve. Incidentally, since 1897, Pennsylvania has acquired more open space than any other state east of the Mississippi River: 2 million acres (800,000 ha) of state forests, more than a million acres (400,000 ha) of state game lands, and almost 300,000 acres (120,000 ha) of state parks (116 of them).

This Appalachian twayblade, a real niche species, grows in the 90,000-acre (36,000-ha) Rothrock State Forest, where it hides alone under the thickest *Rhododendron maximum* tangles, often near water. A characteristic pair of subopposite, sessile leaves on an often short stem gives the twayblades their common name, while an open raceme of small greenish, purplish, or brownish flowers are all lip. This, at least, is the impression one gets because of their extremely tiny, very inconspicuous, linear, reflexed petals and sepals tucked in at the base of the lip. Historically, some species have been confused with each other, but today they are well diagnosed. With reasonably careful examination, all the lips are quite distinctive, either fore or aft (see Figure 3 in Chapter 35). The scientific name of Appalachian twayblade, *Listera smallii,* honors a noted expert on the flora of the southeastern United States, Dr. John K. Small, who first reported the difference between this species and *L. convallarioides.*

Morris and Eames (1929) related in some detail the effort required in crawling around some of these rhododendron thickets and the ease of

Listera smallii, Pennsylvania.

becoming lost. I relived some of their experiences in central Pennsylvania. Essentially nothing grows on the barren, brown floor beneath the rhododendrons and hemlocks other than the occasional well-camouflaged, tan-lipped Appalachian twayblade. It is this tan or light brown color that is so different. (Sometimes the lip is more green than brown or even cream-colored.) The tips of the lobes on the lip are squared off or nearly so instead of being rounded as in some of the other listeras, an important distinction. Two tiny but prominent, round lobes flank the base of the lip, which are also distinctive. The use of a magnifying glass is helpful with this species as it is with the others.

Morris and Eames (1929) complained of the difficulty in photographing this orchid because the lay of the lip is horizontal, "presenting a mere edge instead of their face to the camera." They observed that the lip appeared in outline "like the wings of a rising fly." To me, the overall aspect is angelic: a miniature brown angel with outstretched, skinny arms (petals) poised above the ample, broadly expanded gown (lip), with a tiny head (column) tucked in between the "arms." (See the close-up photographs in Luer 1975 for a good rendition of what I am suggesting.) The lips of other species of *Listera* hang straight down, offering a perpendicular or flat plane of focus to the photographer and thus producing a sharper picture. I echo the conclusion of Morris and Eames (1929), "We doubt if we have ever enjoyed more the sight of a new twayblade than we did that day in the southern mountains."

Besides *Listera smallii, Platanthera peramoena* was another highlight of our all-day field trip. I must confess, however, that the twayblade stole the show, so to speak, for me at least, on this particular July twenty-first.

Speaking of enjoyment, I must mention the background for this foray into the hills of southern Pennsylvania: it was nothing less than the first annual North American Native Orchid Alliance conference in Pittsburgh, 19–21 July 1996. The great three-day meeting was followed by an equally great field trip on Sunday led by the father-son team of Al and Scott Shriver, along with Clete Smith from the Pittsburgh area. Dr. and Mrs. Carlyle Luer, famed author of the "bible" of North American native orchids, were honored guests and the first recipients of the alliance's Education Award. The North American Native Orchid Alliance, founded in 1994, is an organization every native orchid enthusiast should find useful.

CHAPTER 25

The Pine Barrens of New Jersey

THE PINE Barrens of New Jersey mean different things to different people. The city of New York, for example, tried in vain to build an airport there in the 1960s that would have been the largest airport in the world, requiring a new city to support it and essentially destroying the unique pinelands. Philadelphia got into the act when it attempted to divert the water from the barrens for its water supply. Beneath the 2000 square miles (5180 sq km) of sandplains lies one of the world's great aquifers of pure liquid gold—water. Above the ground, the seemingly monotonous landscape of pitch pine and oak is crisscrossed with miles of sandy roads, meandering pristine streams, cedar bogs, and cranberry ponds. Because of this extraordinary natural resource so close to the most densely populated area in the United States, the pine barrens have been set aside as a national preserve, which, for the time being, at least, has stopped most of the commercial inroads. Canoeists, fishermen and fisherwomen, hunters, nature lovers, naturalists, botanists, and conservationists alike have seen their efforts rewarded. To the orchidophile, several rare southern species stop here, notably *Platanthera integra,* the yellow fringeless orchid, and *Cleistes divaricata,* the stately spreading pogonia.

Access is by way of the two major north-south highways, the Jersey Turnpike on the west and the Garden State Parkway to the east. Off the Jersey Turnpike, look for exit 7 and U.S. Route 206, which takes you all the way to the Wharton State Forest and the town of Atsion, after traveling through the heart of the Jersey farmland (yes, there are still farms in New Jersey). Alternatively, you can take the Garden State Parkway and turn off on Route 542 near Gretna, which takes you into Batsto.

Both Atsion and Batsto are good starting points for orchids. I must warn you, however: once on the network of intertwining sandy roads or walking through the woods, everything appears the same wherever you look, making it easy to become turned around and lost without a compass or a good guide, or both. Easier areas to hike alone, on laid-out trails, are to be found near the visitor centers in the State Forest.

On 15 August 1984 my guide, Paul Martin Brown, tracks down almost 100 prime yellow fringeless orchids, *Platanthera integra,* while slogging through ankle-deep water in the sweltering heat of a savannah near the Batsto River. The small cylinders of 50 to 75 golden yellow flowers stand

neatly at attention among the green grasses and rushes. Though the flowers are small, even smaller than those of *P. psycodes,* they are packed tightly in the raceme, which is conical at first when about half the flowers are open, making them easy to see from some distance. Though called fringeless, most flowers do have a slight serration that

Platanthera integra, with yellow crab spider, New Jersey.

Platanthera integra, New Jersey.

is easily seen on close examination. The dorsal sepal and lateral petals connive over the column, as they do in many other orchids. On the wooded edges, a few remnant blooms of *P. cristata* catch our eyes; only the topmost flowers are still a brilliant orange, the others several days past prime.

That night we drive the long haul to Cape May, New Jersey, in preparation for Bennett Bog's showpiece the following morning, the famous snowy orchid, *Platanthera nivea,* Not a bog in the sense of the northern boreal bog, but more accurately a "vernal pond," Bennett Bog was purchased in 1950 by the New Jersey Audubon Society and expanded in the 1980s to the current 24 acres (10 ha). Some years an excess of rainfall reduces the number of snowy orchids, which are the main attraction. Sure enough, only six can be found this morning, but all are in prime condition, helping to compensate for the disappointing numbers.

The same height as *Platanthera integra,* the raceme of the snowy orchid, *P. nivea,* produces fewer and looser flowers, but the pure white color can still be seen from a distance. The most interesting thing about this orchid, perhaps, concerns the arrangement of the flower parts. The flowers are nonresupinate; that is, in most orchids the lip is in the lowest position with the other two petals and three sepals above the lip, but in

the snowy orchid and *Calopogon tuberosus,* the reverse is true. What looks like a lip in the lower position are two lateral petals and a single sepal so close together as to give a three-lobed appearance to the "lip." The other two sepals are falcate-shaped, and curve up, under, and behind the real lip in the upper position (see accompanying plate). The entire flower is pure white (some authors can see a touch of bluish in certain light) except for the yellow column.

"We have no greater favorite than the snowy," is how Morris and Eames (1929) reacted to the beauty of this orchid. Both *Platanthera integra* and *P. nivea* are orchids typical of the Atlantic

Platanthera nivea, showing uppermost lip embraced by lateral sepals, New Jersey.

Coastal Plain, reaching their northern limit in southern New Jersey. They are far more common further south in the Carolinas and Georgia and along the Gulf Coast, where Correll (1950) described large colonies that "form a blanket of white over the landscape." Thirty-five years later, *P. integra* is rare and *P. nivea* infrequent in most of their respective ranges.

Many other new flowers are added to my list in the Cape May area, including the brilliant orange milkwort (*Polygala lutea*), but none more stunning than a non-orchid "weed" with the pedestrian name of horsemint (*Monarda punctata*). The genus name gives you a clue, for it is in the same genus as the ornamental bee-balm garden flower. At any rate, on a 3-foot (90-cm) stem the combination of flower colors is even more eye-catching: yellow rosettes spotted with purple and subtended by larger soft lilac bracts.

About 11:30 A.M. of this second day, on our way back north, we admire several clumps of pink and white-flowered swamp mallows (*Hibiscus palustris*). While driving, Paul spies *Spiranthes tuberosa*, the handsome little ladies'-tresses, on a dry road shoulder in the Pine Barrens. The flowers of this species are the smallest of the genus in eastern North America and perhaps the whitest —certainly the whitest I recall seeing. "An uncommonly clean-cut, charming species," Fred Case (1987) described it. The wiry plant may be as much as 12 inches (30 cm) tall with a spike of up to 30 small flowers, twisted or in a straight row (secund). From southern New England southward, east of the Mississippi, in dry woods and openings, such as this road shoulder, is where to look for it. I get out of the car to photograph the plant. My persistence pays off, I might add, for that picture turns out to be one of the best of the entire trip.

Spiranthes tuberosa, New Jersey.

CHAPTER 26

A New Fringed-orchid on Long Island, New York

LIKE THE proverbial duck hunter, I hear my alarm go off at 3:30 A.M. on the last day of July 1991. Dressing quickly in the dark, I swallow some orange juice and cold cereal, pick up my passenger, Sally Puth, and head south on Interstate 95, connect with Interstate 495, then Interstate 395. Our destination? New London, Connecticut. We are not looking for ducks but for a ferry ride at nine in the morning to Orient Point, Long Island, New York, via Block Island Sound. We have come this long way in the hope of seeing the crippled crane-fly, better known as the crane-fly orchid or *Tipularia discolor*. Long Island represents the northern limit for the genus on the Atlantic coastal plain, except for one site on Martha's Vineyard off the Massachusetts coast. The drive from Dover, New Hampshire, to New London is about three hours, but the combined wait and ferry ride to Orient Point take the same amount of time, believe it or not. In fact, the total time on three ferries, including waiting time, amounts to five hours. Since travel time by vehicle is almost eight hours, we are left with about seven hours for botanizing on the outermost parts of Long Island.

Our first stop is Greenport. Of all things, ten hulking elephants block our way into a wooded sanctuary. They are members of a traveling circus that is performing on an empty lot beside the town ball field. Paul Martin Brown, our group leader, has trouble locating the main trail, so we end up taking a shortcut plowing through a thicket of thorny brambles. Soon the scratches are forgotten. Inside this dark, deciduous woodland, under a small copse of beech (*Fagus grandifolia*) trees, we begin the search. Soon, several "here it is!" shouts are heard over the next several minutes, as at least 100 remarkable crane-fly orchids begin to reveal themselves. They are widely scattered and well-blended across the dark woodland floor, on the protected side of a chain-link fence that separates a mobile home park on the other side, in one corner of the sanctuary.

Despite a 2-foot (60-cm) stem, the thin, willowy plants are difficult to see. Straight as an arrow, fully one-half to two-thirds of the stem is taken up by a loose raceme of up to forty flowers. *Tipularia* is very well named, for the asymmetrical flowers surely could pass for a row of crippled crane-flies stuck on a stem. The overall impression is a plant with gray flowers, the gray relieved by a relatively conspicuous yellowish projecting column. Under a hand lens, the lips and petals are grayish with thin purple lines. Morris and Eames (1929) called the color a "watery purplish green,"

which sums it up in a nutshell. Our time is limited, and to compound matters, I forget my flash equipment back at the car, have the wrong film in the camera, and get mediocre results, I discover later.

One of three native orchids that produces a single leaf in autumn instead of spring, *Tipularia discolor* is the only member of the genus in North America. It is common in places below New York State, especially in the Virginias, the Carolinas, Tennessee, Kentucky, Alabama, and Mississippi. It is the most common woodland orchid in southern Indiana (Homoya 1993). The crane-fly orchid's leaf history is a strange one, unlike all others except for *Aplectrum hyemale,* and to a lesser extent, calypso, the other two orchids that reverse the "normal" spring leaf development. After the trees shed their leaves in autumn, *Tipularia discolor* sends up a solitary, wrinkled, egg-shaped to heart-shaped leaf, dark green above and deep purple below, which spends the winter ex-

Tipularia discolor, New York.

posed on top of the ground. Then when the temperature really gets warm in May, the leaf turns red as if unable to bear the heat of summer and disappears for six months. The process is like reverse hibernation. As a result, the best time to locate the crane-fly orchid is during a stroll in the winter woods, when hundreds can be readily spotted. These hundreds, it is said, send up only a few flowering stems in July and August.

Basically, the same sequence of events happens to *Aplectrum hyemale,* the putty-root. In its case, the leaf is elliptical and heavily pleated above, gray-green with prominent, longitudinal white ribs above and purplish green below. Putty-root presents an interesting conversational piece in the winter woods of North America's eastern deciduous forests, from western New England and the Great Lakes region, south to extreme northern Georgia, Alabama, and Arkansas. Larry Newcomb showed me my only putty-roots, a name derived from the gluelike substance in the paired tubers or corms, which, it is said, was used to repair crockery. Another quaint colloquial name alludes to Adam and Eve. The 8- to 15-inch (20- to 38-cm) stem bears as few as three or four to as many as fifteen or twenty relatively small flowers in a loose raceme, during May. The perianth spreads partially open and is cream-colored with purplish markings, mostly near the tips of the sepals and petals.

Geologically, Long Island consists of two morainal ridges deposited by the last glacier during the Pleistocene Epoch. The island represents the southern terminus of the ice advance. Especially on the eastern half of the island, there is a long sand dune varying in width from less than a mile (1.6 km) to almost 23 miles (37 km) near the middle. Because of this glaciation and the concomitant sand deposits, Long Island ecologically is an extension of the southeastern coastal plain. Therefore, we find several typical coastal plain orchids among the 35 species of orchids that have been recorded on the island. This total has shrunk to about 21 species because of habitat destruction from past and present land-use practices. The population of crane-fly orchids we see today in Greenport is the only existing population for the entire state of New York (Lamont and Beitel 1988). Just northeast of Long Island on Martha's Vineyard, off the coast of Cape Cod, Massachusetts, exists the only station, a well-guarded one, for all of New England.

Surprisingly, there are still six extant stations for *Arethusa* on Long Island, while *Cypripedium acaule* is "widespread and more frequently encountered than any other orchid species" (Lamont and Beitel 1988). Seven sites are still current for *Platanthera ciliaris,* all on the eastern half of the island, while *P. cristata*—at its northern limit here also—is down to seven or fewer locations, again, all on the eastern end. Sixteen sites are still current for *P. blephariglottis.*

On Route 114, several interesting fringed-orchids appear along the road shoulders and ditches. Because of the dry conditions, however, *Platanthera ciliaris* and *P. cristata* are far from prime, looking a bit wilty. One or two cream-colored plants of the hybrid *P. ×canbyi* are noted in the same neighborhood. Both supposed parents are nearby. After a good deal more driving, we finally reach what proves to be the highlight of the day, on the eastern end of Long Island, on Route 27, at an undeveloped state park with the name Napeague.

Trudging up and down sand dunes seems like a strange way to search for orchids, but there they are, scattered under an open growth of pitch pines (*Pinus rigida*), among beautiful carpets of bearberry (*Arctostaphylos uva-ursi*). We count more than a thousand of what look like pale creamy forms of *Platanthera cristata,* but different, we all agree. The lar-

ger size and pale color of the flowers and the reflexed lip petal are obvious differences. These flowers also appear as if wilted by the heat. Several large clumps of *Cypripedium acaule* are growing nearby in this sand dune, yet look fresh and robust. Surprises.

Brown's (1992) efforts ultimately culminate in the description of a new species, *Platanthera pallida,* the pale fringed-orchid, endemic to Long Island. Someone once said that "a man knows no greater excitement than that of discovery."

We call it quits at six o'clock in the evening, celebrate the new discovery with a lobster roll at the popular Lobster Roll Restaurant nearby, and make the long reverse trip back to the Con-

Platanthera pallida, New York.

necticut mainland, by the same ferries. Bidding our adieus, we arrive back in New Hampshire at two o'clock the next morning—almost 24 hours, nonstop, from this morning's start. It is all in a day's work on the orchid trail.

Platanthera pallida, typical habitat, New York.

Platanthera ciliaris, seen here in Connecticut, reaches its greatest abundance in

SOUTHEASTERN STATES

the Cumberland Mountains of Kentucky.

CHAPTER 27

The Magnificent Rosebud in North Carolina

For the orchid lover, many wild orchids evoke powerful thoughts of anticipation before one ever gets to see them. *Cleistes divaricata,* the rosebud orchid, is one of those, thanks in part to Carlyle Luer's magnificent photograph on page forty-one of *The Native Orchids of Florida* (1972). Almost thirty years pass before I finally take advantage of an opportunity to see this orchid, with the help of the staff at the North Carolina Nature Conservancy, especially Katherine Skinner and Ida Phillips. David McAdoo, co-author of *An Annotated Catalog and Distribution Account of the Kentucky Orchidaceae* (Ettman and McAdoo 1979), and Dr. Rick Schneider of Duke University give the go-ahead for the third week of May. So, on 17 May 1990, the long-awaited flight to Wilmington, North Carolina, finally materializes.

The following morning I meet Stan Bentley and Bobby Toler, two Virginia friends, at a motel in Whiteville. The three of us then drive to one of the coastal plain's remaining longleaf pine (*Pinus palustris*) savannas. The sky is clear and the air is hot with temperatures in the nineties—typical of this year's Carolina springtime, a topsy-turvy, harder-than-usual-to-predict season. The heat is no problem, though, because my attention is focused elsewhere to new plants everywhere I step. I am quite aware that here on the coastal plain of North Carolina are some of the most diverse assemblages of plant species per unit of area found anywhere in the world. That world-famous Carolina endemic, the Venus' fly-trap (*Dionaea muscipula*), which Charles Darwin called the "most wonderful plant in the world," is one of the first things to marvel at, close at hand by the roadside. I am also aware of the relentless poaching and consequent destruction of these superb carnivorous plants merely to satisfy the public's appetite for something curious to set on a windowsill, despite the fact they will not survive more than a few weeks. This is another example of self-interest taking precedence over the broader public interest, or is it a case of public indifference and ignorance? I think a little of both perhaps. The North Carolina Nature Conservancy is desperately trying to put a stop to this practice that threatens the entire wild population of Venus' fly-traps.

As we proceed further into the savanna, a clump of striking yellow trumpets (*Sarracenia flava*), also threatened by digging, demands attention. The pure white colicroot (*Aletris farinosa*), on the other hand, is everywhere, especially along the roadside and edges, looking just like a ladies'-tresses from a distance. I must be careful each time I see one until I become used to them. The similarity is quite uncanny in the beginning. On closer inspection, of course, the difference is very pronounced: the surfaces of the pure-white tubular flowers are uniformly covered with tiny "warts" or stipples, unlike any *Spiranthes* species. Colicroot is the most abundant of the dozens of wild flowers in the drier woods and roadsides here.

Another "tricky" flower for identification is *Spiranthes praecox*, the giant ladies'-tresses, which is scattered in the wetter portions of the sa-

Aletris farinosa, illustrating similarity to some *Spiranthes* species at a distance, North Carolina.

vanna. I must again look closely, resorting to a hand lens 90 percent of the time, to catch the faint green veining on the lip, which distinguishes this species from every other *Spiranthes* orchid. Several other rarities in the neighborhood include the red pitcher plant (*Sarracenia rubra*), a rare loosestrife or swamp candles (*Lysimachia asperulaefolia*), and the even rarer spoon flower (*Peltandra sagittaefolia*), with a white spathe similar to the calla lily (*Calla palustris*).

Ah, there it is! Standing tall, graceful, and alert above the surrounding wiregrass, like a Thompson gazelle poised on an African short-grass savanna, is the striking beauty I have come so far to see: a 2-inch (5-cm), horizontal, tubular corolla that is delicate pink on the outside, with a touch of green barring underneath. The corolla is thrown into relief by a spectacular crown of three "horns": upright, partially reflexed, 2-inch (5-cm) mahogany sepals. Inside the flared opening of the tube, the lip is heavily veined with purple on each side of the yellowish, fleshy crest that runs down the center, while the sharply pointed apex is a deeper pink than the rest of the tube. A single, long, lanceolate leaf near the middle of the stem, and a shorter one subtending the remarkable flower, complete the charming portrait.

Cleistes divaricata, pale form, North Carolina.

Cleistes divaricata, typical flower color, North Carolina.

Though not abundant, our search turns up between fifty and a hundred plants, scattered through the grasses. Most are solitary but a few are in pairs. The plants are easy to find because of their stature—up to 3 feet (90 cm) high. One or two are white with just a hint of pink. John Small (1933) noted this orchid "in such abundance as to form seas of pale rose." Radford et al. (1963) considered it infrequent, while today, because of habitat destruction and digging, it is rare and local, from extreme northeastern Florida to extreme southern New Jersey, on the coastal plain. What a pity!

The Latin name is an attractive one for a change. *Cleistes* means "closed" or "tubular" and refers to the union of petals that form the tube, while *divaricata* means "spreading" and refers to the three upright sepals.

Cleistes divaricata, a crossing pair, North Carolina.

The savanna provides a perfect backdrop for these aristocrats. I am struck by the parklike effect of the longleaf pines (*Pinus palustris*) and the aesthetics of the unusual young pine seedlings scattered beneath the taller pines. Longleaf pines have needles longer than any other pine—up to 18 inches (45 cm). The long clusters of three-leaved needles form a tuft at the very top of the 5- to 6-foot (150- to 180-cm) seedling and at the end of each horizontal branch; the spaces between are completely bare on both the branch and trunk. To put it simply, the longleaf pine is just one more example of "I've never seen anything like it." Slow-growing, this pine spends up to ten years in this seedling stage, devoting all energy to root development, which explains one reason, perhaps, for its great resistance to fire. Fires are an important management tool for the optimum survival of the savanna.

Throughout the morning, several pairs of handsome red, white, and black red-headed woodpeckers, one of the most beautiful woodpeckers, noisily cavort around their nesting holes, providing perfect binocular views. We even get to see the famous red-cockaded woodpecker, the one with the zebra back and white cheeks, on a tree trunk close by. This wonderful view does not require the glasses, but is oh so short in duration. This woodpecker is a life bird for me.

The rosebud orchid was one of the earliest orchids described by Carl Linnaeus in 1753, from a discovery made in Virginia by Jan Fredrik Gronovius. One of the early book classics, Stephen Elliott's *A Sketch of the Botany of South Carolina and Georgia,* in 1816 and 1824, listed this orchid for the Carolinas. More than a hundred years after it was described, both in 1860 and 1864, it was discovered in the pine barrens of New Jersey. Another fifty years elapsed before Witmer Stone rediscovered it in Cape May County, New Jersey, in 1909. Sadly, it may be extirpated there today.

Cleistes bifaria, a plant of the Gulf states coastal plain and of the interior highlands, particularly the Cumberland Plateau of eastern Kentucky, eastern Tennessee, and West Virginia, was considered a disjunct form of *C. divaricata* prior to 1992. Studies apparently justify specific status, based mostly on smaller size, paler color, and a difference in fragrance (Catling and Gregg 1992). Originally, R. Fernald thought this smaller form from the mountains migrated to the coastal plain after the regression of the Tertiary seas in prehistoric times, eventually evolving into the larger *C. divaricata*, but Carlyle Luer (1972) suggested the opposite may be true: coastal plain plants may head for the mountains.

Dressler (1993) in his book *Phylogeny and Classification of the Orchid Family* considered the pogonias "primitive orchids of uncertain classification" and put them under his "misfits and leftovers" category. The genus *Cleistes*, along with *Calopogon*, *Isotria*, and *Triphora*, were at one time all included in the genus *Pogonia*. Today, more than fifty species of *Cleistes* occur in South America.

Another new orchid in bloom with *Cleistes* is *Calopogon pallidus*, the pale grass-pink. It is smaller and shorter than the more ubiquitous *C. tuberosus*, with pale pink to white flowers that are usually tinted with pink. The flowers here are mostly white with only a few open at once during what is said to be an extended (several weeks) period of bloom. It is more demure than the other calopogons, I think. *Calopogon barbatus* also occurs here but is earlier and out of bloom. I note only a handful of *Spiranthes vernalis* on the shoulders of the road, probably because of recent mowing, whereas the next day on another road, where no mowing had yet occurred, hundreds waved in the breezes stirred by the passing cars.

After a long, very hot day in the field, we head back to our motel, skirting an isolated thunderstorm. The easy camaraderie of Bobby's jokes and story-telling mixes well with Stan's insightful knowledge, making it difficult to close the evening down. I make a mental note to come back to North Carolina, soon, especially if these guys come with me.

CHAPTER 28

The Flame Orchis
in Kentucky and Connecticut

WHEN IT comes to the most photogenic orchid, the orange-fringed *Platanthera ciliaris* is arguably near the top. The most brilliantly hued of all northern orchids, even rivaling the more glamorous tropical or greenhouse varieties, it epitomizes most people's idea of what an orchid should look like. The color reminds me of *Epidendrum radicans,* a tropical species from Mexico to Colombia and a common sight in northern greenhouses. The dainty, delicate cylinder of flowers belies an unexpected hardiness. Correll (1950) called the orange fringed-orchid "the most rugged terrestrial orchid in our region, especially in the South, where it is almost ubiquitous and has been appropriately designated the 'gentle brute' because of its extreme hardiness and competitive ability."

In some of the southeastern coastal plain savannas of the Carolinas, the orange plumes of *Platanthera ciliaris* light up the landscape. Ettman and McAdoo (1979) noted that this beautiful orchid reaches its greatest abundance in the Cumberland Mountains of Kentucky:

> Invading practically any type of strongly acid open habitat, *P. ciliaris* is especially common above 2000 feet (600 m) in wet or disturbed sites along road shoulders, logging trails, power line clearings and second growth pine thickets. In such sites, this species attains the status of a weed that produces a beautiful yellow cast to the scenery in August.

Alas, it once did the same in parts of southern Connecticut, Long Island, and even around New York City, where thousands could be seen at the turn of the twentieth century. Mabel Osgood Wright (1901) described such a scene: "Each summer two acres in extent are literally overwhelmed and drenched with the splendid color of this barbaric orange flower." She went on to predict,

> Yet its haunt has already been encroached upon by the onion raiser and small farmer who, with growing intelligence, finds the deep rich soil well worth redeeming until, I fear, another half dozen years will see this flower driven to a few uncultivable borders.

In fact, that is just what happened. One need only substitute the words *developer* and *highway engineer* for *the onion raiser* and *small farmer* to get the picture today. Even as recently as 1940, Roy Latham reported that the species was locally common on western Long Island and rare at the eastern end. Now, just a handful of sites remain, all on the eastern end.

The largest remaining stand of *Platanthera ciliaris* north of Virginia is doing well near the coast of Connecticut, in a Flanders field. Plant succession, however, is a problem and regular cutting back of sapling sassafras trees (*Sassafras albidum*), tulip trees (*Liriodendron tulipifera*), and various shrubs is the only thing keeping the stand healthy.

I expect to see this orange landscape on a visit 2 August 1988, similar to the one Mabel Osgood Wright described almost a hundred years before. Reality quickly dispels that fantasy. Most of the orange plumes are hidden by the chopped off tops of various woody vegetation. There are, however, pockets of wetter, more open spaces that display some remnants of massed color, especially along the earthen vehicle track winding through the middle of a two-acre (less than 1-ha) parcel that borders an apple orchard. The two-hour opportunity—with permission—to photograph this beauty is worth any inconvenience, not the least of which, during the dog days of midsummer, are the blistering heat and humidity that turn my shirt into a clinging, soaking wet sheet. The predictable thirst and brilliant orange color remind me of my predilection for orange freeze drinks on just such a hot New England orchid expedition as this one.

In the best inflorescences, the oblong lip is edged with evenly spaced orange eyelashes of a lighter color than the deeper orange of the rest of the flower, which includes the main body of the lip, the large cupped dorsal sepal above it, and the drawn back ear lobes of the lateral sepals flanking it. The combination produces a delicious two-tone orange sherbet effect. The two tiny, linear, lateral petals, only 1.5 mm wide, hug the

Platanthera ciliaris, Connecticut.

Platanthera ciliaris, Connecticut.

edges of the much larger dorsal sepal. Few natives are so striking in close-up. Luer (1972) thought "the blossoms seem to possess a personality of their own."

Why most authors persist in calling this orchid the yellow fringed-orchid I cannot understand, for surely it is more orange than yellow. No such ambivalence, however, with *Platanthera cristata,* a deeper and rich-er orange than *P. ciliaris,* with a flower about half the size, wider petals, and more fringing on those petals. Otherwise the two species are quite similar. *Platanthera cristata* is less common and restricted to the coastal

Platanthera cristata, New York.

plain more than its cousin, who travels to the slopes of the Appalachians and beyond in all kinds of habitats. It is strange, however, how *P. ciliaris* leaps several hundred miles from Kentucky and extreme southern Ohio habitats to northwestern Indiana and southern Michigan sites. It is also interesting to note the similarities between the orange fringed and the white fringed, which prompted some early botanists to consider the latter merely a white form of *P. ciliaris,* on the basis of dried herbarium material and lack of field experience.

Speaking of *Platanthera blephariglottis,* the white fringed-orchid, we find two distinct varieties, the smaller northern *P. blephariglottis* var. *blephariglottis,* and the more robust southeastern variant, *P. blephariglottis* var. *conspicua.* Even Correll (1950), who was conservative when it came to splitting names, had no problem with the separation based on the larger flower, more open raceme, and longer spur of variety *conspicua.* The

Platanthera blephariglottis, New Hampshire.

Platanthera blephariglottis, profile of single flower, New Hampshire.

latter is often an associate of the Venus' fly-trap (*Dionaea muscipula*) on the coastal plain of the Carolinas, while its northern "cousin" is almost exclusively at home in New England's cranberry bogs. Interestingly, variety *blephariglottis* is not found in most of New England's cranberry bogs. For some reason it picks and chooses where it wants to be. One of the best such bogs in the Northeast is the classic Philbrick-Cricenti Bog in New London, New Hampshire. On or about 1 August each year, one corner of the open bog becomes a green blanket decorated with compact white candles of the purest white, like cotton-grass plumes in other open situations. The uniform green backdrop is made up of dwarf tamaracks (*Larix laricina*), bog rosemary

(*Andromeda glaucophylla*), rhodora (*Rhododendron canadense*), and leatherleaf (*Chamaedaphne calyculata*) shrubs, which provide different shades of green and blue-green. The question remains, why does *P. blephariglottis* var. *blephariglottis* choose to grow only in this one corner?

Both *Platanthera ciliaris* and *P. cristata* hybridize with *P. blephariglottis* var. *conspicua* and each other, producing lighter offspring. These hybrids are treated in more detail in Chapter 38, with charts showing their relationships. What was formerly the hybrid *P.* ×*chapmanii* is now the species, *P. chapmanii,* restricted mostly to the panhandle of Florida on the Gulf of Mexico.

Cypripedium californicum, Oregon.

WESTERN STATES

CHAPTER 29

Three California Ladies

RON Coleman's four-wheel-drive Blazer is the best kind of vehicle for exploring the western slope of the mighty Sierra Nevada, where it connects with the southern terminus of the Cascades, southeast of Lassen Peak National Park in northeastern California. The beautiful Plumas National Forest keeps us company most of the way as does the Feather River and its tributaries.

"The week of June 15th looks good," Ron writes way back in February, when I am still dreaming of the day I get to see what in my mind's-eye is one of our most spectacular orchids, the sensational *Cypripedium californicum*. This belief has been nurtured for many years by Luer's (1975) photographs in his *The Orchids of the United States and Canada*: a vision to conjure in the mind, while waiting for the day to come, then store in memory when the day is done.

Four months later, in perfect weather, the day finally arrives. "At about the 5000 foot (1500 m) level we are certain to be able to see them," he assures me. Without warning, he slows, pulls over, and points, "Look there!" Beside the road, at the base of a small waterfall, above which is a jumble of rocks in the middle of a small stream coming down the mountainside through blooming western azaleas (*Rhododendron occidentale*) and alders, sits a single clump of *Cypripedium californicum*, a second would-be clump clearly outlined beside it by an empty shovel hole, one of the perennial perils of a lady's-slipper.

"These are diminutive plants, Ron, unlike the pictures in Luer's book," I say. (Nevertheless, the photos of this clump turn out to be some of the best in my entire collection of cyps.)

Cypripedium californicum, taller clump in shade, California.

"Come follow me," he says, almost running up the steep path beside the brook for another 100 feet (30 m) or so. There, in the deep shade of the early evening shadows, stands a clump of several 4-foot (120-cm) stems strung with vertical strands of evenly spaced small white slippers. "The long rows of flowers seemed to dangle like lanterns in the checkered sunlight. What they lacked in individual beauty was amply compensated by numbers," Luer (1972) so beautifully phrased it.

In the Smith River drainage further northwest and at a much lower

Cypripedium californicum, shorter clump in sun, California.

Cypripedium californicum, California.

elevation, *Cypripedium californicum* is in full bloom a month earlier. J. A. Fowlie (1982) described the extremely interesting ecology and botanical history of this orchid and its common companion, the famous cobra plant (*Darlingtonia californica*), a member of the pitcher plant family. The two species are usually found in the serpentine regions of northern California and extreme southwestern Oregon and nowhere else in the world, making the pair unique.

The sun drops behind the mountain, making photography increasingly difficult, so Ron suggests looking for a campsite for the night before it gets dark. We will come back early in the morning at sun up. Ron and his sure-footed Blazer track a long, lonely, climbing and winding dirt road for many miles, to the 5000-foot (1500-m) level, where he pulls off at the only opportunity we see and we call it a day. He heats a can of Dinty Moore stew while I pitch the tent. In the remaining few minutes of dissipating light I hear and spot a diving nighthawk, zooming high among the stars, while a white-headed woodpecker shimmies up a monster tree trunk, too far away for a very good look, and an owl hoots his two-cents' worth further up the slope.

Ron sleeps in the Blazer; I lay in the tent, but not in sleep, as the ground is too hard and I'm thinking too much cyps and "listening" to the absolute stillness of the wilderness, so far from "civilization." Finally the sky lightens above, the darkness below slowly dissipates, and I dress to greet the first rays of a new day. The air is chilly and still, until a steller's jay alights on the point of the tallest nearby conifer and adds his salute to a new day. Several beautiful western dogwoods or Nuttall's dogwood (*Cornus occidentalis*) punctuate the slope with the largest white bracts in the dogwood family. This dogwood is impressive only in the size of the individual flower (bracts actually), which is 8 inches (20 cm) wide, but it can't compare in beauty with the more floriferous eastern dogwood (*C. florida*). Incense cedar (*Calocedrus decurrens*) is also impressive among the trees with its deeply furrowed chocolate-brown shredded bark and immense size. Miniature pale yellow irises (*Iris hartwegii*?) are scattered all over a mostly barren, dry and very hard red soil.

After a hasty breakfast of cold cereal, off we go, backtracking down the mountain road, which is wide enough for only a single vehicle. Ron says not to fear, the narrow road probably sees only one or two vehicles a week. Back at the shaded lady's-slipper site, the cyps are in dapple light, which is as much light as they are ever going to see, and my aluminum foil reflector comes in handy once again. What a picture! Twelve flowers—fourteen are the most Ron has ever counted—yes, twelve white slippers, set off elegantly by four perfectly balanced, flat, greenish yellow sepals and petals, the wider upper sepal straight up with a slight arch, the two narrower lateral petals straight out to the sides, looking like yellow shoelaces tied in bows. I use my 8× loupe to get a closer look at the lip-pouch and find the inside floor stacked with a thick growth of white hairs, while the bottom of the pouch on the outside glows with bright drops of liquid gold, like the forty-niners gold of one hundred and fifty years ago, still occasionally panned for in the Feather River below us. The staminode is equally colorful—yellow with a median green stripe. The flower stem is evenly spaced with flowers at the axils of the leaves and bracts, all twelve slippers in almost perfect balance.

The California lady's-slipper (surprisingly, I find no other common name for this striking lady's-slipper) is found in California, along with several hundred other plant species, mostly because of the isolating factors of the Pacific Ocean on one side and the Sierras on the other. I want to spend the entire morning here, but unfortunately time is in charge and can't be ignored. Before leaving for good, however, we note and photograph several stream orchids, *Epipactis gigantea,* in the ditch along the road.

The second of three ladies that call California home and the opposite of *Cypripedium californicum* in many ways is another unique lady's-slipper, the brownie or clustered lady's-slipper, *C. fasciculatum,* found as far east as the western edge of the Rocky Mountains in Montana, Wyoming, and Colorado, and north into Utah, Idaho, and extreme southwestern

Oregon. Most occurrences are in U.S. national forests, not surprisingly. Management plans will require careful monitoring of the relatively few and scattered populations in these national forests to prevent their destruction by indiscriminate clear-cutting. After all, one of the original tenets of national forests is multiple use and that should include protection for unique flora as well as fauna.

Inconspicuous and the homeliest of North American cyps, to some people at any rate but not to me, *Cypripedium fasciculatum* amazes by the lay of the flowers and their color. The short clustered raceme of three or four flowers is so heavy or the stem so weak that everything droops down close to the ground, requiring a prone position to see it well. Lifting the flowers helps. Only 6 inches (15 cm) or so tall, the leaves, subopposite half way up the short stem, almost look as if they are basal. Contributing to the disheveled appearance are the relatively large petals and sepals (tepals), which do their part in hiding the lip-pouches if the leaves haven't already done enough. The usual color of the flower is a unique purple-brown, but another form is pale green with purplish lines and

Cypripedium fasciculatum, typical flower color, California.

Cypripedium fasciculatum, pale form, California.

Cypripedium fasciculatum, green form, California.

markings. Both forms are in front of us as we take turns photographing in the hot sun, sweat rolling down our faces. Because of the extraordinary diversity and beauty of color forms all around us, we are reluctant to move into the shade.

Ted Elliman and Anne Dalton (1995), describing the ecology of *Cypripedium fasciculatum* in western Montana, stated that "as an adult in favorable habitat, each plant lives for a number of years. A few sites observed over time appear to indicate that individual populations survive for many decades." They also indicate that this orchid cannot survive severe burn-overs or clear-cuts, but does adapt in selective cuts that do not significantly alter shade or moisture conditions. It was the last North American lady's-slipper species to be described, in 1882, almost one hundred years after *C. acaule* (1789), reflecting, of course, the difference in human exploration and settlement between the East and West. *Cypripedium californicum* was first described in 1868, fourteen years ahead of *C. fasciculatum*, while *C. montanum* was discovered as early as 1840. *Cypripedium guttatum*, in Alaska, and Asiatic in origin, was named in 1800.

Yet another California native, the startling snow plant (*Sarcodes sanguinea*), looms up out of the brown needle duff not far from the several scattered clumps of *Cypripedium fasciculatum*. Twelve inches (30 cm) of scarlet nudity, it literally commands attention. I have never seen anything quite like it, nor have I seen anything like the pine cones of the sugar pine (*Pinus lambertiana*) all around us. Eighteen inches long (45 cm), these cones are the world's longest. They litter the ground and surround the small clumps of brownie lady's-slippers. I am tempted to take a few home with me, but give up the idea because of their size and the difficulty of carrying them in a packed suitcase. John Muir declared the sugar pine to be the king of all pines, surpassing all others not just in size "but in lordly beauty and majesty." It is the fourth largest American tree. At 200 feet (60 m) high with a trunk circumference of 30 feet (9 m), it ranks behind only the California redwood (*Sequoia sempervirens*), giant sequoia (*Sequoiadendron giganteum*), and Douglas-fir (*Pseudotsuga menziesii*). In the northern Sierras, where we are, we first meet this noble giant at around 2000 feet (600 m). Here and in Yosemite National Park many of the conifers are decked out in resplendent, hanging tufts or beards of the yellow-green staghorn lichen (*Evernia vulpina*), which impart a strangely beautiful dimension to these marvelous trees. This narrow ravine of magnificent sugar pines is surrounded by an ugly clearcut, which fortunately spared the ravine and its remarkable collection of unique plants. I understand from Ron that the Native Plant Society of California deserves the credit for saving this priceless ravine.

We drive many more miles up a mountain road, negotiable only by four-wheel drive and littered with small rocks and boulders that slow us down, until we come to a boggy opening on yet another steep slope. It is here that the California lady's-slipper and the marvelous pitcher plant grow so close together in a very wet seep that it is difficult to avoid stepping on one or the other while getting into position to photograph. The hundreds of California lady's-slippers at this site grow fully exposed to the sun, which reduces their size. Most are still in yellow bud, because of the higher elevation and recently melted snow. Some will surely be in bloom early in July. The pristine beauty of the newly emerging bright yellow-green pitcher plants with their natty bows is tainted by the dead remains of last year's stalks, which clutter an otherwise splendid seepage slope. Another hour here is not enough to fully savor or explore all the beauty that surrounds us, which includes several tall, tapered ball-heads of bear-grass (*Xerophyllum tenax*), not a grass at all but a member of the lily family.

In several different areas throughout these mountains, one of the most common orchids I notice is *Goodyera oblongifolia,* unfortunately not a June bloomer, except on Vancouver Island further north off the British Columbia coast. The leaves, however, are very large relative to the other goodyeras and very attractive with their broken white lines down the center.

In one coniferous woods marked by some tremendous orange-plated trunks of the mighty ponderosa pine (*Pinus ponderosa*), the most common and widely distributed of all western conifers, piperias in leaf only are all over the ground, along with *Corallorhiza maculata* and several clumps of the bright yellow form of *C. maculata.* Ron is not sure which *Piperia* species we are looking at because of the difficulty in separating them out of bloom. *Piperia colemanii,* named after Ron, is found in northern California and southern Oregon. The remaining nine species range up and down the state, some in restricted niches, with *P. unalas-*

censis the most widespread of all, including a disjunct station thousands of miles east on Flowerpot Island off the Bruce Peninsula in southern Ontario. New research on this disjunct station may actually reveal a different species.

It is interesting to note the changes in *Piperia* nomenclature since the turn of the twentieth century. In 1901 P. A. Rydberg listed nine species, but fifty years later D. S. Correll reduced the number to one, with two varieties, and in 1975 C. Luer recognized three species, *P. unalascensis, P. elegans,* and *P. maritima* (now a synonym of *P. elegans*). The monumental *Flora of California* (Jepson 1979), also known as the Jepson Manual, brought the total back to nine in 1993. The newly named *P. colemanii* was added shortly after publication to bring the current total to ten species. The flowers of *Piperia* closely resemble those of *Malaxis,* but that genus usually has a single leaf on a shorter stem, while *Piperia* has several on a taller plant.

The third California lady, *Cypripedium montanum,* the mountain lady's-slipper, requires a long hard drive to Yosemite National Park, via Interstate 395, south through Reno and Carson City, Nevada. The eastern slope of the Sierra Nevada—a 2-mile (3-km) high uplift of the so-called Sierra block, which occurred along a fault line on the other or western side of the range more than two million years ago—rises abruptly to our right off the floor of the Great Basin as we hurry southward. The still snow-capped mountain peaks are back-lit with the afternoon sun on our right. The view is imposing mile after mile. We finally pick up Route 120, head west, and climb the road to Tioga Pass, at the east entrance to Yosemite National Park. The pass is 10,000 feet (3,000 m) above sea level and still covered with snow. Dozens of skiers still enjoy the slopes to our left. The pass has been open only a week and streamlets of water lap across the hot blacktop in wavering bands.

Before nightfall, Ron shows me several mountain ladies behind a campground inside the park, most in good condition for so late in their season, he says. It is a tall, stately and handsome slipper orchid, with some plants reaching 2 feet (60 cm) or more. The smartly contrasting combination of mahogany sepals and white lip is very attractive. *Cypripedium montanum* has a distribution in the northwestern mountains similar to that of *C. fasciculatum* except that it also extends through most of British Columbia. Ron, along with my friend Joe Welch, a retired Fish and

Cypripedium montanum, with flash, California.

Wildlife Service Refuge manager, formerly of Oregon and now living in Arizona, and that most famous of all conservationists, John Muir, the father of Yosemite National Park, consider this orchid the most beautiful of the three lady's-slippers in California. I respectfully demur, however, and vote for the California lady (*C. californicum*).

We camp outside the park as the park service's reduction in staffing in recent years means fewer campsites available this early in the season. At 6:30 the next morning, we reenter the park for a whirlwind stop at the two most famous waterfalls—Bridal Veil and Yosemite—before almost anyone else stirs in the valley campgrounds; several mule deer eat their breakfast along the way. The mad Merced River boils and spills over its banks on its rush to exit the valley floor; Ron has never seen it so high. The last stop at Inspiration Point, just as the sun makes its appearance above Half Dome, recalls the last time I was here in 1956. It is my most favored view in the park. After a late breakfast in the city of Merced, reading the paper for the first time in almost a week, we hit the road one last time, crossing the wide-open spaces of the interior valley of California, already clothed in summer tans, part of the endless diversity of California.

It is no wonder that Galen Rowell, the famous landscape photographer and adventurer to most of the wild places on the globe, has confessed that "more of what I am seeking in the wilds is right here in my home state of California than anywhere else on earth."

CHAPTER 30

The Ghost Orchid in the Columbia River Gorge, Washington

From our base in Seattle, Washington, we gather yet another early morning in front of our motel on this first day of July. With the final "All aboard," we drive south along Interstate 5 to Vancouver, Washington, two and a half hours away. We have an appointment with Mike and Nancy Fahey, retirees who have promised to show us the elusive phantom orchid, *Cephalanthera austiniae.* One of the secrets to successful botanizing is knowing the right people in the right places, especially if they are as generous and pleasant as the Faheys.

Our new destination is the famed Columbia River Gorge, which straddles the Washington-Oregon border along Interstate 84. Geologically, historically, scenically, and botanically, this 85-mile (136-km) long gorge has much to offer. I had the pleasure of first seeing it forty years ago on a solo eleven-week auto trip that remains to this day as one of the highlights of my lifetime. Some things have changed, sadly. One of the most noticeable changes is the inability to see the magnificent snow-covered volcanic cone of Mount Hood from the Washington side of the gorge on Route 14 because of the polluted atmosphere.

On my first trip out here, the city of Portland, Oregon, was a favorite, thanks in large part to the symmetrical beauty of snow-covered Mount Hood in the Cascade Range. At over 11,000 feet (3300 m), Mount Hood is the highest mountain in Oregon, the third highest in the Northwest, and North America's most frequently climbed glaciated peak, second worldwide to Japan's famous Mount Fuji. It has a lot going for it.

Earlier this morning, I could barely discern the massive bulk of Mount Rainier, the Northwest's highest mountain at over 14,000 feet (4200 m) and the fifth highest in the lower 48 states. Multnomah Falls still plunges 620 feet (186 m) over the same basalt cliffs, the second highest year-round waterfall in the United States. We have time for only a glimpse as we drive by on the adjacent interstate. This is an orchid trip, remember. The Columbia River Gorge represented the only significant break in the magnificent Cascade–Sierra Nevada range, a sea-level mountain pass that figured prominently in the attempts of early pioneers to access the Pacific Ocean. The Columbia River ranks as the largest and longest river in the Pacific Northwest.

Despite the drought conditions this season, the Faheys lead us to a third-growth Douglas-fir (*Pseudotsuga menziesii*) forest in Klikitat County off Route 14 on the Washington side of the gorge. Pausing first to stretch after another long ride from Vancouver, we scramble up the bank to begin our search. The floor of the forest appears barren and very dry in all directions. A call rings out from another quarter. I pick up the pace under the heavy gear and heat of the early afternoon sun, and soon come upon several people squatting in front of white stems sticking up all over the place. At a distance, these naked stems resemble the Indian pipes

Cephalanthera austiniae, Washington.

(*Monotropa uniflora*) back east. Actually, though, there is little similarity except in the ghostly white color.

Over two hundred ghost orchids are scattered, some in small clumps of a few stems and others singly. Up to twenty-four flowers are held loosely in a raceme that opens gradually from the bottom up and slowly diminishes in beauty. By the time the last few flowers open, the stem is a bit sad looking. Though the majority of plants are past prime, enough are in good condition to produce some excellent images. Up close this orchid wears a redeeming golden-yellow spot near the end of the downcurved heart-shaped lip, a beauty spot on an otherwise somewhat disappointing flower.

Having said that, I recall Leonard Wiley (1969) insisting that the "cold language of botany cannot describe the ineffable beauty of the delicate petals and the graceful flowers." Carlyle Luer (1975) called it North America's weirdest native orchid. One gets the impression the flowers are only half open, which is a correct perception because the sepals and petals are almost connivent around the white column.

This phantom of the fir forest is restricted to mostly coniferous forests in parts of Washington, Oregon, northern Idaho, and the mountains of central and northern California. We find some *Corallorhiza maculata* (spotted coralroot) clumping alone across the road. This saprophyte turns up almost anywhere across the United States, wherever there are mixed and coniferous woods, it seems; I have seen it from near sea level in the moist Northeast to over 10,000 feet (3,000 m) in dry New Mexico.

We learn from the Faheys of the impending logging that this woodlot faces by the local municipality, which will use the proceeds to help defray the school budget. This refrain is familiar wherever one goes these days.

Back on Route 14, we come across a dried up gully lined with jumbled basaltic rocks. Normally it would be a stream bed in wetter seasons. We are surprised to see several clumps of the pale golden *Spiranthes porrifolia,* the western ladies-tresses, in the dry gully. These are in full bloom, though partially hidden by the blending, parched grasses of the same golden color. With these blended orchids are several splendid blue brodieas, adding heavenly blue pastels to the golden scene, the perfect palette for a Monet. One would never have bet his last wooden nickel that anything like this would be blooming here under such parched conditions, but seeing is believing. *Spiranthes porrifolia* was treated by Correll (1978) as a western variety of the very widespread *S. romanzoffiana,* but Luer (1975) treated it as the original species described by John Lindley in 1840.

The lip of *Spiranthes porrifolia* is ovate and tapered, while the golden straw color of the flowers is quite distinctive in the field; it is clearly different from any of the other "yellow" *Spiranthes* species. *Spiranthes romanzoffiana,* on the other hand, has a distinctive fiddle-shaped (panduriform) lip when flattened out and is essentially white in color. Several dozen tightly spiraled flowers, in several ranks, crowd the spike of *S. porrifolia* almost 2 feet (60 cm) tall. All the flower parts (calyx and corolla) of the western ladies'-tresses are equally flared at the apex. The range

Spiranthes porrifolia, Washington.

Spiranthes romanzoffiana, depicting "receding chin" of floret, Vermont.

of this species is centered in the mountains of northern California and southern Oregon, thence narrowing to a point that terminates just across the southern border of Washington, almost exactly where we are today.

Across the road another pretty example of *Piperia elegans,* the elegant piperia, rests under the precious shade of an isolated tree. It is, perhaps, the finest *Piperia* specimen of the whole weekend. As usual, however, time has become a factor and we must head back to Seattle. It is not a pleasant thought in terms of keeping the driver awake late at night on the road after a long, tiring day.

The five-hour ride back to Seattle is softened by good conversation and a late stop for dinner at one of the chain motel dining rooms along the way. Twelve congenial members of the study group relax at the table and take turns commenting on the highs and lows of the two-week excursion, enjoying the last bit of camaraderie. It is just before the strike of midnight when we arrive back at the motel; some of us say our goodbyes and prepare to fly out of Seattle at six o'clock the following morning.

Piperia elegans, showing vertical spur, Washington.

CHAPTER 31

Olympic National Park, Washington

Olympic National Park is a first-rate orchid stop, and *Listera caurina* and *Corallorhiza mertensiana* are first-rate finds. No surprise there, but it is hard to believe that originally the Olympic Mountains were denied national park status because some thought they lacked sufficient grandeur. After Teddy Roosevelt's initial National Monument designation succeeded in 1909, it took cousin Franklin Roosevelt to finally persuade Congress to take the final step twenty-nine years later in 1938. Olympic National Park is now one of the largest national parks in the contiguous forty-eight states, comprising close to a million acres (400,000 ha).

One of the most memorable panoramas in the park is best observed while walking the Hurricane Hill Trail at the terminus of the Hurricane Ridge Road. Sloping wildflower meadows blend into an unbroken sweep of inspiring dark green firs, which front a massive black-walled, snow-capped, serrated mountain range, remindful of grade school days when students made serrated paper cutouts on folded white paper. On the north side of the trail, clumps of subalpine firs (*Abies lasiocarpa*), accented by strategically placed bright white snow banks, guarantee perfect landscape pictures. We oblige. The most famous wildflowers in this part of the park are both lilies—the glacier (*Erythronium grandiflorum*) and avalanche (*E. montanum*). Neither is as plentiful this year as the guide book pictures suggest they should be, at least on 28 June.

The dominant colors along this section of the path are an appropriately patriotic red, white, and blue, represented by two species of Indian paint-brush—a brilliant scarlet (*Castilleja miniata*) and an unusual magenta (*C. parviflora*)—the intense blue rockslide larkspur (*Delphinium glareosum*), and the aforementioned white avalanche lily. No orchids grace these higher slopes on Hurricane Hill. We must descend to lower levels, where on the side of the road and down in the ditches, the tall white spikes of bog candle, *Platanthera dilatata,* beckon us to stop and investigate.

Platanthera dilatata is divided into several varieties and forms. One variation, the so-called Sierra rein-orchid, differs from *P. dilatata* primarily in a longer spur and a smaller column, which we see some examples of here. The same situation applies to the so-called *P. hyperborea* complex (see Chapter 35 for more details). Seeing the group prowling the roadside prompts one or two cars to stop and ask what we are taking pictures of, and then move on. When, however, the object of interest is the ubiquitous mule deer, with the tell-tale black median stripe on the stubby tail, people stop and pull out their cameras en masse. The glamour of the mammals is demonstrated again.

In these ditches, several species of the little known genus *Piperia* (pronounced pie-per´-ee-ah) luxuriate with little notice because of their tiny, demure, greenish flowers, and, until recently, confusion in taxonomic treatment. These plants were originally included in the genus *Habenaria* until P. A. Rydberg formed a separate genus in 1901, named in honor of C. V. Piper of Pullman, Washington. Oakes Ames of Harvard University returned them to *Habenaria* in 1910, while at the same time recognizing only two species of Rydberg's original nine. In 1950 D. S. Correll even lumped these two into a single species, *P. unalascensis,* considering all others mere variants. Carlyle Luer in 1975 again split them, this time into four species. Finally, Morgan and Ackerman, in 1990 and 1993, proved beyond doubt, it is hoped, the existence of ten bona fide species.

Several of these *Piperia* species are endemic to California, the center of distribution, while all of them are confined to the Pacific coast except for *P. unalascensis,* which travels all the way to Alaska and jumps eastward to disjunct stations in Ontario and Québec. The ten-member genus constitutes almost one-third of the total number of orchid species in California. The diagnostic differences between *Piperia* and *Habenaria* (now *Platanthera* for the most part) are pretty clear-cut: the leaves of *Piperia* are basal and wither at anthesis, while those of *Habenaria* are arranged along the stem and remain green through. Furthermore, the lateral sepals of *Piperia* unite with the lip and the anther cells show some technical differences from their counterparts in *Habenaria*.

Separating the individual species of *Piperia* from each other can sometimes be tricky, however. We will see four species during the next few days in Washington and Oregon: *P. candida*, *P. elegans*, *P. transversa*, and *P. unalascensis*. *Piperia candida* is essentially whitish and has a short spur. Both *P. elegans* and *P. transversa* have a long spur and are green and whitish in flower color, but the spur of *P. transversa* is usually (though not always) carried in a horizontal position, while that of *P. elegans* is vertically oriented. The flowers of *P. transversa* are usually more spaced out along the extended raceme than those of *P. elegans*.

Piperias are tall plants up to 2–3 feet (60–90 cm). The individual flowers, however, are so tiny that a loupe is very helpful in identification. Differences in scent can be diagnostic, especially at night; unfortunately I have lost some of my olfactory powers and have never done any night viewing. An excellent source for reference on this group is Ron Coleman's *Wild Orchids of California* (1995).

The "best" orchids, however, are reserved for some of the trails at low elevations in the park. Two notable ones are Heart of the Hills and Sol Duc. In both cases we walk under massive Douglas-fir (*Pseudotsuga taxifolia*), western hemlock (*Tsuga plicata*), and western cedar (*Thuja plicata*) in a magnificent climax forest, where I stand in awe looking up at the trunks, 20 feet (6 m) in circumference, and crowns of 300-year-old trees. It is akin to walking down the hushed aisle of a darkened

Piperia transversa, Oregon.

300-year-old cathedral, but here the dimensions are even greater and the treasures are all alive.

Olympic National Park as a whole protects the largest virgin temperate rain forest in the Western Hemisphere and the largest stand of coniferous forest in the lower 48 states. One hundred and forty inches (355 cm) of rain fall in the famous Hoh rain forest on the western or oceanside of the park, while Port Angeles lying in the so-called rain-shadow of the Olympic Mountains on the "dry" northern side receives only 25 inches (62 cm). As a result, this amazing temperate forest officially became a biosphere reserve in 1976 and a world heritage site in 1981. The only other such example in North America is the world's first national park, Yellowstone in Wyoming.

The Northwest twayblade, *Listera caurina,* is my favorite twayblade. The Latin name *caurina,* meaning "of the northwind," evokes just such a place as the Heart of the Forest Trail. The flower has a rich green lip with two deeper emerald-green lines running down each side of the lip

Piperia transversa, revealing horizontal spur, Oregon.

Piperia unalascensis, Washington.

and terminating basally in two beady black "eyes." It conjures up in my mind, especially as I write this on Halloween eve, a miniature Darth Vader cloaked in green, the vertical sepals and petals flaring above the lip-cloak, like arms posed to strike any intruder or photographer daring to approach too closely. The 6- to 10-inch (15- to 25-cm) stem supports as many as two dozen or more of these little green Darth Vaders. This neat twayblade is the only *Listera* species whose lip is essentially entire with no cleft, although some specimens exhibit a slight indentation. The plants prefer a reclusive existence (in keeping with their other-worldly looks) and are usually well separated from each other while still within "ear-shot."

The western coralroot, *Corallorhiza mertensiana*, is often a companion of *Listera caurina* on these forest trails, as is *L. cordata*, the latter long out of bloom. The coralroot is here more prolific than the Northwest

twayblade. It tends to grow in clumps like most of the coralroots. One clump we saw had almost 100 closely packed stems. The colors vary a great

Listera caurina, Washington.

Listera caurina, Washington.

deal but are mostly some shade of red-purple, which pervades the entire plant. The lip, which is the most colorful part of the plant, hangs down quite abruptly. It is spotted, streaked, or solidly brilliant red-purple, while the lateral petals, often coalesced with the dorsal sepal, stand erect above and behind the equally elongated and erect column. The lateral sepals fold down in back of these front-runners. The entire aspect of the flower differs from the spotted coralroot, *C. maculata*, the other coral root commonly found in these mountains. The western coralroot is tall and narrow, while the spotted coralroot is more squat and rounded. The column of the western coralroot is more elongated than the column of spotted coralroot, and all the petals and sepals are spotted with the same red-purple.

Carlyle Luer (1975) related a remarkable anecdote of the energy stored in the rhizome of this orchid. He had stopped his car to investigate something coming up through the asphalt:

> A layer of asphalt perhaps an inch thick was being cracked and lifted by a reddish plant beneath. I was amazed to discover a husky, doubled-over stem of *C. mertensiana*, the lower flowers of which were already opened in their cramped quarters.

Surprisingly, both the Northwest twayblade and the western coralroot have almost identical distributions, which form an inverted open-end wrench shape on a map. Yellowstone, Wyoming, forms one tip to the right as you look at the map, and northwestern California the other on the left. The "handle" extends into western British Columbia. *Corallorhiza mertensiana*, incidentally, is the orchid that changed Ron Coleman's life in 1972, while hiking one of these trails in Olympic National Park.

Crescent Lake, on the perimeter of Olympic National Park, alongside U.S. Route 101, is our last stop on this 29th day of June. Here, near a small public beach, hundreds of prime stream orchids, *Epipactis gigantea*, blend in with the rock boulders at the edge of the water. They are tucked in between the rocks. To get the best picture, therefore, one must step down into the water, but no matter, for again my waterproof Asolos keep me dry. The lips on these plants are more intensely colored than one normally sees. A bright orange suffuses the lower half of the uniquely hinged lip, the so-called epichile portion, which moves about in the breeze, prompting that delightful epithet, chatterbox, just one among a long list of colloquial names. A loose raceme of ten to fifteen blooms is the usual complement of flowers, with ten or more alternate leaves attached to a 3-foot (90-cm), and occasionally up to 5-foot (150-cm), stem. The flower, not a giant, measures about 2 inches (5 cm) in diameter. Often locally abundant and persistent, the stream orchid is usually associated with water and often inundated in the spring.

W. H. A. Preece (1937) summed up the feelings of many who have come to love this orchid: "It is a treasure that scorns to advertise itself and that so blends with its surroundings as to be passed unnoticed by the multitude." This situation we witness first-hand at Crescent Lake, for

Corallorhiza mertensiana, large clump of pale form, Washington.

not one of the dozens of bathers on this warm, sunny day is curious enough to come over and see what our group is doing. Perhaps that is just as well for the stream orchid.

It may be relevant to note here the criteria for the establishment of national and state parks. Alfred Runte (1979) lists the following four criteria: scenic wonders (e.g., Grand Canyon National Park); curiosities (e.g., Yellowstone National Park—geysers and thermal activity); utilitarian (e.g., Adirondack Park—New York City water supply); and recreational (e.g., Coulee Dam Recreational Area). Worthy of note also is that the Olympic Mountains are an excellent example of more recent mountain building (3 to 12 million years ago) as the result of plate tectonics. Simply put, the offshore oceanic Pacific Plate, with its accumulated sedimentary deposits, later metamorphosed by the earth's interior heat into sandstone and shale, collided with the North American Continental Plate, pushing under it while folding and uplifting the rock material into a tremendous dome, which then underwent glaciation and erosion to form the present configuration of peaks and valleys.

Unlike the Cascade Range, the Olympic Mountains were built inde-

Corallorhiza mertensiana, typical flower color, Washington.

Corallorhiza mertensiana, spotted variation, Washington.

pendently of the volcanic cones. Olympic National Park contains the largest remaining stand of coniferous forest in the United States outside of Alaska and has the longest stretch of undeveloped coastline—57 miles (91 km)—in the lower 48 states. These are just some of the amazing wonders under permanent protection, it is hoped, in this national park.

To conclude this chapter on the treasures of the Pacific Northwest, we cannot leave without at least a mention of yet another jewel. On another day we visited Lake Elizabeth, in the Baker-Snoqualmie National Forest, east of Seattle, off U.S. Route 2. I was shown an extraordinary clump of *Listera caurina* on the shore of this little gem. The plants were more than 10 inches (25 cm) tall, with leaves exceeding 2 inches (5 cm) in diameter and the flowers proportionate. This orchid surpassed all the dimensions in the books, hidden in the shade of trees among a jumble of small boulders above the boggy edges of Lake Elizabeth. Down below on the open boggy apron of the lake, we also found *Platanthera chorisiana*, one of North America's smallest and rarest platantheras. Unfortunately, it was several days away from opening on this 27th day of June. When open, the flower is a tiny globe, the sepals and petals barely crack open. Until fairly recently it was known only from the islands of Japan, across the Aleutian Islands, and on the coastal islands of British Columbia. It is now also known from extreme northwestern Washington and may be less rare than suspected.

To get to Lake Elizabeth requires an almost 7-mile (11-km) drive over a very bumpy gravel road that climbs several thousand feet into the subalpine forest where firs like the subalpine fir (*Abies lasiocarpa*) dominate. Along this road, choking the wet ditch and hiding the water from view, are a lush growth of very tall slender bog-orchids (*Platanthera stricta*), many western red columbines (*Aquilegia formosa*) looking like varieties back east, the dangling creamy white "catkins" of the goat's beard (*Aruncus formosa*), the bright orange Columbia lily (*Lilium columbianum*) with maroon spots, and tremendous clumps of the handsome, shining deer fern (*Blechnum spicant*). That roadside display is only a prelude to the main show up at the lake.

On the boggy edges of beautiful Lake Elizabeth are striking examples of the monstrous—3-foot (90-cm) long and 1-foot (30-cm) wide—and lustrous green leaves of the western skunk cabbage (*Lysichitum ameri-*

canum), the yellow "flowers" long since departed in springtime. This happens to be the largest native wildflower of the Pacific Northwest. The fascinating little elephantheads (*Pedicularis groenlandica*), with reddish purple flowers shaped exactly like the head of an elephant in profile, including the trunk, clump happily beside the water where they have come down to drink (of course). The amazing diversity continues with the circumpolar carnivore, the blue butterwort, (*Pinguicula vulgaris*), and the subalpine spiraea (*Spiraea densiflora*), its tiny fuzzy red flowers forming a dense flat-topped head.

The five hours we spend here in isolation and stillness are priceless. Not another soul or vehicle disturbs us during the entire afternoon. Only the ubiquitous dam and gate at the outlet of the lake tarnish an otherwise beautiful wilderness experience on a perfect day and indicate that we are in a national forest.

CHAPTER 32

Helleborines in Zion National Park, Utah

THREE species of the genus *Epipactis* occur in North America. One is a native, *E. gigantea,* confined to the western states from the Rocky Mountains to the Pacific, while the other two are European imports, *E. helleborine* and *E. atrorubens,* found in the Northeast. The generic name, *Epipactis,* comes from an ancient Greek word used for a medicinal plant dating back to 350 B.C. or thereabouts. The specific name of the western representative, *gigantea,* means "gigantic," though neither the plant nor the flowers are gigantic in size. The common names are decidedly more appropriate; the best known are stream orchid and chatterbox, the latter a local colloquialism derived from the effect of the wind on the hinged lip, which flops around in the breeze. False lady's-slipper is another interesting name reflecting the similarity of the leafy plant to members of the genus *Cypripedium* when out of bloom.

Epipactis gigantea is neither common nor rare, but often locally abundant. It is also persistent, unlike some other native orchids, coming up each year in the same locale; mountain streams in California are a typical site. Also typical but less well known are microclimates in otherwise dry almost semi-desert conditions. As an example, consider our experience in Zion National Park in July 1994.

As one drives into the park from the east, everyone is required to stop at a mile (1.6-km) long tunnel before proceeding through because of the one-way traffic. One of the more popular one-hour hiking trails begins here, with a great view of Zion Canyon itself. Halfway up the trail there is a cavelike overhang called an alcove, where seepage maintains constant moisture summer-long, producing a beautiful "hanging garden." There are several of these hanging gardens in the park, created by percolating water from the rain and snow, which permeates the porous sandstone layers until stopped by an impermeable layer of shale, which then forces the water to move laterally on this hard surface, until it eventually finds an opening and forms the seep. I counted several hundred stream orchids at this one, closely bunched, green and robust, but out of bloom, of course. I could imagine the sight a month before. Lush maidenhair fern (*Adiantum capillus-veneris*) and the Zion daisy (*Erigeron sionis*), a narrow endemic (growing only in Zion National Park) and still with a few flowers, are companion plants to the stream orchid here. These seeps are like oases in the desert. The alcove also provided a fine resting place for the other climbers and me on a day where the temperature reached 105°F (41°C).

The heat is a typically dry one that characterizes the Southwest in the summertime. Many people are discouraged from traveling to this part of the country at this time of year because of the heat. If would-be travelers pay close attention to the weather maps every day, as I do, they will soon learn that only the southern parts of Arizona and New Mexico suffer the daily onslaught of 115°F (46°C) heat. Up in the northern part of these states and in southern Utah, where the national parks are concen-

Epipactis gigantea, habitat with beach in background, Washington.

Epipactis gigantea, highly colored variant, Washington.

trated, the terrain is usually between 5,000 and 10,000 feet (1500 to 3000 m) above sea level so the temperature is quite comfortable. Our five-week excursion bore this out very pleasantly.

There are only a handful of orchid species in Zion National Park, but there is an almost endless number of wildflowers in bloom, even at this season of the year, throughout northern New Mexico and Arizona. Particularly evident are members of the genus *Penstemon,* the largest in North America with more than 250 species—all essentially western and many cultivated in gardens —and *Castilleja* (Indian paintbrush). Both genera belong to the beautiful snapdragon family (Scrophulariaceae). Things like scarlet and pink skyrockets (*Ipomopsis aggregata* and *I. tenuituba,* respectively), the rich deep blue bellflower (*Campanula parryi*), and many others too numerous to mention here line the roadside on the way to the north rim of the Grand Canyon at 8000 feet (2400 m) above sea level. The road meanders through shallow meadows bordering beautiful Engelmann spruce (*Picea engelmannii*) and subalpine fir (*Abies lasiocarpa*) forests.

On the edges of the forest near the north rim, I found my favorite lily, the glamorously beautiful sego or mariposa lily (*Calochortus nuttallii*), with three large waxy, creamy white petals marked with purple and yellow at the base. Over sixty species of *Calochortus,* in a wealth of colors, are found throughout the Southwest and Far West, as well as Mexico. One species or another is in bloom from April to October in a variety of habitats and altitudes. Lacking orchids, this lily will satisfy the most discriminating wildflower enthusiast, I assure you. The road to the north rim is still snowbound early in June, which accounts for the late showing of wildflowers at this altitude.

Incidentally, of the three major parks in southwestern Utah and northern Arizona—Zion, Bryce, and the Grand Canyon—Zion rates number one, especially for the diversity of views, plants, and birds. The views at all the lookouts on the south rim of Grand Canyon are quite similar, in my opinion, with one or two exceptions, and, unless you make the arduous trip down into the heart of the canyon, which the vast majority of visitors don't, the park is a disappointment, at least to me. After years of reading and examining photographs, it was obvious early on that air pollution has significantly increased in recent years as has the overcrowding. Finding a parking spot within a reasonable distance from the visitor's center, for example, was impossible the day we were there, and the traffic, construction, and congestion destroyed any sense of pristine wildness. On top of this, there were the helicopters landing and taking off. All these factors contribute to a once-is-enough experience for me.

Two other members of the genus *Epipactis* in North America come to us from Eurasia, where nearly two dozen other kinds make their home. One is the common helleborine, *E. helleborine,* apparently so-called because of a resemblance to a buttercup in the genus *Helleborus.* It was first discovered near Syracuse, New York, in 1879. How it landed there is still conjectural, but seed stowaway of some sort is a logical bet. The species has since spread throughout most of the southern Great Lakes region, eastern Ontario, New York (where it is quite common), and most of New England. It has even shown up in Missouri and Montana and perhaps, by now, the West Coast. Almost a weed in some areas where it is abundant, it seems to prefer somewhat neutral soil. The leaves resemble those of *Cypripedium parviflorum,* the yellow lady's-slipper, and are easily mistaken for that orchid when not in bloom. The color variation of the up to fifty or more flowers is substantial, ranging from green to purple with tints of pink and yellow, and albinos for good measure. As a result of this variation, several color forms have been named. The lip in both species has the look of a "sauce boat" (Morris and Eames 1929). The individual flowers, when examined closely are quite colorful, while from a distance, aside from the fact that you know you are looking at an orchid, the plant is rather inconspicuous, considering its 2-foot (60-cm) bulk. Bloom period is late July and early August in most of its range. I have found it most abundant in parts of Vermont. There, in one locale it grows in the hundreds across the road from a fine stand of ram's-head lady's-slippers

(*Cypripedium arietinum*). The number of fat seed pods produced at this site was the most phenomenal I've ever seen and is obviously an important reason for its rapid expansion.

The second European import is the red helleborine, *Epipactis atrorubens*. It was discovered in August 1990 in an abandoned serpentine quar-

Epipactis helleborine, Maine.

ry in northern Vermont. Paul Martin Brown believes its unusual habitat will restrict it. The plant is 8–12 inches (20–30 cm) tall, which makes it shorter than *E. helleborine,* with cranberry-red flowers less than 1 inch (2.5 cm) in diameter. It will be interesting to see if this vagabond succeeds in establishing a permanent footing in Vermont.

Epipactis helleborine, green form, Maine.

Epipactis helleborine, Maine.

CHAPTER 33

The California Lady's-slipper in the Klamath Knot

THE LONG ride is over. Doug, our guide, steps carefully into the uneven wooded slope along a small but active brook, hidden by enormous clumps of maidenhair fern and fallen tree trunks bleached silver in the more open enclaves. Rocks composed of peridotite and serpentine jut up from this same cover. It is easy to turn an ankle or fall headfirst into the maze, hopscotching over the logs and rocks, in the haste to see our botanical prize.

At first I barely can make out the clumps of *Cypripedium californicum*, even from a relatively short distance directly in front of me, because of the smallish flowers. Then they hit me, up close—huge clumps, some exceeding a hundred plants, each 4-foot (120-cm), ramrod-straight stem displaying a multitude of small white flowers like a string of miniature hanging white lanterns, the upper part dipped in honey. Usually, the dorsal sepal and straight-out lateral petals are a lemon and lime color, but not here. The degree of bronzing differs slightly from clump to clump, with the very last clump I photograph the darkest honey-brown of all. Only the extreme basal portion is green.

From the first moment on the scene, I know this is something special, so special that my stomach begins to ache from the excitement of the scene and the haste to set up and photograph. Moments later, this feeling is exacerbated when someone beckons us further down the brook to a small opening where the sun and moisture combine to produce an even greater spectacle, if that is possible, and it is here. The air is calm, the sun in and out of the clouds. Shooting conditions are perfect. Relax, I tell myself, after the initial burst of intensity, since that is the only way to stop this stomach ache. So I take a moment to count some inflorescences.

Cypripedium californicum, Oregon.

Correll (1978) and Luer (1975) listed twelve flowers as the maximum, Coleman (1995) fourteen. Here, I count seventeen and nineteen, while Paul Martin Brown finds one stem with a record twenty-one blooms, all open at once and in prime condition. Incredible! In contrast, there is even one small plant with a single flower. Some of the flower nodes produce two flowers instead of the usual one. An unscientific count of stems in an area of less than an acre (0.4 ha) produces at least 5000 plants and 50,000 blooms! Again, incredible! No wonder this experience ranks among the greatest in my thirty years in the field.

The question can be asked: Why is *Cypripedium californicum* so bountiful and luxurious in this southwestern Oregon site, coincidentally the home of the legendary Bigfoot? Is this station typical of other southwestern Oregon sites? For example, on another day, at a lower elevation, in a *Darlingtonia californica* bog, with hundreds, if not thousands, of spectacular cobra plants, only a dozen or two relatively anemic-looking California lady's-slippers are blooming. This latter site is in a typical "red rocks" section of the Siskiyous. There, the typical tree species is the Port Orford cedar (*Chamaecyparis lawsoniana*), while further north and at a higher elevation, the incense cedar (*Calocedrus decurrens*) replaces the Port Orford. The Jeffrey pine (*Pinus jeffreyi*) and Douglas-fir (*Pseudotsuga menziesii*) also associate with the incense cedar.

Cypripedium californicum, bronze variation on sepals, Oregon.

The Klamath Mountains extend into northwestern California and produce several endemics along with *Cypripedium californicum* and *Darlingtonia californica*. This is reason enough to seek permanent protection for these unique habitats. The so-called Klamath Knot is made up of the Siskiyous and Trinity "Alps," among others, where mountain-building millions of years ago took a more complex and tortuous turn than it did with the Cascades and Coast Ranges nearby, exposing older rocks normally found below the massive basalts deep in the earth's crust. None of the peaks in the Klamath Knot are over 10,000 feet (3,000 m) high; they are a jumble of jagged tops and deep V-shaped river canyons (hence the name knot), which were never subjected to the familiar continental glaciation of the northeastern Appalachians where typical U-shaped valleys are the rule. Peridotite and serpentine rocks are characteristic of much of the Klamaths. Green when freshly broken, serpentine weathers a reddish brown from oxidation of its high metal content: magnesium, iron, nickel, and chromium. These heavy metals "tie" up the calcium in the soil and are toxic to most plants. Because calcium is a vital element in plant growth, only those plants that are resistant to calcium starvation succeed well in serpentine regions. According to Ron Coleman, the California lady's-slipper is always found in serpentine.

Another one of the most successful plants in this regard is the aforementioned spectacular cobra plant (*Darlingtonia californica*). In one remote area among the red-rock canyons, certain serpentine seepage slopes (calcium deficiency is apparently less of a problem when the soil is soaked) are wall to wall with these pitcher plants. Several years' worth of ugly blackened skeletons stand massed among the contrastingly beautiful new green tubes, covered with tiny, translucent, squarish "picture windows" (to let light in) especially near the expanded "head." The most remarkable aspect of the plant, perhaps, is the snakelike forked appendage (tongue), splashed with flashes of brilliant scarlet, that hangs from the "mouth" of the downcurved tube. To those less interested in the snake analogy, this appendage is remindful of a bow-tie. It is impossible to step without noisily crunching the dry, dead, old growth, still remaining stiffly upright. David Wallace (1983), in his classic book, *The Klamath Knot,* expresses the scene well:

> There's no more arresting sight in the Klamaths than a patch of
> cobra plants . . . I half expected the plants to writhe and hiss like
> man-eating flowers in jungle movies. It is a plant that acts like an
> animal, rearing snakelike from red-rock swamps to devour insects.

It would seem more at home, perhaps, in the swamps of the southeastern coastal plain of the United States. Like its orchid neighbor, however, it is found nowhere else in the world but here in southwestern Oregon and northern California.

The golden asphodel (*Narthecium californicum*), another serpentine endemic, is common in one of these seeps, as is *Platanthera sparsiflora*, the so-called sparsely flowered bog-orchid. Here the latter is not sparse at all, but rather densely flowered, with a definite yellow tone to the yellowish green flowers in the bright sunshine. The linear spur of these plants exceeds the length of the linear lip, but otherwise, the sparsely flowered bog-orchid is just one more species from a large group of variable green platantheras.

I would be remiss not to mention a couple of other wonderful non-orchid plants in bloom here: two lovely mariposa lilies (*Calochortus tolmiei*), the so-called pussy-ears, remarkable for its thick fringing of white hairs across the petals, and *C. howellii*. The genus *Calochortus* is confined to the Far West, all sixty some odd species. Then there is the beautiful Bolander's lily (*Lilium bolanderi*), a nodding, deep raspberry-colored lily with darker maroon spotting inside the petals, growing sporadically along the gravel roadside. It is yet another endemic of these red rock mountain canyons, which only superficially appear barren and desolate but in reality are a unique botanical corner of the world where the plant life far outshines the animal life (essentially no animal endemics here at all and relatively few fish).

We are fortunate to experience these wonders under such ideal conditions, thanks to Joe Welch, a former National Wildlife Refuge manager from Medford, Oregon, now retired in Arizona, and the fine people at the U.S. Bureau of Land Management.

CHAPTER 34

The Remarkable Sky Islands of Southeastern Arizona

Sky Island! The perfect metaphor for a region of the country unsurpassed for its rich biodiversity, and as biologically grand for its richness of species as the Grand Canyon is for its scenic grandeur and geology. In this vast corner of southeastern Arizona, four great biomes (biogeographical regions) meet: the Rocky Mountains from the north, the Sierra Madres from Mexico, the Sonoran Desert in the west, and the Chiricahuan Desert to the east-southeast. The major sky islands rise boldly from the deserts and are represented by the Santa Rita, Huachuca (pronounced war-CHEW-cah), and the Chiricahua (cheery-CAR-wah) Mountains, among others, trending more or less north to south.

It is in these three mountain ranges in particular that the Mexican element of orchid and bird species contributes so many remarkable new species to one's life list. Six new species of orchids (Arizona has a total of approximately 25 species) and two dozen new birds (including the gorgeous red-faced warbler, the flamboyant painted redstart, and the elegant trogon which some people consider the most beautiful bird in the world), all from Mexico, a mere 50 miles (80 km) or so to the south, were some of the results of our three-week stay in this memorable region. *Malaxis corymbosa, M. porphyrea* (formerly *M. ehrenbergii*), *M. soulei, M. tenuis, Platanthera limosa,* and *Hexalectris warnockii* were all in bloom on the weekend of 15–18 August during the second annual meeting of the North American Native Orchid Alliance, which highlighted these "Mexican" species on three field trips.

Incidentally, we can thank the Gadsden Purchase of 1853 for adding 55,000 square miles (256 ha) to southern Arizona and New Mexico including these magnificent sky islands of southeastern Arizona. This purchase proved to be the last in U.S. history and it was made primarily for the construction of a southern transcontinental railroad, still in use today, paralleling Interstate 10.

Ron Coleman's trusty old Blazer negotiates the final two miles (3 km) through one of the Sky Islands. The "road" here is nothing but a rocky outcropping on the edge of a steep mountain in the famed Chiricahuas, the final stronghold of the Apache chiefs Cochise and Geronimo. Joseph Welch, now retired in Tucson, is the fellow birder on this trip. Ron is the orchid expert, with the go-anywhere four-wheel drive. One could not ask for a more knowledgeable and complementary pair.

Malaxis porphyrea, Arizona.

We find three *Malaxis* species growing in protected mountain meadows, in damper mossy spots in the forest, and near small streams. We are now in the Canadian life zone of ponderosa pine (*Pinus ponderosa*), Douglas-fir (*Pseudotsuga menziesii*), and the southernmost station for Engelmann spruce (*Picea engelmannii*). A meadow of sunflower, delphinium, beebalms, and many other wildflowers is beginning to bloom behind us. These high meadows are famous for their hummingbirds.

Malaxis porphyrea is my favorite among the malaxis because of the deep ruby red or red-purple color. The stature of the plant is surprisingly tall—nearly 18 inches (45 cm) in some cases—considering how tiny the individual flowers are—the lip is 3 mm × 2 mm approximately. On one 14-inch (35-cm) plant, there are 95 flowers, of which 75 are open and 20 are in tight bud. The flowers are beautifully balanced and almost perfectly spaced

Malaxis tenuis, Arizona.

Malaxis porphyrea (left) and *M. tenuis* (right), Arizona.

along a 6-inch (15-cm) flowering stem, which slightly arcs as it matures (i.e., when most of the flowers are open). A purplish haze in microcosm. Other than the color difference, *M. porphyrea* is almost identical to *M. brachypoda.* Both are easily overlooked in the landscape, as are all the *Malaxis* species, because of their diminutive size, although the single leaves are not small and remind me of the leaf of the Canada mayflower (*Maianthemum canadense*), so abundant back home. That is why a hand lens is an essential part of the orchidist's equipment. With it, one sees the pulled back (recurved), filiform lateral petals and the delightful deeper purple edges on the lip, which is lowermost (resupinate) in this species. Even better than a hand lens is a stereo microscope.

In terms of size, *Malaxis tenuis,* the so-called bottlebrush adder's-mouth orchid, is also diminutive, but the inflorescence often appears bedraggled because the individual flowers project horizontally on rather longish pedicels. This creates a narrow, one-plane effect, which is quite different from anything else I can recall. The Latin name *tenuis* refers to this strange shape. The uppermost (non-resupinate) pale green lip is not only edged with deeper green but also graced with two additional dark green stripes down the middle of the approximately 3 × 2 mm triangular lip. Note the difference in the photo between these two species that happened to be growing side by side (photo on previous page).

Malaxis soulei, the well-named rat-tail or mountain malaxis completes the trio we find here in this spot. It reminds me at once of our lawn weed back home, the common plantain (*Plantago major*), with its tightly packed spike of tiny flowers. It is unmistakable. The greenish yellow uppermost, notched lips with basal "ears" hug the stem and on close examination reveal two darker stripes of green down the middle. This species is perhaps the more common of the four "Mexicans" that immigrate to these sky islands.

Malaxis soulei, Arizona.

The temperature, a delightful 70°F (21°C) up here at 9000 feet (2700 m), is flirting with 100°F (38°C) down among the cacti, where just about every living thing has taken cover under the blistering noontime sun. For every 1000 feet (300 m) we climb in altitude, the temperature drops about four degrees. By the same token, the vegetation change is the equivalent of driving 300 miles (480 km) north for each 1000 feet (300 m), effectively putting us in the boreal forest of Canada.

We find our fourth adder's-mouth, *Malaxis corymbosa,* on another day and another mountain—the eastern slope of the Huachucas—in Miller Canyon, just above the Upper Sonoran life zone, which is distinguished by the unique chocolate-colored stems of the manzanita (*Arctostaphylos pungens*) and the alligator-checkered trunk of the alligator juniper (*Juniperus deppeana*). Superficially resembling *M. unifolia* of U.S. eastern woodlands, the headed or corymbed malaxis has a more compact, flat-topped inflorescence than the former and the flowers are comparatively larger. The ovate lateral sepals on *M. corymbosa* closely flank the lip, making the lip appear larger than it actually is. Because of the neat look (the sunburst effect noted by Luer) of the corymb, the inflorescence photographs well.

The only real disappointment of my orchid hunting involved *Hexalectris warnockii*. We finally caught it in bloom on the seventeenth of August in the Chiricahua National Monument, in very dry oak woods beside an equally dried up creek bed, after an agonizing two-week wait for the traditional monsoon rains to stimulate its opening. Some authors describe the flower as spectacular. The ones we saw could hardly be called that. Deep maroon-purple spreading sepals and petals contrast with the three-lobed lip petal, the two lateral lobes incurving and pinkish, and the floor of the lip whitish and purple, with three raised yellow crests. Only one flower was open on each of the two blooming plants we saw this day instead of the usual three or four, apparently. It would be a safe assumption, then, that this is not a good year for them. *Hexalectris warnockii*, incidentally, was not described until 1943 from a collection made in the Chisos Mountains of extreme southwestern Texas.

The so-called monsoonal rains occur during July and August, providing a welcome relief and inspiration to the Southwest's vegetation, as well as its people population. Thunderstorms, many severe enough to cause rapid flooding and washouts, pop up almost every late afternoon or early evening. Because of the sudden and unexpected nature of the dark clouds and curtains of rain, these storms are dubbed popcorn storms. Drivers sometimes must wait hours for these "washes" to subside before crossing the otherwise dry

Malaxis corymbosa, Arizona.

dips in the road. Every year, an impatient one will chance it too soon and either lose his or her vehicle—or life.

We found *Platanthera limosa,* the so-called Thurber's bog-orchid, on 10,000-foot (3000-m) Mount Lemmon just east of Tucson in the Santa Catalina Mountains. Yet another Mexican immigrant in the Southwest, it looks at first glance much like the ubiquitous tall leafy green orchid, *P. hyperborea,* of the far north (barely reaching northern Arizona). *Platanthera limosa* has a much longer and whitish spur and a yellowish green lip that contrasts noticeably with the gray-green sepals and lateral petals. Mount Lemmon is a great ride but only on a weekday. The weekends are much too crowded and the traffic becomes hazardous, particularly on the drive down after an afternoon of partying, high above the desert heat. Despite these "hazards," Arizona is the second fastest growing state in the United States. It is easy to understand why.

BOTANIST'S NOTEBOOK

Malaxis brachypoda, Vermont.

CHAPTER 35

The Other Green Orchids

SOME orchids spend their lives quietly out of the spotlight, attracting little or no attention, except from dyed-in-the-wool orchid lovers who can easily tell the difference between an ordinary, inconspicuous, greenish flower and an inconspicuous and greenish orchid flower that is not ordinary. Upon examination, of course, all the diagnostics are there, even the feel. Happily, a minority of North American orchids fit this category. Wright (1901) expressed the feelings of many beginners or those in the early stages of orchid madness: "I am not quite reconciled to calling such a pale mite of a flower an orchid. The word implies something magnificent in itself, or rich in its massed coloring, like the orange fringed-orchid."

One of those little greens is the so-called auricled twayblade, *Listera auriculata*. The story of this twayblade begins on 25 June 1991 in extreme northern New Hampshire near the Canadian border. It is a long four and a half hour drive from my home on the coast; I stop for lunch in Howard's, a small Colebrook restaurant and familiar stop over the years. The pie is very good. East Inlet is many miles north of Pittsburgh, which in turn is north of Colebrook, between the Second and Third Connecticut Lakes. Following directions, I park on the side of a dirt logging road and walk down a short "path" to an alder-bordered stream. Shod with Wellington boots, I quickly learn why I need them. The water's edge is so thickly crowded with stiff, multistemmed alders that it is impossible to reach the orchids over dry ground. Into the water I go, equipment and all, some on my shoulder, some in my pockets, and some in my hands.

The orchids are just where they're supposed to be, in the sand around the alders, just above the summer high water line. This habitat is subject to inundation from springtime flooding every year, yet the orchid apparently flourishes. It is a struggle to move the alder branches in very cramped quarters to position the tripod and camera in such a way that I can use the reflector properly. Dozens of arrogant and persistent deer flies—worse than black flies—attack throughout the strenuous two-hour session. Deer flies do bother me. Thankfully the seventy-degree temperature poses no problem. As I prepare to climb out of the water, plop drops the expensive Olympus telescoping macro lens. While retrieving that, my T32 flash follows into the drink. Finally, from under my arm, the aluminum reflector slips out of my grasp and floats away. When it rains it pours. I am able to salvage the costly equipment, but can no longer use it. Thankfully, all this happens after the successful photo shoot.

Not only is the habitat of *Listera auriculata* distinctive, but the base of the lip petal is distinctive and must be looked at closely to distinguish it from some other look-alikes, like *L. borealis*. The latter, however, is northwestern in distribution while *L. auriculata* is northeastern. Once seen up close, the lip easily separates it from the other twayblades. The word *auriculata* means "auricled" and refers to the pair of incurved lobes or ears, which "hug" the column, like curved pincers, at the base of the lip. The flower parts are whitish green, and the lip a translucent watery pale green with a darker green groove down the middle of it, producing a two-tone look. *Listera auriculata* was the last species in the genus to be discovered, in 1899.

Coming home, I always stop at Dixville Notch just south of The Balsams, a famous year-round resort. Dixville is the smallest of the four famous New Hampshire notches—mountain valleys shaped by the last glacial period. There is little traffic on this Tuesday afternoon as I set up the tripod to photograph the last glints of sun bouncing off the cliff turrets 1000 feet (300 m) above the road. "Not a creature is stirring, not even a mouse," until several heavenly flute strains of the hermit thrush float down from a shadowed perch high above the road. This is no ordinary music, but the finest in all of birding. If you are not familiar with it, learn it; you have a real treat in store. Neither Alexander Wilson, the father of American ornithology, nor John James Audubon, the great American painter of birds, ever heard this song because the hermit performs only on its northern nesting grounds. In the text of his *The Birds of America*, Audubon praised the song of the wood thrush as "my greatest favorite," while dismissing the hermit's song as "sometimes agreeable," a non sequitur. The hermit's song consists of a series of ethereal phrases, each successively higher in pitch, the notes sweet and flutelike. Those of us privileged to have heard the song for many years recall pleasurable memory associations each time we hear it anew. My earliest involves family blueberry outings late on a Sunday afternoon during the dog days of July and August. The hermit thrush and red-eyed vireo are the only consistently regular singers during the hottest part of the New Hampshire summer.

Platanthera flava, the tubercled orchid, is another of those tiny green nondescripts. It is well named, too, with a tiny pimple on the basal half of the lolling lip, easily noticed once you become used to bending over for a closer look. Botanists have speculated for years as to the purpose of this nodule; the consensus seems to be that it is a device for shunting or deflecting the pollinator, most likely a tiny insect like a mosquito, to the

Platanthera flava, detail of tubercle on lip, New Hampshire.

Platanthera flava, with crab spider, New Hampshire.

precious pollen on the column. The flowers of this little orchid age more slowly than most, following almost two weeks of good color. After that the various floral parts begin to blacken, with the ovary the last to do so.

Until the 1980s, this very inconspicuous orchid was considered quite rare in New England (Crow 1982). Then it was my good fortune to discover nine new stations, three each in York County, Maine; Rockingham County, New Hampshire; and Strafford County, New Hampshire. One in Madbury, New Hampshire, contained more than 2000 plants within an area approximately 50×100 feet (15×30 m). This was the largest station in New Hampshire at the time. The sensitive fern (*Onoclea sensibilis*) was a good indicator plant in each of the nine new stations, all wet meadows or ditches. Since then, however, plant succession has disrupted one or two stations, and a third has been destroyed by draining and commercial development.

The largest site also just happens to be an excellent deer habitat, resulting in several ticks hitching rides on me over the years. Fortunately, they have all been dog ticks rather than deer ticks (*Ixodes dammini*), the notorious Lyme disease carrier. Lyme disease is now found throughout the United States, with heaviest concentrations in the three southern New England states, New York, New Jersey, Pennsylvania, Delaware, Maryland, Wisconsin, Minnesota, and coastal California. The deer tick is very tiny, almost microscopic, no more than a black speck. A careful and thorough body check, particularly on the hairy portions, should be made after a day in the field, especially in the states mentioned above. The dog tick, on the other hand, is large enough to see relatively easily. It is dark brown with a pale collar and pale scriggling on the back. Besides a body check, one should tuck pants inside boots, apply tick repellent, wear light clothing to better see the black speck, and shower or bathe.

If a tick is found embedded in the skin, use tweezers to carefully grasp the tick's head, and gently pull it straight out. The idea is not to leave the tick's biting parts in your skin. The other alternative is to have your doctor do it, as I did with one lodged behind an ear lobe. This is serious stuff. If symptoms (pink rash or flu) do occur—and they don't always—the correct antibiotic quickly applied is crucial. I have recently read where permethrin is effective against ticks, as well as chiggers and mosquitoes. The brand name repellant Duranon is claimed to give two weeks of complete protection, including two launderings, when sprayed on your clothes and allowed to dry. The American Birding Association is the only source I am aware of at this writing, and it is worth investigating.

Another good habitat for some of these little green orchids, particularly *Platanthera clavellata,* the little club spur orchid, is a ski slope. Also known as the small green wood orchid, reflecting its fondness for wooded swamps, *P. clavellata* has a rather long spur thickened toward the end, which accounts for the Latin name. The flower is also different in the way it is carried on the raceme at an angle, as the accompanying photograph emphasizes.

A few years back, on one of the hottest days in late July, with the temperature above 90°F (32°C), I was climbing Moose Mountain, a relatively small hill of less than 2000 feet (600 m) in Wakefield, New Hampshire. I had just finished a photo session with *Platanthera clavellata* halfway up the ski slope. My face was dripping wet, my clothes soaked to the skin, and I had no hat or drinking water under a relentless sun. In a few minutes, my heart started to pound rapidly. I stopped and sat down to rest a moment. When the pounding subsided, I resumed climbing, only to have

the same thing happen again almost instantly. I realized now that maybe the good Lord was trying to tell me something. I gave up the idea of reaching the top, rested again, and walked down the mountain without further complications. Heat stroke and heat exhaustion are very real dangers at this time of year without proper preparation, and so this experience—the first one in my sixty years—served as a reminder to include a hat and water jug from now on when it's hot.

The smallest North American native orchids, at least in this part of the world, are the three little malaxis or adder's-mouth orchids, starting with *Malaxis paludosa,* the bog malaxis of northwestern Canada and Alaska. The lip, believe it or not, is a mere ¹⁄₁₆ inch (1.5

Platanthera clavellata, showing angled spur, New Hampshire.

mm). The eastern *M. brachypoda* and *M. unifolia* have lips approximately ¹/₁₀ inch (2.5 mm) in size.

Malaxis unifolia, the green malaxis, is deep green in color, with long-pediceled flowers that are distant on the lower end of the raceme and crowded near the top and flat-topped. The whole cylinder of florets is about ¹/₂ inch (13 mm) in width. On the other hand, *M. brachypoda*, the white malaxis, is whitish green, with short pedicels, and the florets are arranged uniformly on the tall raceme, looking something like a stretched out spike of the common plantain of weedy lawns. The green malaxis likes the dark, strongly acid, wooded swamps, while the white malaxis prefers a more neutral soil in its swampy, wooded environment. Of all places, I was shown a railroad cut in Vermont that was rich in ferns and several of these tiny white malaxis. The orchids were hiding in the shaded nooks and crannies halfway up the sheer rock wall that was dripping with moisture. The green malaxis requires intense searching among the green, wet vegetation, sighting on its level at 6–12 inches (15–30 cm) off the ground. Even then the tiny green, long-pediceled flowers are very hard to isolate.

Paul Catling (1991) segregated *Malaxis bayardii* from *M. unifolia* on the basis of the following differences: longer-lasting yellowish green flowers on shorter pedicels, with a more elongated spike instead of the crowded, flat-topped spike in *M. unifolia;* the base of the lip with relatively prominent lobes; and drier habitats such as dry oak and pine barrens, on the coastal plain from Virginia to Massachusetts. *Malaxis bayardii* has a much more restricted range than *M. unifolia,* which can be found from Central America all the way to Newfoundland and Manitoba.

Malaxis unifolia, with green caterpillar, New Hampshire.

Listera convallarioides, the broad-lipped twayblade, has two centers of abundance, the dark swampy alluvial soils and seeps of Aroostook County in northern Maine, and the sand dune thickets on the shores of Lake Superior near Grand Marais, Michigan. Both locations produce thousands of plants. This species differs from the others in the genus by the shape of the lip, which expands to a broader apex, with a small indentation. The shape of the lip is diagnostic in all native listeras (see Figure 3).

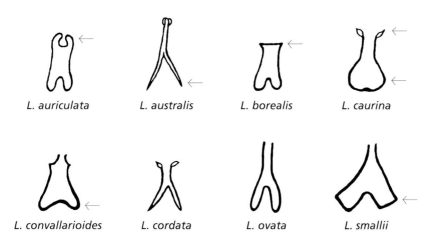

L. auriculata	L. australis	L. borealis	L. caurina

L. convallarioides	L. cordata	L. ovata	L. smallii

Figure 3. Lip shapes of *Listera* species, showing outstanding feature(s): *L. auriculata*, incurved basal "ears" (northeastern species); *L. australis*, longer fork (eastern species); *L. borealis*, outpointed (northern species); *L. caurina*, rounded lip (northwestern species); *L. convallarioides*, wider apex (northern species); *L. cordata* (northern species); *L. ovata*, largest flower, plant and lip (Bruce Peninsula); and *L. smallii*, squared lobes (Appalachian-Southern species).

Listera convallarioides, Maine.

Listera convallarioides, Maine.

One of the smallest and hardest to find of all native orchids—North America seems to have many of these—is the diminutive southern twayblade, *Listera australis,* which blooms in January in Florida and from late June to July in New York, Vermont, and Québec. It is so uncommon and difficult to find that the wide distribution is very misleading. One must crawl on hands and knees in the open bogs of the North or the deeply shaded wet deciduous woods in the South to see it, even when accompanied by a guide. That's exactly how Herm Willey showed it to me twenty-five years ago in a classic northern coniferous bog in Morristown, Vermont.

Usually less than 6–8 inches (15–20 cm) high, *Listera australis* is similar to *L. cordata* in general aspect when one first looks at it superficially, except for the significantly longer and linear lip whose distal half is cleft or split into longer, threadlike lobes. The color of the visible lip is greenish purple generally, but sometimes beet red, but never all greenish like the lip of *L. cordata* sometimes is. *Listera cordata,* the heart-leaved twayblade, is described in more depth in Chapter 6 and elsewhere, as are *L. borealis, L. caurina, L. ovata,* and *L. smallii.*

Though the genus *Liparis* comprises about two hundred fifty species in other parts of the temperate and tropical world, only two are found in North America north of Florida. Closely related to the genus *Malaxis,* these two twayblades have two opposite shiny green leaves that sheath the lower end of the relatively short stem, which is usually less than 10 inches (25 cm).

Liparis loeselii, showing shield, Vermont.

Liparis loeselii, the Loesel's twayblade (named after a seventeenth-century German botanist) or fen orchid (for one choice of habitat), is another of those very inconspicuous tiny green orchids, in this case with more yellow mixed in, that are frequently overlooked in the green vegetation around them. Also like many of these orchids, it prefers sterile, alkaline, and moist conditions with little other competition, especially raw, disturbed areas. In Vermont it is most readily seen on the banks of ditches, brooks, and seepage areas. It is the northern counter-part of the more attractive southern lily-leaved twayblade, *L. liliifolia*. Having said that, I must admit a certain attachment to the fen orchid. It was one of the first Vermont orchids introduced to me by Herm Willey back in the 1970s. The flower reminds me of a miniature knight with shield, from the Middle Ages: the protective shield held out in front is

Liparis loeselii, Vermont.

the "arcuate-recurved, cuneate-orbicular" lip, and the spreading, filiform sepals and petals are the warriors' flaring arms and sword, as he prepares to do combat with the adversary. There are usually several of these "knights" scattered around the wet seepage. Use your hand lens on this one, too.

The lily-leaved twayblade, *Liparis liliifolia,* though not one of the inconspicuous so-called green orchids, is included here for convenience and because it is in the same genus as the fen orchid. It inhabits the mesic deciduous forest of the eastern states, most commonly in ravines and lightly cutover forest mostly north of South Carolina, Georgia, Alabama, and Arkansas. It does not inhabit heavily shaded interiors where it soon dies out. It is noted for great population fluctuations in successional plant communities in the states below the Great Lakes, where it also ranks among the most common of all woodland orchids. The large and broad, dull purple lip—a huge "shield," if you will—contrasts conspicuously with the short, threadlike lateral petals, on a nicely proportioned stem of up to two dozen, long-pediceled flowers, in May and June. It is much larger than the fen orchid with a different color, and is a real charmer to those who know it well.

CHAPTER 36

The Spiranthes *Story*

ON ROADCUTS, pastures, and disturbed areas in general along the Canadian border from Nova Scotia to Wisconsin, *Spiranthes casei*, Case's ladies'-tresses, masqueraded for years as one of the several variations of *S. cernua*, the nodding ladies'-tresses, and *S. ochroleuca*, the yellow ladies'-tresses. Then in 1974 Catling and Cruise proved it worthy of specific status and named it for Fred Case, author of the excellent *Orchids of the Western Great Lakes Region*. *Spiranthes casei* has the least obvious two-lipped profile of any *Spiranthes* species because the sepals and petals, particularly the dorsal sepal, are quite straightforward in aspect, rather than reflexed at the tip. The plant is also smaller, more loosely flowered, off-white or cream in color, and rather plain and ordinary looking, without the frills and curves of most other *Spiranthes* species.

Of the other two that make up the confusing threesome of the Northeast, *Spiranthes cernua* is the whitest, largest, and most variable, while *S. ochroleuca* is the creamiest, especially in the trough of the lip above and below. The three are often found together in these northern parts, from the Canadian Shield of southern Ontario, to Nova Scotia, playing hopscotch back and forth across the United States border. *Spiranthes casei* prefers dry roadcuts and fields, *S. cernua* the wetter ditches and meadows, and *S. ochroleuca* the higher, slightly drier ground, but frequently overlapping with *S. cernua*. Roadcuts are shared habitat for all three of these look-alikes, as it is for *S. lacera*, the green-lipped ladies'-tresses, which blooms earlier in the season than the other three.

My introduction to *Spiranthes casei* came under the direction of two friends, Sally Puth and Shirley Curtis. We became acquainted years ago through my slide shows on wildflowers and orchids, which eventually led to a request to join one of my solo field trips. Needless to say, they had developed orchid fever. On this trip to Coos County in extreme northern New Hampshire to photograph *S. casei*, they took me to a stretch of Route 3 known locally as "moose alley." The two ladies guaranteed to show me my first moose. I had traveled this route many times over the years and never saw a moose, even though, in retrospect, I had noticed the heavily trodden muddy ditches beside the road, but apparently never put two and two together.

This time it is late in the afternoon, the best time to see the moose, since they are most active at dawn and dusk. Two cows have attracted passersby as we arrive on the scene, one of which stands still for her por-

Spiranthes cernua, New Hampshire.

Spiranthes cernua, New Hampshire.

trait while the other ambles out of range into more protective cover. The moose suck up the muddy water in the ditches for the salts they need. I have yet to see a bull, but on a succeeding trip I saw two separate cows, one with calf. If you see vehicles stopped on the side of the road as you approach a long downhill straightaway, it is a sure sign that one or more moose are present. Often, I am told, there can be as many as six or more, including bulls, but the cows always outnumber the males. Amazingly, the moose, the largest member of the deer family, appear to be unperturbed by all this human attention, sometimes allowing approaches to within 50 feet (15 m) or less. If, however, calves are nearby, keep your distance.

Also known as spiral flower or spiral-orchid, *Spiranthes* and "its crystalline white flowers (are) arranged in a dense spiral cone like the thread of a screw," Thoreau wrote. They also remind me of an earlier day when young girls fashioned their long hair into "pigtails" or braids.

Spiranthes casei, showing flat dorsal sepal, New Hampshire.

Spiranthes ochroleuca, Maine.

There are two varieties of the green-lipped *Spiranthes lacera:* the northern *S. lacera* var. *lacera* and the southern *S. lacera* var. *gracilis.* Supposedly, the bottom one or two florets of the northern variety separate from the remaining florets, which creates a gap in the spike. In many instances that appears to be the case, but not always in my experience. This

Spiranthes lacera, New Hampshire.

species has been the subject of much disagreement and discussion regarding the relative merits of a single variable species vis-à-vis two separate species. Since I tend to favor the lumpers, the single variable species gets my vote. To compound the situation, there have been at least three putative hybrids proposed involving *S. lacera, S. cernua, S. magnicamporum,* and *S. romanzoffiana* (see Chapter 38).

In New Hampshire I find *Spiranthes lacera* on almost every roadcut I check out, depending on whether the road crews have beaten me to it with the mower. It is one of the smallest native orchids for flower size and wire-thin stem. It is extremely difficult to find in busy vegetation (again, the advice is to get down on its level while sighting), despite a stem that may go to 2 feet (60 cm). The basal rosette of leaves usually disappears at anthesis. It is amazing how the stem resists the effects of wind and rain, unlike so many "strong" garden plants that sulk; I think of glads, peonies, poppies, and many more. *Spiranthes lacera* blooms during blueberry season in late July, which makes the search more fruitful and enjoyable.

Low-bush blueberry (*Vaccinium angustifolium*) is one of its frequent associates, along with checkerberry (*Gaultheria procumbens*) and the ubiquitous cow wheat (*Melampyrum lineare*), a member of the figwort or snapdragon family.

I have written the New Hampshire highway department regarding their practice of frequently mowing highway road shoulders during the summer months, suggesting that taxpayers' money could be saved—as well as the flowers—by suspending mowing until after the season of bloom. Apparently this idea gets a mixed reception in that half the letters they receive complain about the unkempt appearance of the unmown grass, while half prefer the blooming of the summer flowers. In the past few years, a compromise seems

Spiranthes lacera, displaying "diamond-dusted" flowers, New Hampshire.

to have been worked out, where only a narrow 5- to 10-foot (150- to 300-cm) strip is mowed, in the majority of cases at least.

Herm Willey showed me my first *Spiranthes lucida*, the yellow-lipped ladies'-tresses, easily recognized by that feature. A lover of stream banks, ditches, meadows, and roadcut seepages, especially in early stages of disturbance, this orchid prefers calcareous conditions. Fred Case (1987) related the following interesting story:

> At a lake in Kent County, Michigan, a resident filled the low lake shore with yellow sand to raise it for a better lawn. Within 2 to 3 years hundreds of *S. lucida* appeared. They persisted for a season or two and then gradually disappeared.

I looked forward with great interest to seeing the southern giant ladies'-tresses, *Spiranthes praecox* because of my predilection for green markings in flower colors. When I got to North Carolina, a few years back, I saw plenty of specimens in the open grassy savannas, but only a few individuals had pronounced green veining marks on the lip. In fact, I had to closely examine almost all the plants to verify that they indeed were *S. praecox*

Spiranthes lucida, Vermont.

Spiranthes praecox, North Carolina.

because of the pale, almost nonexistent green stippling on the lips. The arrangement of the green veining is similar to the fruiting dots on the underside of some fern leaves. Morris and Eames (1929) surprisingly did not mention any green veining in their description of the flower. To complicate matters, the ubiquitous colicroot (*Aletris farinosa*) was everywhere looking just like the *Spiranthes*. Close examination, of course, revealed the surface bumps and "warts" on the pure white, tubular, racemose flowers of colicroot.

The early flowering *Spiranthes vernalis* also was in full bloom on 16 May 1990, especially noticeable on the way to Orton Plantation where the road shoulders had not yet been mowed. Hundreds if not thousands of individuals grew along one stretch of the road. *Spiranthes vernalis* can usually be distinguished by the narrow lateral petals that separate and flare a bit on the sides of the flower instead of being somewhat tightly appressed. As happens with the *Spiranthes* species, however, diagnostic features do not always hold true in any given region, or with all individual plants, leading to much confusion, as we have already seen.

Spiranthes species have a long season of bloom from south to north. In northern latitudes, they close out the orchid season in September and early October, but in southern latitudes, other species can be found into November and beyond: *Spiranthes ovalis,* and *S. odorata,* for example. On the prairie, *S. magnicamporum* also extends into November. About this time of the year, we of the northern branch of the fraternity deeply regret the shutdown of another orchid season. Joseph Wood Krutch, I believe, said, "The most serious charge which can be brought against New England is not Puritanism but February." I might add January and March to that sentiment.

Spiranthes vernalis, North Carolina.

CHAPTER 37

Goodyeras—How Long Is Evergreen?

THE GENUS *Goodyera* is named after the English botanist John Goodyer, who lived in the 1600s. The common name of rattlesnake plantain, on the other hand, is conjectured to stem either from an early belief that the leaves were an antidote for the bite of a rattlesnake or that the leaf reticulations resemble the skin patterns of a rattlesnake. Similarly marked species in the Asian genus *Anoectochilus* have the more elegant name of jewel orchids. Even so, I have for many years been curious about the longevity of the evergreen leaves in the four North American representatives of *Goodyera: G. oblongifolia, G. pubescens, G. repens,* and *G. tesselata.*

My simple experiment involved tying two or three newly emerging leaves of *Goodyera pubescens* from different plants with strips of plastic from a sandwich bag, at the beginning of the growing season in late May and June. Each year I checked the condition of the marked plants two or three times. It took four years to get an answer. From June 1985 to June 1989 the tagged leaves remained in first-class condition. As the summer of 1989 progressed, however, these leaves rapidly deteriorated and decomposed. I had enjoyed four full years of green color, four years of leaf longevity.

The rosette of leaves is produced over a period of years by an extremely shallow creeping rhizome, through terminal extension and branching. The creeping rhizome runs over the top of the ground. A flowering stem emerges from the center of a mature rosette. Apparently, only mature rosettes produce a flowering stem in each colony, which accounts for the relatively few flower stems one sees in a colony from year to year. Approximately seven to thirteen leaves make up a mature rosette, in my experience at least.

I repeated the leaf tagging experiment with *Goodyera tesselata*. This species produces much smaller rosettes than *G. pubescens* and does not establish such large colonies, leading me to suspect from the beginning that its leaves were much shorter-lived than those of *G. pubescens*. The result? The leaves lasted only one year, from summer to summer. I have seen all four North American goodyeras but do not live close enough to

Goodyera pubescens, New Hampshire.

Goodyera pubescens, detail of dramatic veining in leaves, New Hampshire.

Goodyera pubescens, detail revealing green tints in flowers, New Hampshire.

G. repens or *G. oblongifolia* to conduct leaf tagging experiments with them. Perhaps someone else will be able to do so.

Goodyera pubescens, the rattlesnake plantain, is confined almost entirely to the eastern United States and southern Ontario. It is the most southern of the four species. It is "exceedingly" common in the mountains and plateau region of Kentucky, and the mountainous regions of Virginia and North Carolina, while barely getting into northern Maine. *Goodyera repens,* on the other hand, grows clear across the Northern Hemisphere, mostly in Canada in North America. *Goodyera tesselata,* the tessellated goodyera, is found primarily in the extreme Northeast, from Newfoundland, Québec, and southern Ontario, and along the border states to Minnesota and extreme northern Maine. *Goodyera oblongifolia,* the largest member of the genus, travels from extreme northern Maine and southeastern Québec, through the Great Lakes region, and then follows a narrow path to British Columbia; it also follows portions of the Rocky Mountains to Arizona; from British Columbia it follows the coast along the Cascades and Coast Mountains to the Sierras in central California.

Goodyera tesselata, the tessellated goodyera, was first described in 1824 but remained in limbo for almost one hundred years because of confusion with the other three members of the genus. It was thought to be a hybrid between *G. oblongifolia* and *G. repens* by Fuller in 1933, but studies by Kallunki in 1976 and thereafter finally unraveled much of the morphological complexities of the group. Intermediates between *G. tesselata* and *G. repens* are known as well as those between *G. tesselata* and *G. oblongifolia. Goodyera repens,* in contrast, first described by Carl Linnaeus in 1753, has a long and relatively quiet taxonomic history.

Goodyera tesselata, Maine.

Goodyera tesselata, with typical subdued veining, Maine.

Another interesting observation concerns the amount of white on the leaves of all four species. *Goodyera oblongifolia* and *G. repens,* in parts of western North American and in Eurasia, occasionally have no reticulations at all, while *G. pubescens* rarely sports an almost all-white leaf surface, a highly unusual but quite attractive condition. As mentioned in the Preface of this book, I bought a woodlot many years ago because of its mountain laurel and large clumps of "white" *G. pubescens.* In all the literature I have read, only Henry Baldwin (1884) mentions this color "form." He found "a very beautiful group of *G. pubescens,* the leaves of which were a dull blue with scarcely a tinge of green, and instead of the usual network of veins, there was a silvery frost-work over them." The tiny flowers, which are similar in all four species, resemble some form of an old-fashioned pitcher, with bulbous-saccate lips—actually scrotiform in *G. pubescens*—and a spout at the apex. The spikes are densely flowered with up to eighty florets in *G. pubescens* and as few as twenty in *G. repens.* The color is white with tints of green (very pretty under a good hand lens), especially in *G. pubescens,* in July and August, and even later for *G. oblongifolia.*

When snow covers the ground in winter, the dried flower stalks of *Goodyera pubescens* are persistent and strong enough to remain above the snow, cluing the naturalist on a winter hike where to remove the snow for a look at the evergreen leaves. Unfortunately, the beautiful leaves are the object of yet another type of plant thief who digs the rosettes, along with the trailing, evergreen, red-berried partridgeberry (*Mitchella repens*), to decorate terrariums and bowls for the Christmas trade. They do not survive in a home for long, but for some people are hard to resist during the holiday season. Please, don't be a part of this destruction.

CHAPTER 38

An Introduction to Hybrids and New Combinations

THERE are thousands of cultivated hybrids of all kinds to entice or confuse hobbyists. In the real world of species orchids, on the other hand, there are far fewer natural hybrids, but these few do cause a certain amount of confusion to botanists. In addition, taxonomists (also known as systematists) occasionally change the rank of a variety to that of a species, and vice versa, when new research indicates the need. It is here then that the value and need of synonymy are realized.

It may be of interest to explain some of the rules governing those who change the Latin names of plants. These rules are spelled out in the taxonomist's "bible," the *International Code of Botanical Nomenclature.* One of the crucial requirements for a legitimate name is that it be published with a description written in Latin. The description is based on the so-called type specimen, which is nothing more than the newly discovered plant itself that has been deposited in a herbarium by the collector. The problem arises when mistakes are made by earlier authorities or ongoing research turns up older names that were applied to the same plant. The so-called Rule of Priority then requires that the earliest name be used.

The *Code* provides a way of retaining a current name despite the discovery of an earlier name that normally would have priority. This is called "conserving a name." An example involves the genus *Paphiopedilum,* the Asiatic lady's-slippers. Two other names pre-dated *Paphiopedilum,* but were never used, ostensibly because of the horticultural importance of *Paphiopedilum.* In some circles, however, the feeling persists that the real reason was a dislike for C. S. Rafinesque, an eccentric, early nineteenth-century naturalist-botanist who published both earlier names. (Politics do indeed enter the world of orchids.) John James Audubon, the birder, relates how Rafinesque began running around his room late one night banging on the wall, using the bow of Audubon's violin to subdue bats flying around, not from any concern over his safety but in hopes of discovering a new species. Rafinesque had developed a reputation of becoming a monomaniac, a person completely obsessed with one idea or subject, in his case that of describing new genera and species of anything that moves or grows. Nonetheless, he "anticipated most of his contemporaries in the discovery of new genera and species" according to the great Louis Agassiz. Published more than nine hundred times, in a variety of biological subjects, Rafinesque's genuine genius under the right guidance would have placed him among the best scientists of his day. He was also an inveterate slob, according to his critics. He died of stomach cancer at the young age of fifty-seven in 1840.

Perhaps the most difficult taxonomic problem among North American orchids involves certain species within three particular genera: the purple and orange fringed-orchids of the genus *Platanthera,* the yellow lady's-slippers complex of the genus *Cypripedium,* and several members of the genus *Spiranthes,* notably the *cernua* complex. To help the reader understand some of these changes more clearly, the following discussion is accompanied by a series of graphic representations of the hybrids in these three genera (Figures 4 to 7).

In the orange fringed-orchid group, there appear to be three major hybrids. One of these involves *Platanthera blephariglottis* var. *conspicua* and *P. ciliaris,* which produces offspring with either lemon or cream flowers, or bicolored flowers (pale orange with white lips). This hybrid is known as *P.* ×*bicolor* (Figure 4). A second combination involves *P. cristata* with *P. blephariglottis* var. *conspicua,* which forms the hybrid *P.* ×*canbyi,* a paler intermediate of the two (Figure 4). The third cross links the two orange fringed species to form *P.* ×*channellii,* again intermediate (Figure 4). The latter two hybrid epithets are named in honor of two American botanists. *Platanthera chapmanii,* originally included in this hybrid complex, recently attained the status of species (Folsom 1984). It sports bright orange flowers and is found in a very restricted range from southeastern Georgia through the Florida panhandle into extreme eastern Texas, in mixed populations with *P. ciliaris* and *P. cristata,* its putative hybrid parents before the separation. One must remember that these natural hy-

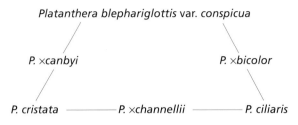

Platanthera blephariglottis var. *conspicua*

P. ×*canbyi*   *P.* ×*bicolor*

P. cristata ——————*P.* ×*channellii* ——————*P. ciliaris*

Figure 4. Orange fringed-orchid hybrids

brids are putative, which is botanical lingo for "supposed"; that is, they have not been proven experimentally under controlled conditions.

In addition to primary hybrids or crosses, there are also back crosses, which, in the case of the purple fringed-orchids, *Platanthera psycodes* and *P. grandiflora,* and the green fringed orchid, *P. lacera,* produce all degrees of fringing and colors ranging from green to combinations of pink, green, and lavender. Genetics (the world of genes, chromosomes, diploids, and triploids) assumes a more important role in the classification of orchids today than it did a few years ago. There has been a shift of emphasis away from the traditional system of differences in physical ap-

Platanthera psycodes, detail with raindrops, New Hampshire.

Platanthera lacera, New Hampshire.

Platanthera grandiflora, Maine.

pearance to that of the genetic makeup and evolution of the plant, a study called "phylogeny," in determining the relationships between species, genera, and other groups and subgroups of orchids.

D. S. Correll as early as 1939 considered the purple fringed group to consist of one species, namely, *Platanthera psycodes*, with *P. grandiflora* treated as a variety. When either of these two taxa crossed with *P. lacera*, the ragged or green fringed-orchid, the resulting hybrids were all called *P. ×andrewsii* by Correll and other workers for years. Stoutamire (1974), however, showed that *P. psycodes* and *P. grandiflora* were separate species based on significant differences in column structure, shape of the spur opening, and overall size. Consequently, their status as separate species has been accepted since 1974. The husband and wife team of the Catlings (1994) made a strong case for recognizing two distinct hybrids instead of maintaining the broad concept of *P. ×andrewsii* for both of them. The "new" hybrid, *P. ×keenanii*, was named by Brown in 1993 (Figure 5).

Regarding the *Cypripedium calceolus* complex, Sheviak (1994) clari-

Platanthera ×*andrewsii*, showing lavender, green and white colors, Maine.

Platanthera ×*keenanii*.

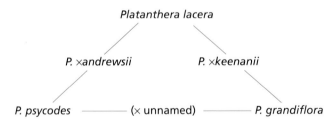

Figure 5. Purple fringed-orchid hybrids

fied the taxonomy in that group. The North American yellow lady's-slippers often have been lumped together with the Eurasian yellow lady's-slipper and assumed the name *C. calceolus*, as part of a circumboreal species—one of only a few circumboreal orchids—distributed across the Northern Hemisphere. The North American yellow lady's-slipper has traditionally been split into three or four varieties of that species by many botanists, thus: *C. calceolus* var. *pubescens, C. calceolus* var. *parviflorum,* and *C. calceolus* var. *planipetalum.* The typical European variety then, is

C. calceolus var. *calceolus*. Sheviak now recognizes important distinctions between the European and American plants, based on differences in the structure and color of the column, for example, and has renamed North American plants as follows:

1. *Cypripedium parviflorum* var. *pubescens* (the most widely distributed, formerly known as *C. calceolus* var. *pubescens*). Note: var. *planipetalum* is now considered merely an extreme expression of var. *pubescens,* no longer a separate variety.
2. *Cypripedium parviflorum* var. *parviflorum* (the southern variety, formerly included in *C. calceolus* var. *pubescens,* which now enters the synonymy).
3. *Cypripedium parviflorum* var. *makasin* (the northern variety of cedar bogs—with mahogany sepals—previously known as *C. calceolus* var. *parviflorum*).

Note that the species name *calceolus* is dropped from the American taxon in favor of Salisbury's species name *parviflorum,* which has priority according to the rules of nomenclature (Figure 6).

Work is also progressing on the *Spiranthes* complex (Figure 7), which can be partially summarized by Sheviak's conclusion in a December 1991 issue of *Lindleyana:*

The great morphological variability of *Spiranthes cernua* arises, ultimately, in concert with its intrinsic colonizing habit. It acquires

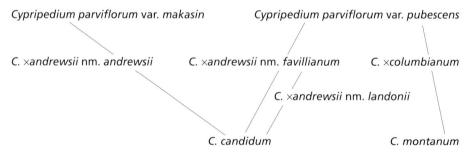

Figure 6. Yellow lady's-slipper hybrids. Based on latest changes in nomenclature of yellow lady's-slippers. nm = notomorph, a botanical term referring to hybrids between varieties of species, and back crosses, rather than just species. When only one hybrid name is used, *C.* ×*andrewsii* is the favored name of a hybrid swarm (all the crosses between the yellow and white lady's-slipper).

genes from related diploids and utilizes these genes adaptively . . .
under some conditions, such as roadcuts in the Northeast, gene
flow may be occurring at the present time in response to the availability of a new habitat within a regional context. Elsewhere, as in
the prairies, the regional occurrence of *S. cernua* is dependent
upon genes evidently acquired in the distant past . . . a most interesting evolutionary story.

All of these complexities may be a bit technical and confusing to the
lay person, at times. In that context, you may empathize with the reac-
tion of William H. Gibson (1905) almost a hundred years ago:

> In the bother of mentally calculating whether a certain specimen
> of purple-fringed orchis is a large specimen of [*Platanthera
> psycodes*], or a small one of [*Platanthera grandiflora*], one is dis-
> tracted from an enjoyment of its beauty, and is tempted to feel a
> trifle of impatience at the naming of names, and to wish one were
> back in the Garden of Eden, where, according to the little boy's
> version, "Adam called the elephant an elephant because it looked
> like an elephant."

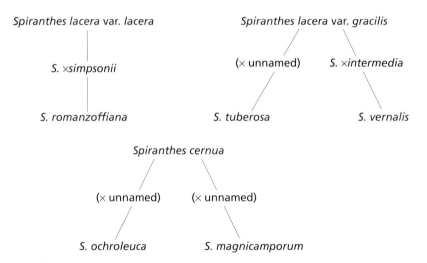

Figure 7. Ladies'-tresses orchid hybrids. One other unnamed hybrid (not
mentioned here) occurs between *S. laciniata* and *S. praecox*, and probably
some others in the *S. cernua* complex.

Afterword

NORTH American native orchids are fighting a losing battle. We hear and read many horror stories detailing the continued destruction of orchid stations. Les Eastman, former president of the Josselyn Society and for twenty years one of the leading plant people in Maine, relates an experience that highlights this battle. During a survey for a mining company, he discovered the largest stand of *Goodyera oblongifolia* in Maine, an orchid barely extending southward into northernmost Aroostook County. Upon notification of his find, the company agreed to set aside a 2-acre (0.8-ha) stand for protection. A year later, while checking back on the woodlot, Eastman was startled to see nothing but devastation. The entire stand of virgin, 400-year-old trees and the orchids had been clearcut out of existence. Four hundred years of life destroyed in a matter of hours! Maurice Brooks (1965) described a meadow in West Virginia's Appalachian Mountains where *Platanthera peramoena* (purple fringeless orchid) and *P. ciliaris* (yellow fringed-orchid) once grew. Today this woods-bordered meadow has become an artificial lake for the sport of fishing.

Do you see the problem here? Orchid lovers and plant lovers in general do not have the clout of those who fish and hunt for sport, even though we probably outnumber them if the truth were known. It is the larger mammals and birds that get the most attention and protection because of their glamour status in the minds of most people.

In the 1980s I discovered several new stations of *Platanthera flava*. One of them—in York County—turned out to be the largest station in the state of Maine, yet only a few years later it was destroyed by another commercial development.

Collecting and digging continue to be perennial problems. The temptation to take it home prevails among many people. Negative results are almost guaranteed each time this occurs. In a rare case in Michigan, a foreign visitor was arrested for digging a truckload of orchids to send back home for commercial sale. He ended up paying the token fine of approximately two thousand dollars, but he is still in business. Sometimes, even people who sign up for orchid field trips have been known to return to the site and dig up some of the plants. Some wildflower nurseries sell wild-collected (that means "dug") orchids, advertising them as nursery propagated (a euphemism for plants collected in the wild and held at the nursery for a year or two before being sold to an unsuspecting public). Until an informed public stops this practice, the unprincipled dealers will continue to supply the demand.

Ron Coleman (1992) related the story of an albino clump of *Calypso bulbosa* var. *occidentalis* that he and a friend discovered on a Sunday afternoon, only to find them dug up the next morning when he went back to take more pictures. A favored habitat for these extraordinary orchids is the coast redwood forests of northern California where, out of an original two million acres (800,000 ha), only 3 percent (mostly in Redwoods National Park) have been saved from the ax. Poaching is believed to have extirpated the queenly *Cypripedium reginae* from Acadia National Park. Lest anyone believes that our parks protect our priceless plant heritage, consider that since 1960 the system has more than doubled in size, from 30 million (thanks to Alaska) to 80 million acres (from 12 million to 32 million hectares), while the number of field rangers dropped more than 11 percent. The current visitor to ranger ratios is estimated at 84,000 to 1! Incredible! Even when caught, poachers pay fines of only $25 to $250.

Natural plant succession is another cause of orchid destruction. This occurs when ideal habitat for one or two species gradually deteriorates as the result of maturing vegetation, such as when a meadow becomes overgrown and gradually succeeds to forest. Of course, the opposite is true, when human intervention beneficially keeps that meadow from going to forest by regular mowing. Animals, notably deer and rodents, account for a certain amount of destruction as they graze for food.

One of the most potentially destructive aspects of human intervention, of course, is reflected in the many ongoing studies of global warming, which strongly suggest that industrial and agricultural gases, chiefly carbon dioxide, methane, and chloroflourocarbons, are affecting the ozone layer and contributing to what some scientists believe will be devastating consequences for Earth if it continues. Since 1870, for example, the average temperature of our planet has risen 1.6°F (0.6°C), and the increase is speeding up. The warmest year in recorded history was 1990, and the ten warmest years ever recorded have occurred since 1973. As a result, many plants and animals are moving north from more southern homes, while some northern plants and animals have been moving even further north. Botanists in Michigan have documented the retreat northward of *Calypso* by as much as 100 miles (160 km) in recent years. In Vermont, I used to see *Platanthera obtusata,* a northern orchid of cold sites, annually in arbor-vitae (*Thuja occidentalis*) swamps. It has disappeared since the mid 1980s because, I suspect, of this global warming trend.

Not all the news is bad, however. The Nature Conservancy is probably accomplishing more in terms of saving plants and animals than any other conservation organization in the world. It has been responsible for the protection of almost 8 million acres (3.2 million hectares) in the United States and Canada, and it is the largest private system of nature sanctuaries in the world. The primary focus of this organization is entire ecosystems, especially with the "Last Great Places" effort. As an example of the Nature Conservancy's latest innovative technique in helping to protect the most valuable ecosystems, witness "a new course for forest management" as Interior Secretary Bruce Babbitt called an equal partnership agreement with Georgia-Pacific involving 21,000 acres (8,400 ha) along the Roanoke River in North Carolina. The company will set aside nearly 7000 of the most sensitive acres (2800 ha) while co-managing the remainder with the Nature Conservancy. No new roads will be built and the timber will be taken out only by helicopter to eliminate as much damage to the forest as possible. Now that's innovation!

Another encouraging corporate donation involved one of the rarest North American orchids, *Isotria medeoloides.* Wheelabrator Technologies, an environmental services company, gave $15,000 to the New Hampshire chapter of Nature Conservancy to help preserve and protect the small whorled pogonia in that state, which happens to be the home of more of these orchids than anywhere else in North America. Wheelabrator has been a major supporter of Nature Conservancy for several years in their mission to protect the earth's unique biodiversity. In the words of the company president, "This grant restates Wheelabrator's deep interest in securing active partnerships between business and conservation programs across the country."

Many other companies, large and small, support conservation organizations, but there are many more that don't and others that pollute and get away with it. One of America's greatest conservationists, Aldo Leopold, maintained that what we need to do is to "examine each question in terms of what is ethically and esthetically right—as well as what is economically expedient." Unfortunately, for too many companies, the bottom line is all that counts. Wendell Berry, who lives and farms in Kentucky, points out two laws that must be taken as absolute. "First, we cannot exempt ourselves from living in this world and therefore using it, and the second law is that if we want to continue living, we cannot exempt that use from care." We have a critical choice between caring and not caring. Increasing numbers of religious groups now emphasize the growing need for conservation of the earth's resources, after some of them previously maintained that our natural resources were put here for us to exploit. Honoring the Creator of the earth does not equate with the destruction of it.

Ecotourisn, which simply means nature-based tourism, is the kind of sustainable economic development of which we need more. Just ask Snoody Borowiec, the Chamber of Commerce director of Sierra Vista in southeastern Arizona. Visitors to the 56,000-acre (22,400-ha) San Pedro Riparian National Conservation Area and Nature Conservancy's 300-acre (120-ha) Ramsey Canyon Preserve pump as much as three million dollars into the regional economy and $890,000 in wages annually. This example can be multiplied a hundred-fold.

In the words of John Burroughs, "I still find each day too short for all the thoughts I want to think, all the walks I want to take, all the books I want to read, and all the friends I want to see." Somebody else said, "Of all manner of men, the plant hunter is the most hopeful."

Glossary

Anthesis. Beginning of bloom, when flower actually opens.

Autogamous. Self-fertilizing.

Calyx. The sepals collectively.

Column. The unique reproductive structure in an orchid flower, consisting of fused stamens and pistils.

Connivent. Sepals and petals partially uniting to form a hood over the lip petal.

Corolla. The petals collectively.

Disk. Upper surface or floor of the lip.

Dorsal. Above or upper.

Ecology. The relationship of a plant and its surrounding environment.

Endemic. Found only in one region and nowhere else.

Epiphyte. A plant that grows on another plant, usually a tree in the case of orchids, without being parasitic.

Fen. An open or treed wetland characterized by a more alkaline source of ground water than a bog.

Filiform. Threadlike.

Fugacious. Withering early.

Glabrous. Smooth.

Habitat. Where a plant lives.

Inflorescence. The part of the plant with flowers, single or multiple.

Lanceolate. Lance-shaped.

Lip. Lowermost petal, except in nonresupinate examples.

Mesic. A moist and rich habitat.

Nonresupinate. Lip petal in uppermost position, as in *Calopogon tuberosus* and *Platanthera nivea*, for example.

Nomenclature. The naming of plants.

Oblong. Longer than wide with parallel sides.

Ovate. Egg-shaped.

Pedicel. The stem that supports a flower; can be either the main stem or smaller stems attaching multiple flowers to the main stem.

Perianth. Combination of both sepals and petals.

Petal. The innermost whorl of flower segments.

Pistil. Female part of flower consisting of the stigma, style, and ovary. Not applicable in orchids usually because the pistil and stamen are fused to form the column.

Pollination. The application of pollen from the male organ (stamen) to the female organ (pistil).

Putative. Supposed but not experimentally proven.

Raceme. An elongated stem of multiple flowers with each floret attached by a short stem of its own.

Resupinate. Lip petal in lowermost position on flower, the normal position in most orchids.

Reticulate. Network of veins.

Rosette. A basal cluster of leaves.

Saccate. Swollen at tip.

Secund. One-sided.

Sepal. The outermost whorl of flower segments.

Spike. An elongated stem of flowers with each floret attached directly to the stem.

Spur. Hollow, tubular extension of the lip.

Stamen. Male part of flower consisting of filament and anther.

Symbiotic. Mutually beneficial.

Taxon. General term for either a species, variety, or color form.

Taxonomy. The science or study of classifying plants in a systematic or orderly way.

Tepal. Combined term for petals and sepals when they look alike.

Tripartite. Divided into three parts.

Xeric. A very dry habitat.

Bibliography

> That every wildflower—even the humblest weed—has a literature
> was news to me then, and, as I have since found, is news to most
> people still. This literature, in many cases, may be no more than a
> bare description published when the name is given . . . or it may be
> a treatise, formal or discursive, on the plant's role in the human
> drama (Saunders 1933).

THERE is no shortage of orchid literature. The bibliography that follows
barely scratches the surface. A few of these sources are technical articles
from botanical and other scientific journals, but most are not. There is a
good sampling of popular articles and books. Increasing numbers of regional and state guide books are beginning to appear, and there is a good
foundation of older books throughout the list.

It may be of interest to some people to mention a few favorites here.
The one indispensable orchid book has been Carl Luer's two-volume set
on North American orchids, *The Native Orchids of Florida* (1972), and *The
Native Orchids of the United States and Canada* (1975). The second vol-
ume has been my vade mecum. The photographs set a new standard at the
time and still are among the best ever done. Many of the distribution maps,
understandably, are off the mark today, and the intervening years have
seen several new taxa described as well as other taxonomic changes. Out
of print now, I believe these two volumes will become collectibles, and
someday, if there ever is a Hall of Fame for books, these two will be in it
under orchids. In my opinion, Luer has done for North American orchids
what Roger Tory Peterson did for birds, on a smaller scale, of course.

I have a special feeling, as do most native orchid enthusiasts, for Morris and Eames' 1929 classic, *Our Wild Orchids*. The bountiful enthusiasm and the elegant prose have never been surpassed. The 1987 edition of Fred Case's *Orchids of the Western Great Lakes Region* is the best of the regional books. The ecology section of the introductory portion is as good as it gets. In state books, I believe Ron Coleman's *The Wild Orchids of California* (1995) sets a high standard, with special emphasis on the conservation outlook for each species. *Orchids of Indiana* by Michael Homoya (1993) is sumptuously produced on heavy glossy paper. Though out of print, I must mention Petrie's *Guide to Orchids of North America*. This handsome gem of a pocket-size fieldguide to all the species in North America north of Florida is outdated, of course, but the format, size, and photos were great.

Aiken, G. D. 1935. *Pioneering with Wildflowers.* Published by the author. 131 p.

Audubon, J. J. 1840. *The Birds of America.* 5 volumes.

Bailey, W. W. 1897. *New England Wild Flowers.* Preston and Rounds, Providence, Rhode Island. 150 p.

Baldwin, H. 1884. *The Orchids of New England.* Wiley, New York. 158 p.

Bechtel, H., P. Cribb, and E. Launert. 1986. *The Manual of Cultivated Orchid Species.* The MIT Press, Cambridge, Massachusetts. 444 p.

Boland, T. 1994. Orchids in Newfoundland. *American Orchid Society Bulletin* 63(4): 396–405.

Brackley, F. E. 1985. The orchids of New Hampshire. *Rhodora* 87: 1–117.

Brooks, M. 1965. *The Appalachians.* Houghton Mifflin Company, Boston. 346 p.

Brown, P. M. 1992. *Platanthera pallida*, a new species of fringed orchis from Long Island, New York, U.S.A. *Novon* 2(4): 308–311.

_____. 1995a. *North American Native Orchid Journal* 1(1): 17.

_____. 1995b. *North American Native Orchid Journal* 1(3): 199.

_____. 1997a. *Checklist of the Orchids of North America (North of Mexico).* Special publication of North American Native Orchid Alliance, Jamaica Plain, Massachusetts. 34 p.

_____. 1997b. *Wild Orchids of the Northeastern United States—A Field Guide.* Comstock Publishing Associates, Ithaca, New York, and London. 236 p.

Brownell, V. R., and P. M. Catling. 1987. Notes on the distribution and taxonomy of *Cypripedium fasciculatum* Kellogg ex Watson. *Lindleyana* 2(1): 53–57.

Burnett, J. A., C. T. Dauphine Jr., S. H. McCrindle, and T. Mosquin. 1989. *On the Brink: Endangered Species in Canada.* Western Producer Prairie Books, Saskatoon, Saskatchewan. 192 p.

Burroughs, J. 1901. *The Complete Nature Writings of John Burroughs.* Wm. H. Wise & Company, New York. 9 volumes.

Case, F. W. 1987. *Orchids of the Western Great Lakes Region.* Revised edition. Cranbrook Institute of Science, Bulletin 48. 251 p.

Cash, C. 1991. *The Slipper Orchids.* Timber Press, Portland, Oregon. 228 p.

Catling, P. M. 1991. Systematics of *Malaxis bayardii* and *Malaxis unifolia. Lindleyana* 6(1): 3–23.

Catling, P. M., and V. R. Brownell. 1995. A review of the alvars of the Great Lakes Region: distribution, floristic composition, biogeography, and protection. *The Canadian Field-Naturalist* 109(2): 143–171.

Catling, P. M., and V. R. Catling. 1994. Identification of *Platanthera lacera* hybrids from New Brunswick and Nova Scotia. *Lindleyana* 9(1): 19–32.

Catling, P. M., and K. Gregg. 1992. Systematics of the genus *Cleistes* in North America. *Lindleyana* 7(2): 57–73.

Catling, P. M., and C. J. Sheviak. 1993. Taxonomic notes on some North American orchids. *Lindleyana* 8(2): 77–81.

Cobb, Boughton. 1975. *Field Guide to Ferns and Their Related Families: Northeastern and Central North America.* Houghton Mifflin Company, Boston. 304 p.

Coleman, R. 1992. *American Orchid Society Bulletin* 61(7): 776–781.

———. 1995. *The Wild Orchids of California.* Cornell University Press, Ithaca, New York. 264 p.

Correll, D. S. [1950] 1978. *Native Orchids of North America North of Mexico.* Stanford University Press, Stanford, California. 399 p.

Critical Areas Program. 1981. *Rare Vascular Plants of Maine.* State Planning Office, Augusta, Maine. 656 p.

Crow, G. E. 1982. *New England's Rare, Threatened, and Endangered Plants.* U.S. Government Printing Office, Washington, D.C. 129 p.

Dana, W. S. 1910. *How to Know the Wildflowers.* Charles Scribner's Sons, New York. 346 p.

Dressler, R. L. 1981. *The Orchids: Natural History and Classification.* Harvard University Press, Cambridge, Massachusetts. 352 p.

———. 1993. *Phylogeny and Classification of the Orchid Family.* Dioscorides Press, Portland, Oregon. 314 p.

Elliman, T., and A. Dalton. 1995. *Cypripedium fasciculatum* in Montana. *North American Native Orchid Journal* 1(1): 58–73.

Ettman, J. K., and D. R. McAdoo. 1979. *An Annotated Catalog and Distribution Account of the Kentucky Orchidaceae.* The Kentucky Society of Natural History Charitable Trust, Louisville. 32 p.

Flora of North America Editorial Committee. 1993. *Flora of North America.* Oxford University Press, New York. Volumes 1 and 2.

Folsom, J. P. 1984. A reinterpretation of the status and relationship of taxa of the yellow fringed-orchid complex. *Orquidea* (Mexico) 9(2): 337–345.

Fowlie, J. A. 1982. Notes on the habitat and ecological relationships of *Cypripedium californicum* and *Darlingtonia californica. Orchid Digest* 46(5): 164–167.

Fox, W. S. 1952. *The Bruce Beckons*. University of Toronto Press. 245 p.

Fuller, M. A. 1933. *Studies on the Flora of Wisconsin. Part I: Orchidaceae*. Bulletin Publ. Mus. Milwaukee 14, I: 1–248.

Garay, L. A. 1982. A generic revision of the Spiranthinae. *Botanical Museum Leaflet* (Harvard University) 28(4): 277–425.

Gibson, W. H. 1905. *Our Native Orchids*. Doubleday, Page, and Company, New York. 158 p.

Goldman, D. H. 1995. A new species of *Calopogon* from the midwestern United States. *Lindleyana* 10(1): 37–42.

Gupton, O. W., and F. C. Swope. 1986. *Wild Orchids of the Middle Atlantic States*. The University of Tennessee Press. 112 p.

Hennessy, E. F., and T. A. Hedge. 1989. *The Slipper Orchids*. Acorn Books, Randburg, South Africa. 263 p.

Homoya, M. A. 1993. *Orchids of Indiana*. Indiana University Press, Bloomington and Indianapolis. 276 p.

Jepson, W. L. 1979. *Flora of California*. Jepson Herbarium. 1722 p.

Kallunki, J. A. 1976. Population studies in *Goodyera* (Orchidaceae) with emphasis on the hybrid origin of *G. tesselata*. *Brittonia* 27: 53–75.

Keenan, P. E. 1986a. New stations for *Platanthera flava* and *Triphora triantho-phora* and other observations. *Rhodora* 88: 409–412.

_____. 1986b. Wild orchids in New England. *American Orchid Society Bulletin* 55(7): 696–699.

_____. 1987. The bloom sequence of wild orchids in New England. *American Orchid Society Bulletin* 56(10): 1059–1061.

_____. 1988a. *Calypso bulbosa*: hider of the north. *American Orchid Society Bulletin* 57(4): 375–377.

_____. 1988b. Progress report on *Isotria medeoloides*. *American Orchid Society Bulletin* 57(6): 624–626.

_____. 1989a. Butterflies of the orchid world. *American Orchid Society Bulletin* 58(8): 767–771.

_____. 1989b. The wonderful world of *Cypripedium*. *American Orchid Society Bulletin* 58(5): 450-455.

_____. 1990a. Documentation on longevity of *Goodyera pubescens* leaves and update on *Triphora trianthophora* in New Hampshire. *Rhodora* 92: 126–128.

_____. 1990b. The big little green orchids. *American Orchid Society Bulletin* 59(3): 228–233.

_____. 1990c. The pigtails of the orchid world. *American Orchid Society Bulletin* 59(7): 683–687.

_____. 1991a. The American orchises. *American Orchid Society Bulletin* 6(6): 536–538.

_____. 1991b. The mighty pogonias. *American Orchid Society Bulletin* 60(4): 338–341.

_____. 1992a. A new form of *Triphora trianthophora* (Swartz) Rydberg, and part three of observations on the ecology of *Triphora trianthophora* (Orchidaceae) in New Hampshire. *Rhodora* 94: 38–42.

_____. 1992b. Grass pinks. *American Orchid Society Bulletin* 61(4): 343–347.

_____. 1993. Thoreau's orchids. *American Orchid Society Bulletin* 62(4): 362–371.

_____. 1994a. Pretty in pink. *American Orchid Society Bulletin* 63(3): 250–255.

_____. 1994b. The coral-roots. *American Orchid Society Bulletin* 63(5): 512–517.

_____. 1995. California ladies. *American Orchid Society Bulletin* 64(3): 234–239.

Lamont, E. E., and J. M. Beitel. 1988. Current status of orchids on Long Island, New York. *Torreya* 115(2): 113–121.

Latham, R. 1940. *Distribution of Wild Orchids on Long Island.* Long Island Forum, Bay Shore, New York. 8 p.

Luer, C. A. 1972. *The Native Orchids of Florida.* New York Botanical Garden, Bronx. 293 p.

_____. 1975. *The Native Orchids of the United States and Canada Excluding Florida.* New York Botanical Garden, Bronx. 361 p.

Medley, M. 1979. *Some Aspects of the Life History of Triphora trianthophora (SW) Rydb. (3-birds orchid) with Special Reference to Its Pollination.* Thesis, Andrews University. 1–45.

Moldenke, H. N. 1949. *American Wild Flowers.* D. Van Nostrand Company, Toronto. 453 p.

Morris, F., and E. Eames. 1929. *Our Wild Orchids.* Charles Scribner's Sons, New York. 464 p.

Niles, G. G. 1904. *Bog Trotting for Orchids.* Knickerbocker Press, New York. 310 p.

Nylander, O. O. 1935. *Our Northern Orchids.* 12 p.

Petrie, W. 1981. *Guide to Orchids of North America.* Hancock House Publishers, Blaine, Washington. 128 p.

Plaxton, E. H., editor. 1981. *North American Terrestrial Orchids.* Michigan Orchid Society, Livonia. 143 p.

Preece, W. H. A. 1937. *North American Rock Plants.* Macmillan, New York. 204 p.

Radford, A. E., H. E. Ahles, and C. R. Bell. 1963. *Manual of the Vascular Plants of the Carolinas.* University of North Carolina Press, Chapel Hill. 1183 p.

Reddoch, A. H., and J. M. Reddoch. 1993. The species pair *Platanthera orbiculata* and *P. macrophylla*: taxonomy, morphology, distributions and habitats. *Lindleyana* 8(4): 171–187.

Runte, A. 1979. *National Parks: The American Experience.* University of Nebraska.

Saunders, Charles Francis. 1933. Introduction to *Western Wild Flowers and their Stories.* Garden City, New York: Doubleday, Doran & Company.

Schrenk, W. J. 1978. North American *Platanthera* evolution in the making. *American Orchid Society Bulletin* 47(5): 429–437.

Sheviak, C. J. 1989. A new *Spiranthes* from Ash Meadows, Nevada. *Rhodora* 91: 225–234.

_____. 1990. A new *Spiranthes* from the cienegas of southernmost Arizona. *Rhodora* 92: 213–231.

_____. 1991. Morphological variation in the compilospecies *Spiranthes cernua*: ecologically limited effects of gene flow. *Lindleyana* (6)4: 228–234.

_____. 1994. *Cypripedium parviflorum* Salisb. I: the small-flowered varieties. *American Orchid Society Bulletin* 63(6): 664–669.

Sheviak, C. J., and M. L. Bowles. 1986. The prairie fringed-orchids: a pollinator-isolated species pair. *Rhodora* 88: 267–290.

Small, J. K. 1933. *Manual of the Southeastern Flora.* University of North Carolina Press, Chapel Hill. 1554 p.

Smith, R. M. 1989. *Wild Plants of America.* Wiley, New York. 267 p.

Smith, W. R. 1993. *Orchids of Minnesota.* University of Minnesota Press, Minneapolis. 172 p.

Stoutamire, W. P. 1974. Relationships of the purple fringed-orchid *Platanthera psycodes* and *P. grandiflora. Brittonia* 26: 42–58.

Szczawinski, A. F. 1959. *The Orchids of British Columbia.* British Columbia Provincial Museum Handbook 16, Victoria. 124 p.

Taylor, N. 1915. Flora of the vicinity of New York. *Memoirs of the New York Botanical Garden* 51: 1–683.

Turner, F. 1985. *Rediscovering America: John Muir in His Time and Ours.* Sierra Club Books, San Francisco. 417 p.

Thoreau, H. D. 1962. *The Journal of Henry David Thoreau.* Dover Publications, New York. 1804 p.

Tyler, R. W. 1994. Slips and cuttings. *Wildflower Magazine* (spring issue): 11.

Van Der Pijl, L., and C. H. Dodson. 1966. *Orchid Flowers: Their Pollination and Evolution.* University of Miami Press, Florida.

Wallace, David. 1983. *The Klamath Knot.* Sierra Club Books, San Francisco. 160 p.

Whiting, R. E., and P. M. Catling. 1986. *Orchids of Ontario.* CanaColl Foundation, Ottawa, Ontario. 169 p.

Williams, S. A. 1994. Observations on reproduction in *Triphora trianthophora* (Orchidaceae). *Rhodora* 96: 30–43.

Wiley, L. 1969. *Rare Wildflowers of North America.* Published by the author. 501 p.

Wright, M. O. 1901. *Flowers and Ferns in their Haunts.* Macmillan, New York. 358 p.

APPENDIX 1

Checklist of North American Orchids

North America, excluding Florida and Mexico, is home to approximately 145 orchid species in 35 genera. The names listed here are based on Brown (1997a) with guides to the pronunciation and derivation of the names. All these species are native to the United States (with a few extending into Mexico); 75 of them, marked here with an asterisk (*), are also native to Canada.

Amerorchis (am-er-or´-kiss), American orchis
    * *rotundifolia* (row-tund-e-foe´-lee-a), round leaved
    rotundifolia forma *beckettiae* (beck-et´-ee-a), honors Beckett
    rotundifolia forma *lineata* (lin-e-ay´-ta), marked by fine parallel lines
        (referring to the lip)
Aplectrum (a-plec´-trum), without a spur
    * *hyemale* (hi-e-ma´-lee), of winter (referring to the persistent leaf)
Arethusa (ar-e-thew´-sa), mythical river nymph
    * *bulbosa* (bul-bo´-sa), bulbous corm
Calopogon (cal-o-po´-gon), beautiful beard
    barbatus (bar-bay´-tus), bearded or crested lip
    multiflorus (mul-ti-flor´-us), many flowers
    oklahomensis (oh-kla-home-en´-sis), of Oklahoma
    pallidus (pal´-i-dus), pale or whitish flowers
    * *tuberosus* (tu-ber-o´-sus), tuberlike root
Calypso (ca-lip´-so), sea nymph in Homer's *Odyssey*
    * *bulbosa* (bul-bo´-sa), bulbous corm
    bulbosa var. *americana* (a-mer-i-can´-a), of America
    bulbosa var. *americana* forma *rosea* (roe-zay´-a), pink or pale rose (referring
        to the lips of the flower)
    bulbosa var. *occidentalis* (oks-i-den-tal´-iss), western

Cephalanthera (sef-a-lan´-ther-a), anther and column position
  *austiniae (os-tin´-e), honors Rebecca Austin (1832–1919), a California student of *Darlingtonia*
Cleistes (clye´-steez), closed (referring to the tubelike corolla)
  bifaria (bye-fair´-ee-a), developed in two areas (in this case, mountains and coastal plain)
  divaricata (die-vair-i-cay´-ta), spreading (referring to the sepals)
Coeloglossum (see-lo-gloss´-um), the saccate nectary behind the lip
  *viride (vur´-i-dee), green
  viride var. *virescens* (vur-es´-ens), becoming green
Corallorhiza (cor-a-lo-rye´-sa), coral-like roots
  *maculata (mac-u-lay´-ta), spotted
  *mertensiana (mer-ten-see-a´-na), honors Franz Mertens (1764–1831), a German botanist
  *odontorhiza (oh-don-toe-rye´-za), coral-like roots
  *striata (stry-ay´-ta), striped
  *trifida (trif´-i-da), three-lobed lip
  wisteriana (wis-ter´-ee-a-na), honors Charles Wister (1782–1865), an American botanist
Cypripedium (sip-re-pee´-dee-um), goddess of beauty
  *acaule (a-call´-e), stemless
  *arietinum (ar-ee-tie´-num), ramlike (referring to the appearance and shape of the lip)
  californicum (cal-i-for´-ni-cum), of California
  *candidum (can-dee´-dum), white
  fasciculatum (fas-sick-u-lay´-tum), clustered
  *guttatum (goo-tay´-tum), spotted
  kentuckiense (ken-tuck-ee-en´-see), of Kentucky
  *montanum (mon-ta´-num), of the mountains
  *parviflorum (par-vi-flor´-um), small flower
  parviflorum var. *makasin* (ma´-ka-sin), shoe
  parviflorum var. *pubescens* (poo-bess´-inns), downy
  *passerinum (pass-er-eye´-num), like a sparrow´s egg (referring to the shape of the lip)
  *reginae (re-jye´-nee), beauty of a queen
  yatabeanum (ya-tah-bee´-a-num), honors Ryokichi Yatabe (1851–1899), a Japanese professor of biology
Dactylorhiza (dac-till-o-rye´-za), fingerlike root tubers
  aristata (ar-iss-tay´-ta), pointed (referring to the tip of the tepals)
  aristata var. *kodiakensis* (koe-dee-ack-en´-sis), of Kodiak Island, Alaska
  aristata var. *kodiakensis* forma *perbracteata* (per-bract-e-ay´-ta), bearing many bracts

*cf. *fuchsii* (fuke´-see-eye), magenta

praetermissa (pray-ter-miss´-a), omission of something, in this case spots on the leaves

Deiregnye (deer-reg´-e-nee)

    durangensis (dur-ang-en´-sis), of Durango, Mexico (where first discovered)

Dichromanthus (die-crow-man´-this), two-colored (referring to the red and gold floral parts)

    cinnabarinus (cin-na-bar-ee´-nus), vermilion

Epidendrum (ep-i-den´-drum), growing on trees

    conopseum (con-op´-see-um), gnatlike (referring to the inconspicuous and loosely flowered raceme)

Epipactis (epi-pac´-tis), medicinal herb

    atrorubens (atro-ru´-bins), dark red

    gigantea (gye-gan´-tee-a), gigantic

    helleborine (hell´-bore-een), resembling a hellebore

Erythrodes (err-i-throw´-deez), ruddy (referring to the color of the flowers of the first described species)

    querciticola (quer-sit´-i-cola), inhabitant of *Quercus* (oak) woods

Galearis (gal-ee-ar´-iss), hooded

    spectabilis (spec-ta´-bi-liss), spectacular or showy

Goodyera (good-yer´-a), honors John Goodyer (1592–1664), an English botanist

    oblongifolia (ob-lon-i-foe´-lee-a), oblong leaved

    pubescens (poo-bess´-inns), downy

    repens (ree´-pens), creeping

    tesselata (tess-e-lay´-ta), checkered (referring to the reticulated leaf pattern)

Habenaria (ha-bin-air´-ee-a), a strap-shaped or thong-shaped spur

    quinqueseta (quin-que-set´-a), having five linear or threadlike divisions of petals

    repens (ree´-pens), creeping

Hexalectris (hex-a-lek´-tris), having six ridges on the lip

    nitida (nit´-i-da), shining (referring to "polished" flower parts)

    revoluta (rev-o-loo´-ta), rolled back (referring to the tips of flower parts)

    spicata (spy-cay´-ta), spiked inflorescence

    warnockii (war-knock´-ee-eye), honors Barton Warnock, a Texas botanist

Isotria (eye-sew´-tree-a), three equal sepals

    medeoloides (med-ee-o-loy´-deez), like *Medeola virginiana*

    verticillata (vur-tiss-i-lay´-ta), whorled leaves

Liparis (lip´-ar-iss), greasy (referring to the fleshy leaves)

    liliifolia (lil-i-ee-foe´-lee-a), lilylike (referring to the fleshy leaves)

    loeselii (low-sell´-ee-eye), honors Johann Loesel (1607–1655), a German botanist

Listera (lis´-ter-a), honors Martin Lister (1638–1712), an English naturalist
  *auriculata (o-rick-u-lay´-ta), auricled (referring to the pair of incurved
    lobes or ears)
  *australis (aus-tral´-iss), southern
  *borealis (bor-ee-ay´-lis), northern
  *caurina (caw-ree´-na), northwestern
  *convallarioides (con-val-er-ee-oy´-deez), like *Convallaria*
  *cordata (caw-day´-ta), heart-shaped (referring to the leaves)
  *ovata (o-vay´-ta), egg-shaped (referring to the leaves)
  smallii (small´-ee-eye), honors John Small (1869–1938), an American bota-
    nist
Malaxis (ma-lax´-iss), soft (referring to the leaves)
  *bayardii (bay-ard´-ee-eye), honors Bayard Long (1885–1969), an American
    botanist
  *brachypoda (brack-i-po´-da), short foot (referring to the short pedicels of
    the flowers)
  corymbosa (cor-em-bo´-sa), with flowers in a corymb
  diphyllos (die-phil´-os), two leaves
  *paludosa (pal-u-do´-sa), boggy (referring to the habitat)
  porphyrea (por-phy-ree´-a), purple (referring to flower color)
  soulei (soo´-lee-eye), honors Soule
  spicata (spy-cay´-ta), spicate (referring to the slender raceme)
  tenuis (ten´-u-iss), thin (referring to linear flower parts)
  *unifolia (you-ne-foe´-lee-a), single-leaved
Piperia (pie-per´-ee-a), honors Charles Piper (1867–1926)
  *candida (can-dee´-da), white flowered
  colemanii (col-man´-ee-eye), honors Ron Coleman, a California botanist
  cooperi (coop´-er-eye), honors Cooper
  *elegans (el´-e-gans), elegant
  *elongata (ee-long-ay´-ta), elongated
  leptopetala (lep-toe-pet´-a-la), thin-petaled
  michaelii (my-kell´-ee-eye), honors Michael
  *transversa (trans-ver´-sa), transverse (referring to the oblong viscidia)
  *unalascensis (u-na-las-sen´-sis), of the Aleutian island of Unalaska
  yadonii (ya-doe´-nee-eye), honors Vernal Yadon, a California botanist
Platanthera (pla-tan´-ther-a), broad anthered
  *blephariglottis (blef´-are-e-glot-iss), eyebrow tongued (referring to the
    fringed lip)
  blephariglottis var. *conspicua* (con-spik´-u-a), remarkable or conspicuous
    (referring to the larger flower, more open raceme, and longer spur)
  brevifolia (brev-i-foe´-lee-a), short-leaved (referring to the bracts)
  chapmanii (chap-man´-ee-eye), honors Alvan Chapman (1809–1899), an
    American botanist

chorisiana (core-iss´-ee-a-na), honors Louis Choris (1795–1828), a Russian painter

ciliaris (see-lee-ar´-iss), like an eyelash (referring to the fringed lip)

clavellata (clav-i-lay´-ta), like a club (referring to the club-shaped spur)

cristata (cris-tay´-ta), crested (referring to the fringed lip of the lateral petals)

dilatata (die-la-tay´-ta), widened (referring to the base of the lip)

flava (flay´-va), yellow (referring to the yellow-green flowers)

grandiflora (grand´-i-flor-a), large flowered

hookeri (hook´-er-eye), honors William Hooker (1785–1865), an English botanist

huronensis (yur-on-en´-sis), of Lake Huron

hyperborea (hye-per-bor´-ee-a), beyond the north (referring to inside Arctic Circle)

integra (in-teg´-ra), entire (referring to the unfringed lip)

integrilabia (in-teg-ri-lay´-bee-a), entire lip

lacera (las´-er-a), torn (referring to the deeply fringed lip)

leucophaea (lew-co-fee´-a), whitish (referring to the flowers)

limosa (li-mo´-sa), muddy (referring to the habitat)

macrophylla (mac-ro-phil´-a), large plant

nivea (niv´-ee-a), snowy (referring to the flowers)

obtusata (ob-tu-say´-ta), blunt (referring to the rounded apex of single leaf)

orbiculata (or-bic-u-lay´-ta), round (referring to the leaves)

pallida (pal´-i-da), pale (referring to the flower color)

peramoena (per-a-mee´-na), very lovely (referring to the flowers)

praeclara (pre-clar´-a), bright, beautiful, glorious, and noble

psycodes (sye-co´-deez), butterfly-like (referring to the flowers)

sparsiflora (spar-si-flor´-a), sparsely flowered

stricta (stric´-ta), straight, narrow, and upright

tipuloides (tip-u-loy´-deez), water-spider-like

zothecina (zoth-e-seen´-a), cloistered (referring to hood made by sepals)

Pogonia (po-go´-nee-a), bearded

ophioglossoides (off-ee-o-gloss-oy´-deez), resembling *Ophioglossum* fern leaf (referring to the leaf)

Ponthieva (pon-tee´-va), honors Henri de Ponthieu, a French–West Indian merchant-collector

racemosa (ras-e-mo´-sa), with flowers in racemes

Pseudorchis (sood-or´-kiss), of *Orchis*

straminea (stram´-i-knee-a), straw-yellow flowers

Pteroglossaspis (tear-o-gloss-ass´-piss), referring to the wings of the column merging with the basal margins of the lip

ecristata (ek-ri-stay´-ta), without a crest

Schiedeella (shy-dee´-la), honors Schiedeel, a German botanist
  fauci-sanguinea (fos-e-sang-guin´-ee-a), slashed throat with red (referring to the lip petal)
Spiranthes (spur-ann´-theez), a coiled flower
  brevilabris (brev-i-lay´-bris), short lipped
  *casei (case´-ee-eye), honors Fred Case, American wildflower and orchid author-botanist
  *cernua (cern´-u-a), nodding (referring to the flowers)
  delitescens (del-i-tes´-ens), elusive (referring to rarity)
  diluvialis (di-lu-vee-al´-iss), very wet (referring to habitat)
  infernalis (in-fer-nay´-liss), "hot as hell" (referring to the habitat)
  *lacera (las´-er-a), torn (referring to the lip)
  lacera var. *gracilis* (gra´-sill-iss), slender
  laciniata (la-sin-ee-ay´-ta), slashed (referring to the lip)
  longilabris (lon-gee-lay´-bris), long lip
  *lucida (lew´-se-da), shining (referring to the lip)
  *magnicamporum (mag-ni-cam-por´-um), of the Great Plains
  *ochroleuca (oh-crow-lew´-ca), yellowish white (referring to the flower color)
  parksii (park-see-eye), honors H. B. Parks
  odorata (oh-dor-ay´-ta), fragrant
  ovalis (oh-vay´-lis), oval (referring to the shape of the inflorescence)
  porrifolia (po-ri-foe´-lee-a), leek green leaves
  praecox (pre´-cox), early blooming
  *romanzoffiana (ro-man-zoff´-ee-a-na), honors Russian Nicholas Romanzof (1754–1826)
  tuberosa (too-ber-o´-sa), tuberlike swollen root
  vernalis (vur-nay´-lis), spring blooming
Stenorrhyncos (sten-o-rin´-cos), narrow snout
  michuacanum (mish-wa-can´-um), of Michuacan, Mexico (where first discovered)
Tipularia (tip-u-lair´-ee-a), resembling *Tipula,* a genus of crane flies
  discolor (dis-col´-or), two-colored
Triphora (try´-for-a), threesome (referring to the buds or ridges on the lip)
  *trianthophora (try-an-thof´-o-ra), bearing three flowers
  trianthophora forma *albidoflava* (al-bid-o-flay´-va), white and yellow (referring to the white flower with a yellow crest on the lip)
Zeuxine (zooks´-in-e), "yoking" of the lip and column
  strateumatica (stra-te-mat´-i-ca), a company or clump of plants

APPENDIX 2

Notes on the Photography

We photographers are curious about the work of other photographers, especially their equipment and technique. We are interested in whether someone else knows something we don't or has some piece of equipment that is superior to what we are using. It has been my experience that photographers, professionals included, do not have many secrets. The dozens of magazines and books on the subject will prove that point. Nevertheless, not everyone does it the same way, nor is there one best camera or method, and certainly the perfect camera has yet to be made. Some ideas and opinions are better than others, I've found. I have been published dozens of times over a thirty-year period, with hundreds of photographs and many covers to my credit. I have never been brave enough, however, to try and make a living from photography. Nonetheless, I do have opinions and ideas on how to do certain things, so, for what they are worth, here are some of them.

The camera of choice for the vast majority of wildflower photographers is the 35 mm single lens reflex (SLR). Larger formats are fine for some people, but they are bulky, heavy, and very expensive in terms of equipment and film. In the early years, almost all my picture taking was done with a $2\frac{1}{4}$-inch (6 × 6 cm) Norita SLR using 120 film. There is no question that I had excellent results with this camera, which was made in Japan by the same company that used to make the famous, larger format Speed and Crown Graphics. I still own that Norita, but haven't used it for several years because the larger film size became too expensive (twice as much per picture as the 35 mm), and forced me to go with the smaller format. Some professionals prefer the larger sized transparency for its increased sharpness, especially when enlargements are needed.

Most cameras manufactured by the big five—Canon, Minolta, Nikon, Olympus, and Pentax—will do an equally good job of picture taking. The so-called pro camera is "superior" only because it is built tougher to take the added wear and tear a professional puts its through. At one time or another we all have been tempted by the latest bells and whistles that come with the newer automatic cam-

eras. For most wildflower photographers, these whistles are unnecessary and seldom used. Most images in this book have been taken with the Canon EOS
equipped with a 100 mm $f/2.8$ macro lens, and the Olympus OM 2S equipped
with a 50 mm $f/3.5$ macro lens. I also use the macro lens as my regular lens on
both cameras, for all types of photography. Olympus probably has the best line-
up of lenses and accessories among the major manufacturers for closeup photography. I particularly like their 80 mm $f/4$ macro lens in combination with
their telescopic auto tube. The apertures range from $f/4$ to $f/32$. I also use the
50 mm $f/3.5$ macro with Vivitar's 2× macro focusing teleconverter lens. I tried
a Nikon SLR with their Nikkor macro lens early on, but found no improvement
over the Olympus set-up. Another relatively low-priced optic, which has given
excellent results but which is no longer available except as used equipment, is
the John Shaw recommended Kiron 105 mm $f/2.8$ macro.

A macro lens is expensive, but for anyone serious about closeup photography, it is the best way to go. I do not use bellows for several reasons—too fragile, too bulky, less portable, and too cumbersome on the job. I occasionally use
extension tubes but don't need them very often because both my macro lenses
give life-size images, expressed as 1:1, rather than the usual half life-size (expressed as 1:2) macros. The 100 and 200 macros have the advantage of providing greater working distance between the camera and subject, which is especially
helpful when insects are involved, for example.

Like cameras, films are constantly changing, with new versions coming to
market, it seems, every other month or so. Rivalry between Fuji and Kodak has
increased significantly. Most of my pictures were taken with Kodachrome 64,
but now I have switched to some of the newer film like Ektachrome Elite II 100
and Fujichrome's Provia 100 and Velvia 50. There are forty or more slide films
to choose from out there, so something is bound to suit you. Kodachrome 25 is
probably still the finest grained film, but its speed is too slow, in my opinion, for
most wildflower photography. That's why I have pretty much settled on ASA 100
film. Some of the Fujichrome films, like Velvia, at one time gave a distinct pinkish or magenta cast to many blue and purple flowers, which turned me off. Kodak
Ektachrome films have generally been superior to Fuji in this regard.

The only accessories I use all the time are a tripod and a reflector. Most of the
time I use a cable release and sometimes a lens shade. Like film, there are dozens
of different tripods to choose from. If, like me, you are into much wildlife photography, including birds and animals, you should have two tripods: a relatively heavier and sturdier one for birds and animals and one that almost lays flat
on the ground for wildflowers. The latter tripod should not be the kind where
the center post has to be cranked off, cut off, or turned upside down to get close
to the subject, but rather a Velbon or Benbo type that puts the camera almost
on the ground.

I seldom use filters, except for an occasional polarizer, for the simple reason
that they add another piece of glass between the film and subject thus degrad-

ing the sharpness of the image, however slightly. This applies also to the UV or skylight filter that some photographers use to "protect" their prime lens.

The most important accessory, in my opinion, is the least expensive, a reflector. You can spend good money, as I have, on the commercial fabric that opens and closes like an umbrella, with white, silver, and gold surfaces. The gold surface gives an unnatural gold tint in my experience. The other two surfaces do not reflect enough light for me. I have better success with plain aluminum foil, a piece of which I crumple up in a tight roll, then unroll, flatten out, and tape onto a rectangular piece of cardboard. I prefer a fairly large piece of cardboard, folded in half to make it convenient to carry in the field. I use it in almost all wildflower situations, sun, shade, and overcast.

Light, of course, is the key ingredient in photography. The word *photography* comes from the Greek word meaning "writing with light." There are no fixed rules when it comes to lighting, in my opinion, despite what some authors say to the contrary. Each kind of light—front lighting, side lighting, and back lighting; midday, early, or late; overcast or sunny—has its advantages and disadvantages. In comparing slides taken under cloudy conditions with those in the sun, with a reflector, my preferences vary depending on the subject. Often the shade or dark overcast distorts the true colors and makes the flower dull. On the other hand, pictures in the sun sometimes are too contrasty and glaring. Perhaps the best light is cloudy-bright: an overcast sky with some hazy sun showing through. The reflector works best in side lighting by filling in the shadow side of the flower beautifully. In front lighting the reflector imparts a special glow as long as the sun isn't too bright. In back lighting, remember to shade the lens, either with your hand or a piece of cardboard, making sure neither gets in the picture nor cuts off some of it. When not using the reflector in a backlit situation, open up the lens one or two stops, depending on the color of the flower, or bracket the exposure. Bracketing, which involves varying the exposure one stop above and one below the called-for stop, is like an insurance policy, almost guaranteeing a good shot.

Most of my pictures are done in natural light, but flash is sometimes necessary, or better, because of dark clouds, too much shade, or a breeze. My Olympus OM 2S, equipped with the Olympus T32, used off the camera, to one side or the other, or above and below the subject, has worked well. Incidentally, I use only a single flash, unlike some authors who use two.

Be careful of the backgrounds. In many cases a dark background is superior. In others, a relatively small lens opening throws the background out of focus to improve the shot. I always do a bit of housecleaning, when necessary, around the plant. This simply involves removing distracting twigs and branches on the ground and in the background. Nothing ruins a picture more than these distractions. Finally, I often move in close to fill the viewfinder with the flower or some part of it. To me, the closeup is superior because of the impact and detail.

There certainly is a place for impressionism in flower photography, and selective focus can produce unusual and beautiful results. Here again your objectives determine what you end up doing. Most people, myself included, seek maximum sharpness in their photographs. To this end one has to pay close attention to correct exposure, depth of field, and the various combinations of lens opening and shutter speed. Or you can leave it up to the auto functions on your new auto camera. Most of my flower pictures are taken in manual mode where I make all the camera settings. Even today, though, I sometimes have to review in my mind—while set up in the field—the current combination of lens opening and shutter speed. It has always been confusing to me. The lens barrel has a series of so-called f numbers, from 1.8 to 32, depending on the speed of the particular macro lens, in a sequence of $f/2$, 2.8, 3.5, 4, 5.6, 8, 11, 22, and so forth. To open up the lens does not mean to use a higher number like $f/16$ or $f/22$. Rather, the higher the f number, the smaller the lens opening. Conversely, the smaller the f number, the larger the lens opening such as 1/2, 1/4, 8, 15, 1/30, 1/60, 1/125 second and higher. If the situation calls for a small lens opening to get the required depth of field, and the shutter speed called for is a slow one, then the need for flash arises when the air movement at that slow shutter speed is enough to prevent a sharp exposure. In manual mode, the photographer has to pick the correct combination of f opening and shutter speed. In auto mode, the camera does it automatically. Why not use the auto mode all the time? Because the combination the camera chooses for that particular flower set up may cause an unsharp picture as the result of a lack of depth of field from an arbitrarily too large lens opening or too slow shutter period.

This presents another potential problem in that most lenses have an optimum area of sharpness. This usually lies between $f/5.6$ and $f/11$. When you get to the outer limits on either end of the scale, there is a decided drop off in sharpness. For closeup photography, therefore, when you need as much depth of field of possible—$f/16$ through $f/32$, for example—the sharpness may suffer, introducing the need for compromise settings, the old trade-off principle. I have yet to satisfy in my mind how serious this is in a pragmatic sense. Larger enlargements yes, but for most use probably no. Another perennial argument relates to camera shake when there is no mirror lockup provided by the manufacturer. Some photographers insist there is a significant difference in sharpness. One way to partially obviate this shortcoming is to set your camera on the self-timer setting, which is a gamble in that the breeze may pick up just as the ten-second delay elapses and the shutter releases. I often take two cameras in the field, the other one loaded with color print film.

In closing, I would remind you that one of the joys of photography and orchid hunting is the annual renewal of spring and summer when we get a chance to do it again. I am never complacent and entirely satisfied with my results from year to year. The late Eliot Porter, a great landscaper-photographer, said, "It is always possible to do better. . .this challenge is comforting and sustaining."

APPENDIX 3

A Baker's Dozen of Personal Favorites

Briefly, my favorite orchids are as follows:

Cypripedium acaule, the eastern lady's-slipper, is simply the prettiest bag I ever laid eyes on and is the orchid of first acquaintance.

Cypripedium guttatum, the spotted lady's-slipper, is peerless for its configuration of purple blotches and spectacular dorsal sepal.

Cypripedium reginae, the queen lady's-slipper, is just that—queen of all for sheer beauty.

Cypripedium californicum, the California lady's-slipper, with its string of white and gold "lanterns" is serpentine's finest representative.

Triphora trianthophora, the three-birds orchid, is a miniature classic with the most beguiling ecology.

Calypso bulbosa is the favorite of many.

Cleistes divaricata, with its stature and bearing, epitomizes class in the orchid world.

Corallorhiza striata, striped coralroot, with its backlit fire, is never forgotten once seen.

Platanthera ciliaris is the cream of the fringed orchids with its vivid orange lips and eyelashes.

Arethusa bulbosa, the rosy-pink dragon, is the most exquisitely beautiful of all single-flowered orchids (according to Morris and Eames 1929) and a favorite of many.

Platanthera psycodes, the purple fringed-orchid, has the charm of lavender butterflies.

Goodyera pubescens, rattlesnake plantain, with its superb jewel leaves, provides a twelve-month bonus.

Listera caurina, with its abode of giant dark firs and tiny green, evokes unforgettable wilderness.

APPENDIX 4

Identification Synopsis

To assist readers in the identification of all orchids north of Florida and Mexico, a concise summary of identification aids as well as distribution and months of bloom is provided below. Exact dates of bloom at extreme locations are not given.

Amerorchis rotundifolia. Mostly cold, wet evergreen forests and bogs, limestone barrens across Canada, from Newfoundland to Alaska, to extreme northern Minnesota and extreme northern Maine. June and July. To 30 cm (12 in.), single basal leaf, loose raceme of up to 12 white flowers, three-lobed lip spotted with purple. Forma *beckettiae* has a pure white lip with no purple spotting or bands. Forma *lineata* has confluent purple lines on the lip. Unmistakable.

Aplectrum hyemale. Mostly rich, deciduous open woods, especially beech-sugar maple, southern Ontario and Québec, Vermont, New York to Minnesota, south to extreme northern Arkansas, Alabama, and Georgia, Ohio River valley and mid-Appalachians. May and June. To 50 cm (20 in.), single basal leaf in winter, white-ribbed above, purplish below (withered in summer), loose raceme of 12 or more creamy white flowers with mauve tints.

Arethusa bulbosa. Mostly sphagnous bogs, wooded and open meadows, Newfoundland to Minnesota through Great Lakes region. May and June. To 40 cm (16 in.), single large bright rose flower with erect sepals and petals arching over down-curved, wavy lip, marked with white and deeper pink-purple, and yellow crest. Unmistakable.

Calopogon barbatus. Mostly wet pinelands on coastal plain from North Carolina to Mississippi. February to April. To 40 cm (16 in.), loose raceme of about six mostly light pink flowers, opening simultaneously. Confused with *C. multiflorus,* but lighter color, earlier bloom on average, and wider basal part of petals.

Calopogon multiflorus. Mostly wet pinelands and meadows on coastal plain from Florida to Mississippi. March and April. To 30 cm (12 in.), loose raceme of more than 12 deeper pink flowers, opening quickly and simultaneously. Confused with *C. barbatus,* but more vivid flowers and narrower petals.

Calopogon oklahomensis. Mostly in sandy-loamy prairies of eastern Oklahoma, Arkansas, eastern Kansas, southwestern Missouri, eastern Texas, and western Louisiana. Previously included in *C. tuberosus,* but differs in forked corm, grooved flower bud, lateral sepals reflexed backward, fragrance, and in blooming about three weeks (early May) ahead of *C. tuberosus,* in drier terrain.

Calopogon pallidus. Mostly open pinelands and meadows on coastal plain from Virginia to Florida and Mississippi. March to May. Open successfully and more slowly than *C. barbatus* and *C. multiflorus.* To 50 cm (20 in.), loose raceme of about 12 pale pink or white flowers. Distinguished by broad sepals that reflex backward and narrow lateral petals that project forward; white flowers distinctive.

Calopogon tuberosus. Mostly open wet, boggy meadows, from Newfoundland and eastern Minnesota to Florida and Louisiana. March to August, depending on latitude. To 120 cm (48 in.), tallest of grass-pinks, loose raceme of up to 24 medium pink flowers, opening successively and more slowly than other species. Only *Calopogon* species in northern states.

Calypso bulbosa. Mostly coniferous bogs and forests, from Newfoundland to Alaska, across Canada, plus extreme northern New England and immediate vicinity of Great Lakes. April to June. To 20 cm (8 in.), single basal leaf, and single pink flower with gold beard on white apron (lip), showy ribbonlike sepals and petals wave above the lip. The eastern variety *americana* occurs well inland from the Rockies to Alaska as well as eastward to Newfoundland, mostly in Canada. Forma *rosea* has flowers with pink or pale rose lips. The distinctive western variety *occidentalis* is restricted mostly to coastal northern California, northern Idaho, north to British Columbia, and has whitish hairs instead of yellow and a purple spotted or blotched apron. Unmistakable.

Cephalanthera austiniae. Mostly dry or moist coniferous woods, in a narrow arc from Sierras of central California to northern Idaho. June and July. Up to 60 cm (24 in.), saprophyte, entire plant white, with loose raceme of up to 20 white flowers, and bright yellow spot on lip. Unmistakable.

Cleistes bifaria. Mostly open pine-oak woodlands and meadows, on Cumberland Plateau and adjacent mountains of West Virginia, western Virginia and North Carolina, eastern Kentucky and eastern Tennessee; in addition, pine savannas on coastal plain from North Carolina to Louisiana. Originally thought restricted to interior plateau region but now apparently coexists with *C. divaricata* on coastal plain. April to June. To 60 cm (24 in.), single pale pink tubular flower, very similar to *C. divaricata,* but smaller flower (much shorter lip), paler color, slightly shorter column, different fragrance (vanilla), and earlier bloom.

Cleistes divaricata. Mostly pine savannas on coastal plain from New Jersey to northeastern Florida. April to June. To 70 cm (28 in.), single pink tubular flower, lip veined in purple, with yellow crest, flanked by long (5 cm/2 in.), erect and spreading, mahogany sepals. Distinguished from *C. bifaria* as indicated under that new species, otherwise unmistakable.

Coeloglossum viride. Mostly moist woods, evergreen and deciduous (also meadows and swamps further north), from Newfoundland, across Canada to Alaska, south to Great Lakes region and North Carolina in Appalachians, Colorado in Rockies. April to July, long bloom season due to persistence of floral parts, as in some other green platantheras. To 70 cm (28 in.), loose or dense spike of up to 30, small, greenish, hooded flowers tinged reddish at base of lip, with long floral bracts. The long bract subtending each floret is distinctive. The typical variety is circumpolar with shorter bracts, and mostly Eurasian in distribution. Variety *virescens* is North America's long-bracted green orchid. Unmistakable.

Corallorhiza maculata. Mostly dry or moist evergreen, deciduous, or mixed forests, Newfoundland to British Columbia, south to mountains of California, Rockies to Arizona and New Mexico, and Appalachians to North Carolina, along with the Lakes region. May to September, long season. To 80 cm (32 in.), saprophytic, leafless, up to 40 flowers, variable in color from red-purple to light brownish yellow, with white lip, spotted crimson or magenta. Color forms include an all yellow with unspotted white lip. Unmistakable.

Corallorhiza mertensiana. Moist evergreen forests of Pacific Northwest from extreme northwestern California through most of British Columbia, south to northern Idaho and western Montana and Wyoming. June and July. To 60 cm (24 in.), up to 40 colorful, mostly red-purple flowers with elongated, erect yellowish column and elongated sepals and petals, the lip streaked with claret or uniformly pigmented. Unmistakable.

Corallorhiza odontorhiza. Mostly rich deciduous (beech-sugar maple) or mixed woods, southern Maine to southern Wisconsin, south to Louisiana and Georgia, mostly in mountains. August and September. To 20 cm (8 in.), very inconspicuous, up to 15 pendent, green and purplish flowers with purple-spotted white lip; mostly unopen or half-open (self-fertilized). Slightly similar to *C. wisteriana* (spring coralroot), but smaller and blooms late in the summer and early autumn. Flower parts of *C. maculata* flare wide open on a much larger plant.

Corallorhiza striata. Mostly evergreen or mixed forests, dry or moist, local and scattered in most areas from Great Lakes region to British Columbia and northern California, with outposts in Rockies south to New Mexico, locally abundant in the upper Great Lakes region on limestone pavement. May and June. To 50 cm (20 in.), raceme of up to 35 whitish florets, peppermint-striped red-purple on all petals and sepals, pigment coalesces into solid color on apex of lip. Unmistakable.

Corallorhiza trifida. Mostly aspen-spruce forests, in subarctic Canada from Newfoundland to Alaska, further south in cedar swamps and evergreen woods, to New England and Great Lakes region, also south in Rockies to New Mexico. May and July. To 30 cm (12 in.), raceme of up to 20 yellow-green flowers with contrasting white lip (spotted only in far northern Canada). Unmistakable.

Corallorhiza wisteriana. Mostly deciduous woods in the southeastern United States, with disjunct populations in the Rockies. December in Florida to April and May northward to August in West. To 30 cm (12 in.), raceme of up to 25 yellowish brown to reddish purple stem and flower, and white lip faintly spotted purple, the sepals and petals connive over the lip. Could be confused only with *C. maculata,* but is smaller, paler, with fainter spotting, convergent tepals, and earlier blooming.

Cypripedium acaule. Mostly dry or moist pine woods and open deciduous woods, in northeastern United States and highlands of Appalachia, Great Lakes region (bogs and dunes), and Newfoundland through northern Ontario. May to July (far north). To 40 cm (16 in.), basal pair of opposite leaves and scape with single, showy, large, deep pink, pendent pouch. Unmistakable.

Cypripedium arietinum. Mostly cold cedar-bogs and swamps from northern New England, Québec and Ontario, south through immediate vicinity of Great Lakes region, becoming locally common in jack pine forests and low sand dune areas where limestone is prevalent. Late May and June. To 30 cm (12 in.), with distinctive, small conical white pouch with purple reticulations. Unmistakable.

Cypripedium californicum. Mostly along mountain streams and serpentine seepages in northern California and southwestern Oregon, in shade or sun. May to early July, depending on altitude. To 120 cm (48 in.), very tall, multiflowered stem, up to 21 pure white pouches, from axils of upper leaves. Unmistakable.

Cypripedium candidum. Mostly wet meadows and prairies, marly fens, in open sun, formerly a much less restricted range, now mostly extreme northern Ohio, northern Illinois, southern Michigan, southern Wisconsin, and southern Minnesota, to eastern Nebraska and northern Missouri. Mid-May and early June. To 40 cm (16 in.), a polished white, egg-shaped pouch, with interior purple veining and rim dots. Unmistakable.

Cypripedium fasciculatum. Mostly evergreen forests, adjacent to streams, on slopes, locally in northern California, southwestern Oregon and widely separate localities in northern Idaho, southwestern Montana, and western Wyoming. April to June and early July, depending on altitude. To 20 cm (8 in.), two oversized, opposite, midstem leaves, and up to four purplish brown to greenish, small, drooping flowers (pouches) in a short, crowded raceme that appears to be weighted down, almost wilted. Unmistakable.

Cypripedium guttatum. Mostly open wooded slopes and banks, in narrow arc along Arctic Circle from Canada's Northwest Territory, northern Yukon, to central and southeast Alaska (Kenai Peninsula). June and July. To 30 cm (12 in.), white, with irregular purple spots and blotches on pouch and all sepals and petals. Unmistakable.

Cypripedium kentuckiense. Mostly wooded floodplains, marshes, and seeps from Kentucky to Arkansas. April and May. To 90 cm (36 in.), more robust than other yellows, with larger opening, and larger (over 5 cm/2 in.), blunt, creamcolored pouch. Formerly confused with large yellow (*C. parviflorum*), but size, shape, and pale pouch color distinctive.

Cypripedium montanum. Mostly evergreen forests on mountain slopes, moist or dry, sun or shade, from extreme southeastern Alaska to California, east to Alberta and Wyoming. May to July, depending on altitude. To 70 cm (28 in.), one to three showy flowers with white lip pouch and interior streaks of purple, showy mahogany sepals and petals distinctive. Unmistakable.

Cypripedium parviflorum. Mostly rich, moist, open deciduous or mixed woods from Newfoundland across Canada to the Yukon and British Columbia, south to eastern Washington and Oregon, scattered through Rockies, and eastern United States, away from the coastal plain. Variety *makasin* has a northern distribution in deep cedar swamps, variety *parviflorum* has a southern distribution, and variety *pubescens* is the most widely distributed. April to July, depending on the latitude. To 80 cm (32 in.), leafy, with yellowish green sepals and petals (dark brown in variety *makasin*), and rich yellow lip pouch, spotted inside with maroon. A diverse species with several hybrids that can be confusing (see Chapter 37).

Cypripedium passerinum. Mostly open coniferous forest slopes and gravel outwashes in northern Canada from James Bay northwest through most of Alaska, including most of Alberta. June and July. To 35 cm (14 in.), leafy stem, with small white pouch, green dorsal sepal almost shutting off pouch opening, lateral petals narrow, flat, straight out and pure white. Unmistakable.

Cypripedium reginae. Mostly edges of open wet cedar-spruce-tamarack swamps and bogs rather than deep shade where it peters out, Newfoundland across extreme southern Canada to Manitoba, south in Appalachians to North Carolina, and from Pennsylvania westward to Great Lakes region and Missouri. To 90 cm (36 in.), tall, leafy stem, and one or two showy, globular flowers, white lip pouch suffused in various shades of rosy pink, large snow-white sepals and petals show off lip pouch. Unmistakable.

Cypripedium yatabeanum. Mostly open slopes and meadows facing the sea, Kodiak Island, and Aleutians in Alaska. June and July. To 30 cm (12 in.), two sub-opposite basal leaves, as in *C. guttatum*, with yellowish green, or creamy lip pouch marked with blotches of tan and brown, lateral petals spotted with brownish purple. Unmistakable.

Dactylorhiza aristata. Mostly open meadows and slopes in Alaska peninsula, Kodiak Island, and the Aleutian Islands. June and early July. To 40 cm (16 in.), three or four green leaves, densely flowered raceme of up to 30 magenta flowers, marked with purple spots and streaks. Variety *kodiakensis* with purple markings on leaves, and its forma *perbracteata* with large purple bracts and no flowers.

Dactylorhiza cf. *fuchsii.* Mostly open shores of lake and river in Timmins, Ontario, only North American site. July. To 60 cm (24 in.), up to eight mottled leaves, dense raceme of up to 50 magenta-pink flowers, marked with purple lines. Unmistakable.

Dactylorhiza praetermissa. Mostly meadow in Tilt Cove, Newfoundland, only North American site. July. To 50 cm (20 in.), five unspotted leaves, dense cylinder of up to 50 magenta-pink flowers, marked with darker spots and lines and subtended by long bracts.

Deiregyne durangensis (synonym *Spiranthes durangensis*). A Mexican species of limited distribution in extreme southwestern Texas in the Chisos Mountains of Big Bend National Park, at higher altitudes in rocky areas with some moisture. May through July. To 40 cm (16 in.), two or three leaves absent at anthesis, more than 12 rather large and spectacular flowers with the look of a deflexed *Spiranthes* species, white with a pink flush and stripes of green. Unmistakable.

Dichromanthus cinnabarinus (synonym *Spiranthes cinnabarinus*). A Mexican species that only reaches Big Bend National Park in extreme southwestern Texas, on open grassy slopes. July to October. To 50 cm (20 in.) with three or four lower leaves and a short, dense spike of up to 40 or so bright red or vermilion *Spiranthes*-like flowers uniformly reflexed at the tips, and sporting a gold lip tipped with red. Unmistakable.

Epidendrum conopseum. Epiphytic from extreme coastal southwestern North Carolina, through most of northern half of Florida, and locally west to Louisiana on the coastal plain. Throughout the year sporadically, but mostly in autumn. To 30 cm (12 in.) with two or three dark green leaves and a raceme of 12 to 18 small, spindly yellow-green flowers that are very hard to see from the ground, perched on large limbs of deciduous trees in company with the resurrection fern (*Polypodium polypodioides*), cousin to the northern rock polypody, which makes it even harder to see. Easy to identify as it is the only epiphytic orchid north of Florida.

Epipactis atrorubens. Discovered in 1990 in a serpentine quarry in northern Vermont and nowhere else at this point. August. To 30 cm (12 in.), up to 20 flowers reported to be cranberry-red. A second epipactis import from Europe.

Epipactis gigantea. Mostly gravelly shores, sand-bars, springs, and seepages from Pacific Northwest and extreme southern British Columbia, east to Rockies, south to Mexico. April to July, depending on latitude and altitude. To 90 cm (36 in.), with loose raceme of well-spaced, up to 15 multicolored flowers (greenish yellow to rose, purple, and orange-brown), with unusual hinged, heart-shaped lip. Unmistakable.

Epipactis helleborine. Mostly moist or dry rocky evergreen woods, roadside ditches, river banks, shaded or partly shaded, in a wide band from New England to Great Lakes region, and scattered outposts across the country. July and August. To 90 cm (36 in.), up to ten *Cypripedium*-like leaves and 50 or more multicolored flowers (green, yellow, pink, and purple). Unmistakable.

Erythrodes querciticola. Springs and creek banks in moist heavily wooded forest long the Gulf coast of Mississippi, Louisiana, and eastern Texas, south through Florida. July and August, except through the year in southern Florida. To 30 cm (12 in.), from a leafy stem a raceme of a few to several dozen very small yellowish white flowers, the leafy stem reminful of the dayflower or tradescantia plant, and the flowers a little like habernaria.

Galearis spectabilis. Mostly rich deciduous woods in eastern United States from Maine west through the southern half of Great Lakes region to North Carolina, Tennessee, and Arkansas. April to June. To 35 cm (14 in.), two large, opposite, basal leaves, with up to 15 bicolored flowers in loose raceme, hooded, mauve sepals and petals, white lip, often in congested clumps. Forma *willeyi* has flowers a uniform pink throughout. Unmistakable.

Goodyera oblongifolia. Mostly coniferous, deciduous, or mixed woods, dry or moist from extreme northern Maine, southeastern Québec, skipping to western Great Lakes region, westward in narrow band to most of British Columbia, south in Cascades to Sierras in central California, and through Rockies to Arizona and New Mexico. August and September. To 45 cm (18 in.), basal rosette of three to seven green leaves with broken white center stripe, and loose or dense spike of up to 30 downy, green and white flowers. Unmistakable.

Goodyera pubescens. Mostly rich, rocky, evergreen or mixed woods, from Maine to Minnesota, south to Carolinas, west to Arkansas. Mostly July and August, earlier South. To 50 cm (20 in.), basal rosette of green leaves with wide white center stripe and narrow white reticulations or veins on both sides of center stripe, dense raceme of up to 80 downy, green and white globular-shaped flowers. Unmistakable.

Goodyera repens. Mostly cold, mossy, evergreen woods, from Newfoundland across Canada to Alaska, south through northern Great Lakes region, Appalachians to North Carolina and Rockies to New Mexico. July and August. To 25 cm (10 in.), basal rosette of leaves lacking white center stripe, but heavily reticulated with bright silver-white, with an open or dense spike of up to 40 downy, white flowers. Can be confused with *G. tesselata* near southern edge of range, where some plants appear to be hybrids and cause much difficulty in identification. Further north, unmistakable.

Goodyera tesselata. Mostly rich evergreen or mixed woods, moist or dry, Newfoundland to Ontario, south to New England, New York and northern Great Lakes region. July and August. To 35 cm (14 in.), pale blue-green rosette, with paler reticulations and no center stripe, loose or dense spike of up to 40 narrow, downy, white flowers. Can be confused with *G. repens* where the two species overlap and hybridize.

Habenaria quinqueseta. Mostly low, wet pinelands and flatwoods on coastal plain from southeastern South Carolina to all of Florida, west to extreme southeastern Texas. August to January. To 60 cm (24 in.), three to seven ovate leaves along stem, loose, spindly raceme of up to 15 mostly white flowers, strongly tripartite lip with linear middle division and filiform lateral divisions, lateral petals bipartite, filiform and curved, sepals conventionally shaped and green, and long spur (to 10 cm/4 in.). Unmistakable.

Habenaria repens. Mostly semiaquatic, floating masses on water, swamps, and roadside ditches on coastal plain from southeastern North Carolina to Florida and west to southeastern Texas. April to December, sporadically. To 50 cm

(20 in.), dense raceme of up to 50 yellow-green flowers, miniature edition of *H. quinqueseta,* all parts significantly smaller and green. Unmistakable.

Hexalectris nitida. A Mexican species ranging into extreme southwestern Texas in the Big Bend area, on shaded, rocky oak canyon floors. Mostly July and August. To 30 cm (12 in.), leafless and saprophytic, with a loose or dense raceme of 20 or more small flowers with reflexed tips, purplish white with purple stripes and purple-red on tip of lip. Like a miniature *H. revoluta.*

Hexalectris revoluta. A Mexican species confined to the Big Bend area of Texas, in oak canyons at higher altitudes. July and August. To 50 cm (20 in.), leafless and saprophytic, with a raceme of a dozen or fewer pale brownish purple, loose and widely spaced, striped flowers, and a purple-red tip of the lip. Similar to *H. nitida* but half again larger, especially lip petal.

Hexalectris spicata. Mostly open deciduous woods and streambanks, Maryland and Virginia to northern half of Florida, west to southeastern Missouri, central Texas, into northeastern Mexico and back up to southeastern Arizona. April in South to August in North. To 80 cm (32 in.), saprophyte, loose raceme of up to 25 showy, flowers, all floral parts golden-brown and strongly striped red-purple, sepals and petals flare open. Unmistakable.

Hexalectris warnockii. A Mexican species reaching extreme southwestern Texas and extreme southeastern Arizona, typically in the dappled shade of oak forests beside rock, dried up creek-bed canyons. July and August, dependent on the summer monsoons. To 30 cm (12 in.), leafless and saprophytic, with a raceme of eight or ten loose purple and cream flowers, the lip of which is deeply lobed and incurved above the middle lobe, all flower parts deep maroon except the lip, which is white and yellow with maroon markings.

Isotria medeoloides. Mostly moist, rich deciduous and mixed woods, scattered in isolated stations, Maine to Michigan and southwestern Ontario, south to Missouri and Georgia. May and June. To 25 cm (10 in.), pale, glaucous green stem with whorl of five leaves at top, one or two small yellowish green, tubular flowers with crested, greenish white lip, on short pedicels. Plant similar to sterile Indian cucumber-root (*Medeola virginiana*), but stem thick, glaucous, and hollow, while latter is thin and wiry. Unmistakable in flower.

Isotria verticillata. Mostly deciduous and mixed woods, Maine to Michigan, south to Florida and Louisiana. April to June, depending on latitude. To 30 cm (12 in.), whorl of five leaves at top of thick, hollow, purplish stem, with single greenish yellow, tubular flower, streaked purple inside with fleshy ridge, long (5 cm/2 in.), spreading, purplish sepals frame the gaping flower. Unmistakable.

Liparis liliifolia. Mostly mixed deciduous woods and streambanks, especially open second-growth woods, extreme western New England to southeastern Minnesota, south to Arkansas and extreme northern Gulf states. May and June. To 25 cm (62 in.), two opposite, sheathing, basal leaves, loose raceme of up to 30 flowers, dominated by large, translucent, pale purple, shield-shaped lip. Unmistakable.

Liparis loeselii. Mostly wet meadows, seepages, sandy stream edges, Nova Scotia to Minnesota, south to Pennsylvania and Illinois, Appalachians to Georgia, and several isolated stations in nearby states. June and July. To 25 cm (10 in.), two basally, sheathing leaves, loose raceme of up to 15 very small greenish yellow flowers with larger wedge-shaped or shield-shaped lip. Unmistakable.

Listera auriculata. Mostly in sand under alder thickets at edge of streams, distinctive habitat, Newfoundland, Québec, Ontario, south to Maine, extreme northern New Hampshire, and Upper Michigan. June and July. To 20 cm (8 in.), two opposite, midstem, ovate leaves, loose raceme of up to 20 very small translucent green flowers, dominated by oblong lip, cleft at the tip, and diagnostic, incurved "auricles" at base of lip, curving around base of column. Similar to *L. borealis* except for incurving auricles at base of lip, and northwestern range of *L. borealis*. Some overlap in Ontario.

Listera australis. Mostly open sphagnous bogs in North, and densely shaded, wet, deciduous woods in South, mostly southern, but from extreme southern Québec, north-central Vermont, New York and on coastal plain to Florida and extreme eastern Texas. January in Florida to July in North. To 20 cm (8 in.), loose raceme of up to 25 tiny, greenish to mostly purplish flowers and deeply forked lip petal, deepest of any twayblade, which distinguishes it from *L. cordata.*

Listera borealis. Mostly moist, mossy, coniferous forests of northwestern Canada, from extreme western Newfoundland to Alaska, south in Rockies to Colorado. June and July. To 20 cm (8 in.), loose raceme of up to 20 small green flowers, oblong, translucent green lip, moderately cleft, with basal auricles diverging away from column, instead of converging around it, which distinguishes it from *L. auriculata,* as do its Pacific Northwest distribution and habitat preference.

Listera caurina. Mostly cool, dark, coniferous forests of the Pacific Northwest, British Columbia to extreme northwestern Wyoming, and extreme northwestern California along coastal mountains. June to August, depending on altitude. To 30 cm (12 in.), loose raceme of up to 25 small, rich green flowers with two darker green stripes the length of lip that end as minute, basal, black spots. Most rounded lip tip of all listeras, with only slightest notch in some specimens. Superficially similar to *L. convallarioides,* but essentially unmistakable.

Listera convallarioides. Mostly wet depressions in rich coniferous woods, Newfoundland to British Columbia, south to extreme northern New England, northern Great Lakes region, and south in mountains to northern California, and Rockies to Colorado. June to August. To 35 cm (14 in.), with loose raceme of up to 20 small, translucent, watery green flowers, lip narrowed at base and widened at apex, with shallow notch at tip. Superficially similar to some other listeras but habitat and lip shape should distinguish it.

Listera cordata. Mostly cold, wooded, sphagnum bogs of cedar, spruce, and tamarack, or coniferous forests, Newfoundland to Alaska, south in coastal mountains to northwestern California, in Rockies to New Mexico, and Appalachians to North Carolina. June and July. To 25 cm (10 in.), with loose or dense raceme of up to 25 tiny, greenish or purplish flowers with forked lips second only to *L. australis* in depth.

Listera ovata. Mostly edges of wet, deciduous or mixed woods in one station in Ontario. June and July. To 60 cm (24 in.), with loose or dense raceme of over 50 greenish yellow flowers, deeply cleft lip, linear at base and dilated at apex. Most robust *Listera* species, taller, and with larger flowers than others. Unmistakable.

Listera smallii. Mostly moist, deeply wooded mountain slopes and ravines, especially under rhododendrons in shade, northwestern New Jersey to extreme northern Georgia, in narrow strip along Appalachians. June and July. To 25 cm (10 in.), loose raceme of up to 15 brownish green flowers, and brown lip that forks into two rounded widely angled lobes. Unmistakable.

Malaxis bayardii. Mostly dry pine or oak barrens, shale barrens, rocky hilltops, southeastern Massachusetts (Cape Cod), southeastern New York and on coastal plain to Virginia, also to mountains of North Carolina. July and August. To 25 cm (10 in.), with single sheathing, midstem, ovate leaf, and loose, relatively long raceme of up to 50 relatively long-lasting, yellowish green flowers, on relatively long pedicels. Distinguished from *M. unifolia* by longer pedicels, longer inflorescence (not flattened at top like *M. unifolia*), more prominent basal lip lobes, and drier habitat.

Malaxis brachypoda. Mostly mossy, wooded swamps, often in depressions on footpaths and deer trails, in shade, while further north in open sun of wet meadows, from western Newfoundland, across Canada to southeastern Alaska, south to northern New England, New York and Great Lakes region, and a few isolated sites in Far West. July and August. To 20 cm (8 in.), with single, sheathing, basal leaf, and up to 50 very tiny, greenish white flowers, widely spaced on spike, with minute, broadly triangular lip. Unmistakable.

Malaxis corymbosa. A Mexican species barely ranging into mountains of extreme southeastern Arizona, at relatively high altitudes with three other *Malaxis* species, in mixed forests along creeks. August. To 30 cm (12 in.), single leaf, like *Maianthemum* leaves, with up to 50 small, crowded, green flowers on classically shaped, flat-topped corymb at top of long stem; lip heart-shaped. *Malaxis unifolia* has three-lobed lip with basal auricles, and its inflorescence is much less uniformly flat-topped than that of *M. corymbosa*.

Malaxis diphyllos. Mostly sandy soil behind beaches in Aleutian Islands and Kodiak Island. July. To 30 cm (12 in.), with two opposite, basal leaves, dense spike of up to 100 yellow flowers, nonresupinate lip. Unmistakable.

Malaxis paludosa. Mostly sunny, open sphagnum bogs in Alaska and Yukon, or wet woods further south, in British Columbia, east to western Ontario. June and July. To 15 cm (6 in.), small, fragile plant, two to four small, fleshy, basal leaves, spike of up to 35 dense yellow-green flowers, lip tiny, nonresupinate, and ovate, with several dark green stripes. Unmistakable.

Malaxis porphyrea (synonym *M. ehrenbergii*). A Mexican species extending into southern Arizona and New Mexico mountains, at high altitudes, in cool mixed and coniferous forests, often associated with *M. soulei* and *M. tenuis*. August. To 45 cm (18 in.), with a single sheathing leaf on lower half of stem, similar to many other *Malaxis* species, and a tall, slender raceme of up to 100 very tiny red-purple flowers. Unmistakable.

Malaxis soulei (synonym *M. macrostachya*). A Mexican species extending into extreme southwestern Texas and southern New Mexico and Arizona mountains, at high altitudes, in edges of open mixed and coniferous forests, often near *M. porphyrea* and *M. tenuis*. August and September. To 40 cm (16 in.), with single sheathing leaf and tightly packed, closely appressed, spike of 50 to 100 tiny green to whitish flowers, lip uppermost. Looks like the common plantain weed of lawns. Unmistakable.

Malaxis spicata. Mostly damp, shaded, humusy forests (in Florida, swamps and floating logs), extreme southeastern Virginia and narrow coastal band to Florida and West Indies. July and August in North to January in Florida. To 40 cm (16 in.), two opposite green leaves (one larger than other) near base, loose raceme of up to 50 tiny, nonresupinate, multicolored flowers, greenish brown to reddish orange. Unmistakable.

Malaxis tenuis. A Mexican species reaching southwestern New Mexico and southeastern Arizona mountains, at high altitudes, in open, moist, mixed and coniferous forests. August and September. To 25 cm (10 in.), with single leaf near middle of stem, and cylinder of 30 or so long-pediceled, tiny green flowers, held straight out from the pedicels, the triangular lip petal uppermost and marked with four darker green stripes. Unmistakable.

Malaxis unifolia. Mostly wet, boggy, evergreen and mixed woods, but drier and more open situations further north and in mountains, Newfoundland to extreme southeastern Manitoba, south to extreme eastern Texas and northern Florida. March in South to August in North. To 40 cm (16 in.), with loose spike of up to 50 green flowers, which becomes flattened and congested near top of stem. Distinguished from *M. bayardii* by flattened top, longer pedicels, and relatively shorter-lived flowers, indicated by more wilted flowers at bottom of inflorescence during anthesis.

Piperia candida. Mostly coniferous and mixed forests, open sun or shade, northwestern California north to extreme southeastern Alaska. June to August, depending on altitude. To 60 cm (24 in.), with two *Clintonia*-like nearly basal leaves, sometimes disappearing at anthesis, spike of up to 100 whitish flowers with greenish tints. The essentially white flowers and short spur should identify it.

Piperia colemanii. Mostly open coniferous forests and chaparral in sandy soil, endemic to California, in narrow strip from southern Sierras (Fresno County) to Cascades in extreme northern California (Siskiyou County). July. To 50 cm (20 in.), grasslike leaves wither at anthesis, spike with up to 100 tiny greenish flowers, very short spur (2 mm). Similar to *P. unalascensis*, but has shorter-than-lip spur, is scentless, and is much more uncommon in distribution.

Piperia cooperi. Mostly chaparral-covered hilltops in extreme southern California. April and May. To 90 cm (36 in.), long, basal leaves usually wither at anthesis, spike of up to 100 squat, greenish flowers. Habitat and distribution distinguish it from other piperias.

Piperia elegans. Mostly coastal from southern California to British Columbia, in various habitats, mostly open coastal cliffs and bluffs and open forest inland. May to September. To 80 cm (32 in.), two or three long basal leaves, spike of up to 100 greenish white flowers, spike more dense near coast, the predominantly whitish flowers largest (but still small) of all piperias, spur up to 13 mm. Distinguished from *P. transversa* by vertical spur instead of horizontal, but this does not always hold up.

Piperia elongata. Mostly open mixed or oak forest in North, and chaparral in South, and roadcuts, most of California to British Columbia. May and June in South, July and August in North. To 90 cm (36 in.), basal leaves wither at anthesis, loose or dense spike of up to 100 uniformly green flowers. The green flowers distinguish it from *P. elegans,* and the more narrowly triangular lip from *P. michaelii.*

Piperia leptopetala. Mostly open mixed forest on hillsides and flat terrain alike, especially with poison oak, endemic to California and widely distributed, but rare. May and June. To 40 cm (16 in.), open spike of up to 50 pale green flowers with nearly linear sepals and petals, giving feathery appearance to inflorescence.

Piperia michaelii. Mostly coastal scrub, inland oak woods, grassy hillsides, endemic to California. Long season, May to August. To 50 cm (20 in.), the spike carries up to 60 greenish to yellowish green flowers with wider ovate lip than *P. elongata,* long spur usually under 15 mm. The whitish flowers of *P. elegans* separate it.

Piperia transversa. Mostly dry, open woods of mixed and coniferous forest, road banks, in sun or partial shade, California north to British Columbia. June to August. To 40 cm (16 in.), spike of up to 90 whitish flowers with greenish midvein and yellowish tints, long (11 mm), horizontally (not always) directed spur. Confused with *P. elegans* whose spur is usually vertically oriented.

Piperia unalascensis. Mostly open mixed and coniferous forest, road banks, roadsides, in sun or partial shade, mountains of southern California, north to Alaska's Aleutian Islands, east to Ontario, Québec, and Newfoundland, widest range of any *Piperia* species. May to July, depending on altitude and latitude. To 70 cm (28 in.), spike of up to 100 tiny, well-spaced, yellowish greenish flowers, spur slightly shorter or longer (2 to 4 mm) than lip.

Piperia yadonii. Mostly open pine forests and chaparral, part sun and part shade, a rare endemic of northern Monterey County in California, below 100 meters (320 feet) altitude. July. To 50 cm (20 in.), with loose or dense spike of up to 100 bicolored, green and white flowers, petals falcate and connivent at tips, green with wide white outer edge, dorsal sepal green with white edges, triangular lip white and deflexed.

Platanthera blephariglottis. Mostly quaking bogs in sun, Newfoundland to Michigan, Pennsylvania, and New Jersey (southern variety *conspicua* to Florida and extreme eastern Texas on coastal plain). July and August. To 60 cm (24 in.), mostly dense raceme of up to 50 bright white flowers, heavily fringed, white, tongue-shaped lip, with long spur. Unmistakable.

Platanthera brevifolia. A Mexican immigrant, mostly in extreme southwestern New Mexico, in high altitudes where some moisture exists along dry creeks and neighboring woods. July and August. To 60 cm (24 in.), with three to five small bractlike leaves sheathing the base, and several dozen greenish flowers (sometimes with yellowish lips) beginning low down on the thick raceme. The long, dense raceme and the long, linear lip (which does not widen at the base), as well as the restricted distribution, will identify it. Formerly a variety of *P. sparsiflora.*

Platanthera chapmanii (formerly considered a hybrid between *P. cristata* and *P. ciliaris*). On coastal plain in wet meadows and pinelands from extreme southeastern Georgia, northern Florida, to extreme eastern Texas. July and August. Intermediate in size between *P. ciliaris* and *P. cristata.*

Platanthera chorisiana. Mostly open wet meadows and sphagnum bogs, extreme northwestern Washington, north along coastal British Columbia to extreme southeastern Alaska and Aleutian Islands. July and August. To 20 cm (8 in.), spike of up to 20 tiny, greenish flowers, ball-shaped (flowers barely crack open except lateral sepals, which partially spread). Unmistakable.

Platanthera ciliaris. Mostly bogs, meadows, and open woods, extreme southeastern Massachusetts to southern Michigan, south to northern Florida and extreme eastern Texas. July and August in North, September in South. To 90 cm (36 in.), mostly dense raceme of up to 60 bright yellowish orange flowers, heavily fringed, two-toned orange, tongue-shaped lip and long spur. Unmistakable.

Platanthera clavellata. Mostly wet woods, wooded swamps, wet meadows and ditches, Newfoundland, southern Ontario, to eastern Minnesota, south to Gulf states. July and August. To 40 cm (16 in.), one or two stem leaves below the middle, raceme of up to 15 yellowish green flowers, an oblong and truncated lip, long curved spur, bulbous at the tip, held angled below flower. Unmistakable

Platanthera cristata. Mostly wet meadows and open moist woods and edges, extreme southeastern Massachusetts, south on coastal plain to northern Florida and extreme eastern Texas. July and August. To 80 cm (32 in.), dense raceme of up to 80 small deep orange, fringed flowers, less than half the size of *P. ciliaris,* and deeper orange. Unmistakable.

Platanthera dilatata. Mostly bogs, marshes, and wet meadows, Newfoundland across most of Canada to southeastern Alaska, Aleutian Islands and Kodiak Island, south in mountains to central California, and Rockies to northern New Mexico, and New England, New York, and Great Lakes region. June and July. To 120 cm (48 in.), dense spike of up to 100 white flowers, strongly fragrant. Unmistakable.

Platanthera flava. Mostly wet woods, wet meadows, and ditches, Newfoundland to Minnesota, south to central Florida, west to southeastern Texas. March in Florida to June through August northward, flower parts persist as they blacken. To 60 cm (24 in.), opening to dense spike of up to 50 small yellowish green flowers, down-curved lip petal has diagnostic tubercle or bump near middle. Unmistakable.

Platanthera grandiflora. Mostly open wet woods and ditches, Newfoundland to eastern Ontario, south to New England, Pennsylvania, and Appalachians to North Carolina. June and July. To 120 cm (48 in.), with lax to densely flowered raceme of up to 60 pinkish purple flowers with tripartite fringed lip. Raceme much less dense and fewer-flowered than *P. psycodes,* flowers larger. Key diagnostic is shape of spur opening: round in *P. grandiflora,* horizontal or a transverse dumb-bell in *P. psycodes.* Several hybrids can be confusing (see Chapter 37.)

Platanthera hookeri. Mostly rich evergreen or mixed woods, Newfoundland to southeastern Manitoba, south to extreme northwestern New Jersey and extreme northeastern Iowa. June. To 40 cm (16 in.), two opposite, basal, rounded green leaves, raceme of up to 50 lax or densely flowered yellowish green flowers, shaped like an ice tong in profile (diagnostic), caused by overhanging dorsal sepal and upcurving lip petal. Leaves not as shiny as *P. orbiculata,* and half their size.

Platanthera huronensis. Mostly wet meadows, shores, ditches, or cedar swamps, Newfoundland to Alaska, south to Great Lakes region and mountains to northern California. June to August. To 120 cm (48 on.), tall spike of up to 100 green or yellow-green flowers, very robust in part sun, loose and fewer flowered in deep shade. Variable and causing much confusion in identification, but any tall, robust plant that mimics cornstalks is surely this species.

Platanthera hyperborea. Mostly wet woods, boggy margins, open wet meadows, ditches, Newfoundland across Canada northwest to most of Alaska, south in mountains to northern California, Rockies to New Mexico, and New England to Minnesota through Great Lakes region. June to August, depending on altitude and latitude. To 40 cm (16 in.), with spike of up to 50 loose or dense yellowish green to green flowers. Variable and difficult to separate from other green platantheras.

Platanthera integra. Mostly wet meadows, bogs, pinelands, New Jersey to central Florida, west to extreme southeastern Texas. July and August, blooming with other two orange fringed-orchids. To 60 cm (24 in.), with dense, neatly packed raceme of up to 60 small golden-yellow (not orange) flowers, hood formed from dorsal sepal and petals, while lateral sepals spread out to side, lip essentially entire but with definite serrated edge. Unmistakable.

Platanthera integrilabia. Mostly deep shade of wet deciduous woods, in restricted range, extreme southeastern Kentucky, southwestern North Carolina, northwestern Georgia, eastern Tennessee, northern Alabama, and extreme northeastern Mississippi, mostly small parts of six states. August and September. To

60 cm (24 in.), loose raceme of up to 15 white flowers with finely serrated lip and very long (5 cm/2 in.) spur, usually few plants bloom in any given population. Unmistakable.

Platanthera lacera. Mostly moist meadows, bogs, open wooded swamps, or any field, Newfoundland to extreme southeastern Manitoba, south to Georgia and extreme northeastern Oklahoma. May in South to August in North. To 80 cm (32 in.), open or dense raceme of up to 40 whitish green or greenish white flowers, deeply fringed or lacerated lip tripartite, almost looking "ratty" or ragged compared to *P. leucophaea* and other fringed-orchids. Unmistakable.

Platanthera leucophaea. Mostly wet meadows, rich prairies, bog mats, northern Maine (one station), southern Ontario, Michigan, northwestern Ohio, northern Indiana, Illinois, southern Wisconsin. (Distribution mostly east of the Mississippi as distinguished from *P. praeclara*). June and July. To 100 cm (40 in.), loosely flowered raceme of up to 30 creamy white flowers with tripartite fringed lip. Long pedicellate ovaries and fewer flowers create a more open, airy inflorescence than other fringed-orchids. Creamy color distinctive. Unmistakable.

Platanthera limosa. A Mexican species reaching southeastern Arizona and southwestern New Mexico, at higher altitudes, in moist pockets of forests and along mountain brooks. June to September. To 1.5 m (6 ft.) but usually much shorter, a very leafy stem of 12 or more leaves become bracts above the lower stem, and a densely or occasionally sparsely flowered raceme of green flowers, with a long spur about twice as long as the lip petal. The flowers often bi-toned, a contrasting bright green and grayish green, which, combined with the diagnostic spur length, aids in identification. The distinctive bump at the base of lip needs a glass to see for certain. This species replaces *P. hyperborea* of the North.

Platanthera macrophylla. Mostly shaded evergreen and mixed woods, Newfoundland to extreme southern Ontario and Michigan, south to Pennsylvania and Appalachians to North Carolina. July. To 60 cm (24 in.), with two opposite, very large (average 20 × 15 cm/8 × 6 in.), shiny green, ground-hugging leaves, lax to dense raceme of up to 30 greenish white or whitish green flowers with long spurs on long pedicels. In profile, fanciful flower looks like an elf or gargoyle, with prominent column and drawn back sepals and petals. Leaves nearly twice as large and more round than in *P. orbiculata*, raceme carries twice as many flowers and spur is twice as long. Reddochs (1993), however, say distinguishable only by spur length: more than 28 mm in *P. macrophylla*, less than 28 mm in *P. orbiculata.*

Platanthera nivea. Mostly open bogs, wet meadows, and pinelands, from extreme southern New Jersey on coastal plain to Florida and extreme southeastern Texas. June in Florida to July and August northward. To 60 cm (24 in.), dense raceme of up to 50 nonresupinate, pure white flowers, and long spur. Up close, linear, upper lip deflects backward and is clasped behind at its base by the two twisting lateral sepals, an unusual deployment. Unmistakable.

Platanthera obtusata. Mostly cold, northern, wooded bogs, wet evergreen woods, and open birch-aspen groves further north, from Newfoundland, across all of wooded Canada to Alaska, south to northern New England, northern Great Lakes region, and in Rockies to Colorado. June and July. To 25 cm (10 in.), single basal, oblanceolate-blunt leaf, with raceme of up to 15 well-spaced, whitish green flowers, the narrow strap-shaped lip recurves backward toward stem. Unmistakable.

Platanthera orbiculata. Mostly shade of mixed and evergreen forests, Newfoundland to British Columbia, south to Washington, Great Lakes region, and Appalachians to North Carolina. July and August. To 50 cm (20 in.), two opposite, shiny, basal leaves (average 8 × 10 cm/3 × 4 in.), and raceme of up to 15 whitish green or greenish white flowers. *Platanthera macrophylla* has leaf twice as big and twice the number of flowers, but Reddochs (1993) say the two species are distinguishable, diagnostically, only by spur length: under 28 mm in *P. orbiculata* and more than 28 mm in *P. macrophylla.*

Platanthera pallida. Endemic to interdunal pitch pine hollows of eastern Long Island, New York. Late July to August. To 70 cm (28 in.), dense raceme of up to 100 small, cream-colored flowers. Similar to *P. cristata* and originally called pale cristata, but separated by recurved lip petal, reflexed lateral sepals, cream color, and habitat.

Platanthera peramoena. Mostly meadows, ditches, wet woods and mountain streamsides, extreme southern New Jersey, southern Ohio, west to southeast Missouri, south to northern Mississippi, and extreme northwestern Georgia. July and August. To 90 cm (36 in.), dense to loose raceme of up to 50 rose-purple flowers with tripartite lip not deeply lacerated, but with very shallow teeth on margins, and notch on front edge of widest lobe. Unmistakable.

Platanthera praeclara. Mostly wet prairie soils, from Minnesota and extreme eastern Dakotas and Nebraska to Missouri and Oklahoma. Distribution west of Mississippi River. June and July. To 100 cm (40 in.), short raceme of up to 20 loose creamy flowers. The diagnostic differences: longer spur (35 to 53 mm), shorter raceme and fewer flowers (under twenty usually) in *P. praeclara* compared to shorter spur (20 to 35 mm) and longer raceme of up to 30 flowers in *P. leucophaea.* Comparative distribution should resolve most of the problem.

Platanthera psycodes. Mostly low wet, swampy, shaded deciduous woods, and open wet meadows and ditches, Newfoundland to Minnesota, south to extreme northern New Jersey and Ohio, and Appalachians to North Carolina. July and August. To 100 cm (40 in.), raceme of up to 75 and more mostly dense lavender, red-purple, or purplish pink flowers. Very variable in flower size and color, usually smaller than *P. grandiflora,* and starts to bloom two weeks later. Key diagnostic is shape of spur opening: round in *P. grandiflora,* horizontal or a transverse dumb-bell in *P. psycodes.* You must get down to flower level and look head-on, otherwise flattened opening is not easily noted from a higher angle of view. Several hybrids (see Chapter 37).

Platanthera sparsiflora. Mostly wet meadows, hillsides, seepages and ditches, California (most common of only three green platantheras in California), to extreme southern Washington, also Utah, Arizona, and New Mexico. May to August, depending on altitude and latitude. To 80 cm (32 in.), with raceme of more than 100 green to yellowish green flowers, identified by a large column that fills more than half the hood, which is formed by dorsal sepal and lateral petals, also has linear lip, without dilation at base.

Platanthera stricta. Mostly wet meadows and along streams and ditches, southern Alaska and Aleutian Islands through British Columbia to extreme northern California, into Idaho and western Montana and Wyoming. To 90 cm (36 in.), with spike of up to 60 greenish flowers, and saccate spur about as long as the elliptic (narrow) lip petal. Distinguished from other varieties and forms of *P. hyperborea* complex by the saccate spur and lip shape (not dilated at base) but there are many examples of intergrades making it difficult to always pin it down.

Platanthera tipuloides. Mostly open wet meadows, in North America only in the western Aleutian Islands (also Japan and eastern Asia). July and August. To 20 cm (8 in.), with single lanceolate leaf, spike of up to 20 small yellow flowers, similar to those of the *P. hyperborea-dilatata* complex, but color, size, distribution, and habitat insure no identity problem.

Platanthera zothecina (synonym *P. sparsiflora*). Very restricted bog orchid found in northwestern Colorado (hanging gardens in Dinosaur National Park) near Moab, Utah, and extreme northeastern Arizona (Navajo reservation). Mostly July. Very similar to *P. sparsiflora,* identify by locations above.

Pogonia ophioglossoides. Mostly open wet meadows, bogs, and ditches, Newfoundland to eastern Minnesota, south to Florida and southeastern Texas. March in Florida to August northward. To 40 cm (16 in.), with single, elliptic leaf midway on stem, and one or two terminal rose-pink flowers, the lip spatulate-shape, fringed on all sides but deeply near apex, fleshy bearded crest near apex and yellow bristles behind it. Unmistakable.

Ponthieva racemosa. Mostly wet, shaded woods, streambanks and springs, extreme southeastern Virginia, to Florida (south in tropics), west to extreme southeastern Texas. September and October northward to February in southern Florida. To 60 cm (24 in.), basal rosette of three to eight large, elliptic, satiny leaves, raceme of up to 30 greenish white flowers with nonresupinate lip, sepals and petals striped with green. Long-pediceled, upward-facing flowers are unusual and unmistakable.

Pseudorchis straminea. Mostly vegetation in pockets between barren, broken limestone rocks, in extreme northern tip of Newfoundland and coastal Labrador (also Greenland, Iceland, and Eurasia). July. To 35 cm (14 in.), with three or four elliptic (narrow) leaves sheathing bottom of stem, spike of up to 50 yellowish green flowers, lip with three distinctive lobes that taper to a point at apex. Unmistakable.

Pteroglossaspis ecristata. Mostly dry, open pine barrens, and sandy palmetto fields, extreme southeastern North Carolina, along coast to Florida, west to southern Louisiana. July to September. To 170 cm (68 in.), two or three grasslike leaves to 70 cm (28 in.), raceme of up to 30 green and purple flowers, green hood of sepals and petals hides all but dark maroon lip edged in green. Flowers twisted on stem, as if peeking around it, easily viewed at eye level. Another unusual semitropical orchid of the Southeast. Unmistakable.

Schiedeella fauci-sanguinea (synonym *S. parasitica*). A Mexican immigrant, commonly called the red-spot ladies'-tresses. In rich humus of high coniferous forests on mountains of southwestern New Mexico, southeastern Arizona, and extreme southwestern Texas. June and July. To 30 cm (12 in.), with basal rosette of ovate leaves, absent at anthesis, and loose spike of up to a dozen small white flowers, marked with three pale green stripes on lip and a diagnostic red blotch in the interior center of the lip (as in a slashed throat), which requires getting down on all fours to see.

Spiranthes brevilabris. In open pinelands and meadows from southeastern North Carolina through Florida, west to southeastern Texas. February to May. To 40 cm (16 in.), three or four basal leaves at anthesis, and a spike of 30 or more pale yellowish flowers with a darker yellow center on the lips.

Spiranthes casei. Mostly drier roadcuts, roadsides, and pastures, sometimes moist; a colonizer of disturbed habitats from Nova Scotia to Canadian Shield of Ontario, south to extreme northern New England, upper Michigan and northern Wisconsin. Mid-August to mid-September. To 40 cm (16 in.), spike of up to 50 small white or creamy white flowers. Confused with *S. cernua* complex and not given specific status until 1974. Least two-lipped of all *S. cernua* complex in profile, smaller, more compact flower with blunter dorsal sepal essentially not upturned like most *Spiranthes* species. Usually drier habitat than others.

Spiranthes cernua. Mostly wet meadows, ditches, pastures, and lake shores, from Nova Scotia to southern Ontario, Minnesota and extreme southeastern North Dakota, south to extreme northern Florida and eastern Texas. September in North to November in South. To 50 cm (20 in.), dense raceme of up to 70 fragrant, sparkling white flowers, center of lip with yellowish groove, very variable in size and shape of flowers and fragrance. Similar to *S. ochroleuca,* which has more cream or pale yellowish tinge to entire flower, particularly under surface of lip petal where yellow is most pronounced and most diagnostic. *Spiranthes cernua* has no yellow under lip petal.

Spiranthes delitescens. Around wet, marshy-meadowy areas known as *cienegas,* confined to four populations in southeastern Arizona. July. To 25 cm (10 in.), with 30 or more small white *S. cernua*-type flowers. Originally considered a northern extension of *S. graminea* from Mexico. Identify by distribution.

Spiranthes diluvialis. In wet meadows near springs, streams, or lakes at high elevations in only three areas of North America: the eastern slope of the Rocky Mountains in Colorado and southwestern Wyoming, the Colorado River Basin in northeastern Utah, and the eastern Great Basin of Nevada and Utah. July through September. To 40 cm (16 in.), a basal rosette of leaves, absent at anthesis, persists through winter, with several dozen tubular white flowers similar to *S. magnicamporum*. Considered a distinct species resulting from the ancient hybridization of *S. magnicamporum* and *S. romanzoffiana*.

Spiranthes infernalis. In very hot, seasonally moist springs, streams, and marshes in the desert, isolated from but closely related to *S. romanzoffiana* and *S. porrifolia*. Very rare, possibly endemic to Ash Meadows, Nevada, east of Death Valley, California. May and June. To 40 cm (16 in.), lower leaves lanceolate and remaining at anthesis, spike usually very dense with up to 100 tubular flowers that are brownish yellow, except for the basal one-fourth of sepals and petals, and up to half of lip, which is green, while the apex and middle of the lip are pale orange. The color of the flowers and restrictive distribution are distinctive.

Spiranthes lacera. Mostly old, dry fields, openings in dry woods, dry roadsides, sometimes moist, from Nova Scotia to Manitoba, south to Virginia and Missouri, and in southern variety *gracilis*, to Florida and eastern Texas. To 50 cm (20 in.), with spike of up to 50 tiny, crystalline white flowers, lip with green stripe down the center, spike twisted or secund. Southern variety *gracilis* supposedly has more closely spaced flowers and more twisted spiral, northern variety *lacera* has gap between two lowermost florets, but in my experience this does not always hold true. Ranges of both varieties overlap.

Spiranthes laciniata. Mostly wet meadows, pinelands, roadsides, and ditches, from southern New Jersey to Florida, west to southeastern Texas on coastal plain. April in Florida to August northward. To 60 cm (24 in.), dense spike of up to 50 whitish or yellowish white flowers with yellow center of lip, spike typical of genus—either single rank, spiraled, or secund. Yellow on lip may not distinguish it from look-alike *S. vernalis*, but large, incurved basal tuberosities at base of lip petal should.

Spiranthes longilabris. Mostly wet prairies and pinelands on coastal plain from extreme southeastern Virginia to Florida, west to extreme eastern Texas. November and December. To 50 cm (20 in.), spike with up to 30 white flowers, and yellow centered, long lip, mostly secund. Late blooming separates from look-alikes *S. vernalis* and *S. laciniata*, as will the longer lip.

Spiranthes lucida. Mostly wet meadows, stream sandbars, pastures, and roadcut seepages, from Nova Scotia to extreme southern Ontario, southern Michigan, south to Kentucky and West Virginia and outposts in Wisconsin, Kansas, and Missouri. June and July. To 35 cm (14 in.), three or four fleshy basal leaves, dense but short spike of up to 20 white flowers with bright yellow center, in three-spiraled ranks. Unmistakable.

Spiranthes magnicamporum. Mostly midwestern plains, compact range from North Dakota to central Texas, east to extreme southern Ontario, southern Michigan and Illinois. Mid-September to early November. To 60 cm (24 in.), leaves absent at anthesis, dense spike of up to 60 white or creamy white flowers, tightly spiraled, obliterating ranks, lip yellowish on both upper and lower surfaces, strong fragrance. The freely spreading and ascending "cow's-horn" look of lateral sepals, strong fragrance, habitat, and later bloom help separate it from *S. cernua*.

Spiranthes ochroleuca. Mostly drier road shoulders and fields, Nova Scotia to extreme southern Ontario, lower Michigan, east to Pennsylvania and southern Maine. September to early October. To 50 cm (20 in.), spike dense with up to 60 pale, creamy white flowers. The best field diagnostic in my experience is the consistently yellow lower surface of the lip, which is mostly white in *S. cernua*. When in doubt, turn the lip over and compare.

Spiranthes odorata. Mostly wet prairies and marshes in sun, or wet woods in shade, southern New Jersey to Florida, west to eastern Texas. October in North to January in Florida. To 90 cm (36 in.), dense, spiraled spike of up to 60 white or creamy white flowers, very fragrant. Similar to *S. cernua*, but taller and blooms later.

Spiranthes ovalis. Mostly uncommon and local in shaded, rich wet forests, southern Virginia to southern Illinois, south to northern Florida and eastern Texas. September to November. To 40 cm (16 in.), open spike of up to 50 small spiraled white flowers. Size, tapered inflorescence (oval), and habitat identify it.

Spiranthes parksii. Grassy banks of streams in open scrub woodland, apparently endemic to Brazos County, Texas. Similar to *S. lacera* var. *gracilis*.

Spiranthes porrifolia. Mostly along streams in high grasses, seepage slopes and bogs, endemic to Pacific Northwest, California (one of only two spiranthes) north to extreme south-central Washington, and extreme northwestern Nevada. June to August. To 70 cm (28 in.), dense, spiraled spike of up to 100 creamy yellow flowers. Unmistakable.

Spiranthes praecox. Southern Delaware southward on the coastal plain to Florida and west to eastern Texas, in wet meadows, ditches, and edges of woods. February in Florida to June in the North. To 80 cm (32 in.), up to six keeled and rigid basal leaves, spike of up to 40 white flowers, faintly marked with green stippling on the undulate and crenulate (rounded teeth) lips. The green stippling is usually present and distinctive, but must be looked for up close. One of the tallest *Spiranthes* species.

Spiranthes romanzoffiana. Mostly wet meadows, bogs, seepages (very variable in habitats), transcontinental from Newfoundland to Alaska through most of Canada, south to northern New England, Great Lakes region, and in mountains to California, Rockies to Arizona and New Mexico. August to September. To 50 cm (20 in.), dense spike of up to 60 creamy white flowers with most two-lipped appearance, from a hood composed of all sepals (tip of dorsal sepal upturned) and petals and sharply deflexed lip, which gives a "receding chin" look. The flowers also tip upward instead of usual ninety-degree outward look.

Spiranthes tuberosa. Mostly dry, open woods, roadsides, old grassy fields, from southeastern Massachusetts on coastal plain to Florida and west to eastern Texas, thence north to southern Michigan, southern Indiana and extreme southern Ohio. June in Florida to early September northward. To 30 cm (12 in.), dense spike of up to 30 tiny, sparkling pure white, glabrous flowers, one rank, spiraled, or secund. Smallest flowers in genus, pure white and clean-cut in looks. Unmistakable.

Spiranthes vernalis. Mostly wet grasslands, pinelands, and roadsides, Massachusetts to Florida and eastern Texas on coastal plain, thence to Missouri and Oklahoma and below Ohio River valley. February in southern Florida to August northward. To 60 cm (24 in.), with up to 50 whitish flowers with hints of yellow on lip, lateral sepals flare outward from petals. Flowers densely hairy, the hairs pointed (apparently diagnostic), and one of earliest *Spiranthes* species to bloom.

Stenorrhynchos michuacanum (synonym *Spiranthes michuacana*). A Mexican species barely crossing the border in southwestern Texas and extreme southeastern Arizona, in scrub forests, slopes, and fields. September and October. To 40 cm (16 in.), with basal rosette of lanceolate leaves, and up to 30 or more crowded, handsome *Spiranthes*-type flowers, white with colorful green stripes on all floral parts. Different bloom season than *Deiregyne durangensis*. Unmistakable.

Tipularia discolor. Mostly dark, wet deciduous forest, with deep leaf mold, from extreme southeastern Massachusetts and New York, south to extreme northern Florida, west to extreme eastern Texas, thence northward to southeastern Arkansas, southern Illinois, Indiana, Ohio and Pennsylvania, especially Cumberland Plateau region and Appalachians. July to September. To 70 cm (28 in.), solitary, fugacious leaf (green above, purple below), loose and very slender raceme of up to 40 watery greenish grayish to purplish flowers with long spur and asymmetrical flower on long pedicels giving crane-fly look. Unmistakable.

Triphora trianthophora. Mostly open beech forest and other deciduous or mixed forest, in pockets of deep humus, from southwestern Maine to northwestern Florida, west to extreme eastern Texas, north to extreme southern Wisconsin and Michigan, and New York. Mostly August, later in Deep South. To 30 cm (12 in.), up to eight tiny, ovate, clasping leaves on purplish stem, with raceme of usually three or four small, sparkling white flowers with lavender tips on all parts, floor of lip marked with three bright green crests. Forma *albidoflava* has all white flowers with pure yellow crests on the lip. Unmistakable.

Zeuxine strateumatica. On lawns, roadsides, and swamps in Florida and extreme southeastern Georgia. December and January. To 25 cm (10 in.), with six to twelve dark green, deeply keeled, almost linear leaves, and densely flowered terminal spike of 50 or more small white flowers with prominent yellow lip. Unmistakable.

Index of Plant Names